The SEARCH for VALUE

Financial Management Association Survey and Synthesis Series

The Search for Value: Measuring the Company's Cost of Capital
Michael C. Ehrhardt

The S EARCH *for* VALUE

Measuring the Company's Cost of Capital

Michael C. Ehrhardt

Harvard Business School Press
Boston, Massachusetts

98 97 96 95 94   5 4 3 2

Library of Congress Cataloging-in-Publication Data

Ehrhardt, Michael C., 1955–
    The search for value : measuring the company's cost of capital /
Michael C. Ehrhardt.
        p.   cm.—(Financial Management Association survey and
synthesis series)
    Includes bibliographical references and index.
    ISBN 0-87584-380-8 (acid-free paper)
    1. Corporations—Valuation.   2. Capital investments.   I. Title.
II. Series.
HG4028.V3E37   1994
658.15—dc20   93-21411
                                                            CIP

Text design by Wilson Graphics & Design (Kenneth J. Wilson)

The paper used in this publication meets the requirements of the
American National Standard for Permanence of Paper for Printed
Library Materials Z39.49-1984.

Contents

Preface

One of the Financial Management Association's ongoing activities is the Survey and Synthesis Series. Its primary purpose is to bridge the gap between the financial research literature and the day-to-day concerns of finance practitioners. In other words, the FMA's Survey and Synthesis Series makes it easier for finance practitioners to locate, understand, and apply the financial research that is relevant to their problems.

I have written this book for the financial directors, planners, managers, and analysts who measure their company's cost of capital and who ensure that the cost of capital is used appropriately in issues of corporate finance, including capital budgeting. The book pulls together a large body of financial research related to the cost of capital. This synthesis describes the results and explains the implications of the research. The nature of the topic makes discussion of the research sometimes unavoidably technical and complicated. To make the material easier to understand, I provide numerous examples, showing in detail how to apply the research when measuring the cost of capital.

Organization of the Book

The first chapter identifies the importance of the cost of capital within the context of a firm's overall search for value. Chapter 2 explains why the weighted average cost of capital is an appropriate tool to be used in identifying value-adding projects. This chapter also gives the correct definition of cash flows for a capital budgeting application, given that the weighted average cost of capital is used to discount those cash flows.

Chapter 3 describes the basic steps in estimating the cost of capital. This chapter compares and contrasts different approaches, and illustrates the different techniques with numerous examples. The next two chapters focus on more advanced issues and problems, such as the estimation of divisional costs of capital and the treatment of flotation costs. As in the previous chapters, numerical examples demonstrate the techniques.

Chapter 6 discusses issues associated with estimating the cost of capital for companies affected by regulatory processes such as utilities and financial institutions. Chapter 7 is a discussion of international issues and their effect on the cost of capital.

Chapter 8, the final chapter, identifies situations where the discounted cash flow approach is not an appropriate technique for determining the value of a proposed project. This is important, because misusing the cost of capital in these situations can lead to incorrect decisions with respect to capital budgeting and strategic planning.

Acknowledgments

Although any errors or omissions are my own responsibility, I am grateful to many colleagues for helpful comments and suggestions. I particularly appreciate the time, effort, and inputs of Mike Long and Sam Weaver. I also want to thank Harold Black, Ivan Brick, Cary Collins, Ray DeGennaro, Jim Dunston, Kendall Hoyd, Greg Kuhlmeyer, Charlie Moyer, Jim Reeve, Larry Shao, Ron Shrieves, and Al Tucker. Finally, I especially want to thank my wife, Sallie, and my daughter, Katie, for putting up with me during the time I worked on this project.

The SEARCH *for* VALUE

Chapter *1*

The Search for Value: Measuring the Company's Cost of Capital

Your company is considering a proposed project. A team of members from several different departments, including engineering, marketing, accounting, finance, and production, analyzes the project. The analysis provides estimates of the installation cost and the expected after-tax cash flows associated with the project for each year of the project's life. Should you accept the project?

On the surface, the answer is simple: you should accept the project if it adds value to the firm; you should reject the project if it doesn't add value. Operationalizing this simple rule, however, is not at all simple. First, how do you define "value"? Is this the value of the common equity in the company, or should it include the value to other stakeholders who are affected by company decisions, such as customers, suppliers, employees, and managers? Second, how can you determine whether the project creates value? What methods and techniques are appropriate for measuring value?

I. Value Creation: Stockholders and Stakeholders

Many stakeholders are affected by a company's decisions. There are providers of capital, including equity shareholders, bondholders, and bankers. There are suppliers of raw materials and component parts to the company. There are creators of the product, including employees, independent contractors, and managers. There are customers of the company, including purchasers and users of the product. How should

1

you define the value of a project, given the interests that these diverse stakeholders have in the project?

Legal concepts of private property provide a clear answer to the question concerning the definition of value. You must define value as the value to the owners, who are the shareholders. If managers undertake projects that don't maximize shareholder value, shareholders will rationally exercise their rights to remove the managers and replace them with managers who will undertake value-maximizing projects. Of course, the world we live in is not this simple. The widely dispersed ownership of most major corporations creates enormous monitoring problems on the part of shareholders. In fact, it's not clear whether atomistic shareholders are effective in either monitoring management or applying remedies. There is, however, an increasingly active market for corporate control where external "raiders" apply considerable pressure on managers who don't maximize shareholder value.[1]

From the shareholders' point of view, which is supported by legal concepts of private property, managers are the agents of the shareholders and should act on their behalf. Yet this definition of value in no way implies that managers should ignore other stakeholders. Companies that fail to address their customers' needs and desires are pursuing a strategy that will ultimately destroy value for all stakeholders, including shareholders. To understand this point, it's necessary to understand how stocks are valued by shareholders.

Empirical studies of the stock market indicate that stock value is not just a function of short-term earnings but is determined largely by future cash flows. Rappaport (1983) defines the portion of stock price that is attributable to earnings occurring beyond the immediate five-year horizon as the "Long-Term Value Index." For a large sample of firms, Rappaport finds that this value ranges from 60% to 89%. Put another way, most of a stock's value is not determined by short-term earnings.

Many corporate strategies have a negative impact on short-term earnings and short-term cash flow but offer the potential for significant long-term gains. Research and development, joint ventures, and large capital expenditures are examples of these projects. Despite the negative effect of such investments on short-term earnings, Woolridge (1988) finds that the stock market reacts favorably to announcements that companies are undertaking these types of projects. In other words,

---

[1] See Jensen (1986, 1989) for a more detailed discussion of these issues.

shareholders recognize and value future cash flows, and not just short-term earnings.

Future cash flows depend to a large degree on the constant creation of value for customers. It's important to recognize that customers represent not just a sale today, but rather an "annuity" of cash flows.[2]

Think about the way two automobile manufacturers have handled some of their quality problems. Instead of a traditional recall to repair a problem with some Lexus automobiles, employees went to the customer's house after the customer had returned from work, took the car back to the service department, made the repairs, and returned the car to the customer's house before the customer left for work the next day. When a batch of defective radiator coolant created problems for a group of Saturn automobiles, the company actually replaced the entire car. These are clearly expensive remedies and can't be justified by the profit of a single automobile. But suppose these actions lead to repeat sales? In this case, the expensive remedy is likely to be more than compensated by the future profits from these repeat customers.[3]

Other stakeholders are also important in the creation of value. For example, companies that deceive lenders may pay a lower interest rate on today's loan, but will pay much more when they return to the capital markets for their next round of financing. Companies that ignore employee welfare will typically have greater turnover and lower effort from the employees, which leads to lower future cash flows. The lesson is simple: shareholder value is not independent of stakeholder welfare. In fact, attention to stakeholder welfare is a necessary prerequisite for increasing stockholder value. Unlike formal legal contracts, the relationships between a firm and its stakeholders are often not explicitly or formally codified, even though "implicit" contracts with stakeholders add significant value to the firm.[4]

These implicit contracts allow managers to operationalize the goal of increasing shareholder value. Simply telling an employee to increase stock value usually doesn't do much good, because most people see very little connection between their daily work and the value of the company's stock. In contrast, most employees do understand and are able to implement in their daily work the idea of creating value for their customers, whether those customers are the ultimate consumers

---

[2] Stewart (1991) has an interesting discussion of this concept.

[3] For a more detailed treatment of customer value within a management systems framework, see Stahl and Bounds (1991).

[4] See Cornell and Shapiro (1987) for an interesting discussion of implicit contracting.

or whether they are the company's internal customers that depend on the employee. Shareholder value may be the desired "end," but creating value for customers, employees, and other stakeholders is the "means" to that end.

People are more creative and productive when they feel they are part of an organization that is doing something important and worthwhile. They often get this feeling as a result of a well-articulated and fully enacted corporate vision. Still, achieving superior "return on equity does not, as a goal, mobilize the most noble forces of our soul."[5] In other words, the maximization of shareholder value isn't a particularly effective element in a corporate vision. Implicit contracting, with its emphasis on the creation of value for customers and other stakeholders, can guide managers in shaping an effective vision, a vision that moves people to action.

II. Techniques for Measuring Value Creation

Should you accept the project the management team is analyzing? Before you even think about applying any quantitative techniques for project evaluation, you need to answer the following question: Is the project aligned with your company's strategic goals?

II.A. Strategic Alignment

Prahalad and Hamel (1990) argue that strategic goals should be driven by the company's existing or desired core technologies. For example, Honda Motor Co. Ltd. produces excellent engines, and has built its strategy and product lines around this core technology. Other examples of companies and their core technologies are Casio Computer Co. Ltd. (miniaturization), Minnesota Mining and Manufacturing Co. (substrates, coatings, and adhesives), and Black and Decker Corp. (small electrical motors). Prahalad and Hamel document numerous instances where companies accept projects that are not aligned with their strategic goals, and the projects lead to a reduction rather than an increase in value. Whether or not you agree with Prahalad and Hamel's assertion that a company's strategy should be built around core technologies, you should ensure that any project up for serious consideration should be aligned with your company's strategic goals.

---

[5] See Senge (1990) for a reference to this statement of Lawrence Miller. Senge also provides an interesting discussion of the role of the leader in defining an organizational vision.

If the project is not aligned with your company's goals, you should probably reject the project on that basis. If you do decide to give it further consideration, you should be highly skeptical of the project's projected cash flows; it is very unusual for the actual cash flows from such a project to be as high as the forecasted cash flows.

II.B. Discounted Cash Flow Techniques

Discounted cash flow (DCF) techniques are used by most companies for project evaluation, probably because they are straightforward to apply and because they are intuitively appealing.[6] You forecast the future cash flows, choose the appropriate discount rate, and find the present value of the forecasted cash flows. The net present value (NPV) is defined as the difference between the present value of the future cash flows and the initial cost. If the NPV is positive, then accepting the project adds value to the firm.[7]

Let's assume you have done a good job in estimating the future cash flows of the project.[8] Given accurate estimates of future cash flows, the success of the discounted cash flow technique then will depend on how well you choose the discount rate. If you pick a rate that is too high, you will reject projects that add value to the firm; if you pick a rate that is too low, you will accept projects that subtract value. In a nutshell, here's the primary objective of this book: to help you increase the value of your company by choosing the appropriate discount rate.

III. The Rest of the Book

There are several different types of discounted cash flow approaches, and each has a different specification of cash flows and a

---

[6] See Weaver, Peters, Cason, and Daleiden (1989) for a panel discussion of capital budgeting and discounted cash flow techniques. Kim, Crick, and Kim (1986) conducted a survey of the *Fortune* 1000 firms. Of their 367 respondents, 90% used the discounted cash flow approach in their capital budgeting process, while 70% used the discounted cash flow approach as their primary means of project evaluation.

[7] An alternative discounted cash flow approach is the internal rate of return (IRR) approach. IRR is defined as the discount rate that equates the present value of the future cash flows with the initial cost. If the IRR is higher than the appropriate discount rate (often called the cutoff rate or the hurdle rate), the project adds value. See Bierman (1986) for more details on this and other project evaluation techniques.

[8] Other than cash flows associated with financing costs and depreciation, this book will not discuss how you should estimate expected cash flows. It is true that deciding which cash flows should be included in the analysis and subsequently estimating those cash flows are extremely important. These topics, however, are well-covered elsewhere. For more details, see Bierman (1986), Shapiro (1989), or Brealey and Myers (1988).

different appropriate discount rate. The next chapter explains these different approaches, with an emphasis on the weighted average cost of capital technique. The chapter also explains which techniques are appropriate for certain situations, why they are appropriate in those situations, and how to implement the appropriate technique.

To implement the weighted average cost of capital technique, you must first estimate the costs of the various sources of financing. In general, these costs are a function of: (1) the riskiness of the assets being financed, and (2) the amount of debt used to finance the assets. Chapter 3 explains how to measure the cost of each source and how to use these costs to estimate the weighted average cost of capital.

Keep in mind that the emphasis in Chapter 3 is *not* on the selection of an optimal capital structure. Throughout this book, it is assumed that your capital structure is fixed. The goal of the book is to help you answer the question: Given a particular capital structure, what is your cost of capital? If you are interested in the debt/equity choice, see Masulis (1988), who provides a thorough analysis of this issue.

The cost of capital depends on the riskiness of the project. Therefore, it's not always appropriate to use the same cost of capital for all divisions or all projects within a firm. Chapter 4 defines the situations that require a project-specific cost of capital and shows how to estimate such a cost of capital.

Many situations are more complicated than the scenarios of Chapters 2–4. For example, what about flotation costs associated with new issues of capital? Should you have a different cost of capital for short- and long-term projects? What about cases where capital is rationed, when there are fixed limits on expenditures? Chapter 5 discusses issues such as these and shows how to accommodate these complications.

There are also special issues associated with regulated industries such as utilities and deposit-taking financial institutions. Chapter 6 shows how to estimate the cost of capital for companies in these industries.

Most companies face a global marketplace and increasingly intense global competition. What effect does this have on the cost of capital when projects are located outside the company's home country? What effects do international capital markets have on the cost of capital? Chapter 7 examines these international issues.

Finally, it's important to understand that not all projects should be evaluated with discounted cash flow techniques. For such projects, usually there is no well-accepted method for identifying the appropriate discount rate. An example is a project that involves a real option such as the option to abandon the project or the option to expand the scale of the project if the market grows faster than anticipated. Chapter 8 discusses this issue, because it is important to understand the limitations of the discounted cash flow techniques.

References

Bierman, H., Jr. *Implementation of Capital Budgeting Techniques*. Tampa: Financial Management Association, 1986.

Brealey, R. A., and S. C. Myers. *Principles of Corporate Finance*, 3rd ed. New York: McGraw-Hill, 1988.

Cornell, B., and A. C. Shapiro, "Corporate Stakeholders and Corporate Finance." *Financial Management* 16(1) (Spring 1987): 5–14.

Jensen, M. C. "The Takeover Controversy: Analysis and Evidence." *Midland Corporate Finance Journal* 4(2) (Summer 1986): 6–32.

———. "Eclipse of the Public Corporation." *Harvard Business Review* (September–October 1989): 61–74.

Kim, S. H., T. Crick, and S. H. Kim. "Do Executives Practice What Academics Preach?" *Management Accounting* (November 1986): 49–52.

Masulis, R. W. *The Debt/Equity Choice*. Cambridge, Mass.: Ballinger, 1988.

Prahalad, C. K., and G. Hamel. "The Core Competence of the Corporation." *Harvard Business Review* (May–June 1990): 79–91.

Rappaport, A. "Don't Sell Stock Market Horizons Short." *The Wall Street Journal* (June 27, 1983): 24.

Senge, P. "The Leader's New Work: Building Learning Organizations." *Sloan Management Review* (Fall 1990): 7–23.

Shapiro, A. C. *Modern Corporate Finance*. New York: Macmillan, 1989.

Stahl, M. J., and G. M. Bounds (eds.). *Competing Globally Through Customer Value*. New York: Quorum Books, 1991.

Stewart, D. W. "The Customer as Annuity." *USC Business* (Summer 1991): 48–52.

Weaver, S. C., D. Peters, R. Cason, and J. Daleiden. "Panel Discussion on Corporate Investment: Capital Budgeting," *Financial Management* 18(1) (Spring 1989): 10–17.

Woolridge, J. R. "Competitive Decline and Corporate Restructuring: Is a Myopic Stock Market to Blame?" *Journal of Applied Corporate Finance* 1(1) (Spring 1988): 26–36.

Chapter **2**

Why You Should Use the Weighted Average Cost of Capital

Suppose you must decide whether to accept or reject a proposed project. Your team of analysts has provided you with the project's estimated cash flows, and you've decided to evaluate the project using a discounted cash flow approach.[1] To determine the value of the project, you will find the present value of the future cash flows and compare this with the initial cash outlays. This can be written as:

$$NPV = CF_0 + \sum_{t=1}^{T} \frac{CF_t}{(1 + r_c)^t} \qquad (2.1)$$

where NPV is the net present value, CF_0 is the cash flow due to installation incurred at the beginning of the project, T is the number of periods that the project will last, CF_t is the expected after-tax cash flow at period t, and r_c is the discount rate appropriate for this project.

But how do you choose r_c, the discount rate? That's the primary question this chapter addresses. At the risk of making the rest of the chapter anticlimactic, here's the answer. First, you estimate the current cost of each source of funds; this is not the historical cost of the capital you have already raised, but instead the marginal cost of any incremental funds that you will raise. Second, you find the weighted average

---

[1] The DCF approach is not appropriate for all projects. Chapter 8 characterizes the types of projects that can be evaluated with DCF methods and the types of projects that should not be evaluated with DCF methods. Chapter 8 also offers some suggestions on how to evaluate those projects for which DCF methods are not appropriate.

of the costs of these separate sources of capital, with the weights based on the market values of the sources of financing. The result is the "weighted average cost of capital."[2] You should use this weighted average cost of capital, r_c, to discount the appropriate after-tax cash flows of the project in equation (2.1).

Suppose there are N different sources of capital used to finance the project. If M_j is the market value of the jth source of financing, then the market-weighted percentage of the project financed by source j, w_j, is defined as:

$$w_j = \frac{M_j}{\sum\limits_{j=1}^{N} M_j} \qquad (2.2)$$

If r_j is the marginal cost of source j, the weighted average cost of capital, r_c, is defined:

$$r_c = \sum_{j=1}^{N} w_j r_j \qquad (2.3)$$

This weighted average cost of capital, as defined by equation (2.3), is often called the "traditional" cost of capital, because analysts have used it for at least 30 years.[3] It's also called the "textbook" cost of capital, because many textbooks discuss it.[4]

The rest of this chapter explains *why* you should use the weighted average cost of capital. This understanding not only will give you more confidence in your results, but also help you to apply the method to your particular company.

As you might expect, proving that the weighted average cost of capital is the correct discount rate requires a good bit of algebra. It's easiest to start with the simplest case, and that's what Section I does. Section II relaxes the restrictive assumptions of Section I and shows that the weighted average cost of capital is appropriate under realistic conditions.

---

[2] Strictly speaking, this should be called the "market-weighted average of the marginal costs of capital."

[3] It's not clear exactly when the concept of the weighted average cost of capital was first developed. Nantell and Carlson (1975) credit Solomon (1963) with its first formal development. Boness (1964) indicates that Bierman and Smidt (1960) and Durand (1959) each used a very similar concept.

[4] See Shapiro (1989) for an example.

I. The Simplest Case: Perpetual Constant Cash Flows

Here are the assumptions for the simplest case:

1. the firm and the project last forever;

2. the cash flows of the firm (CF_F) and the expected cash flows of the project (CF_P) are constant in every period;

3. the firm is financed with common equity and debt in a fixed proportion, and the project will be financed in the same proportions as the firm itself;

4. the debt of the firm, D, has an interest rate of i, never matures (it is a consol bond), and is issued at par; similar debt will be issued for the project;

5. the corporate tax rate is τ;

6. at least one of two assumptions holds: (1) all cash flows net of interest payments are distributed to shareholders; or (2) dividend policy does not affect the value of the firm; and

7. the project is identical to the firm with respect to riskiness.

The primary objective of this chapter is to show you why you should use the weighted average cost of capital when you estimate the present value of a project. However, it's easier to start with the cost of capital for the entire firm, so that's what Section I.A does. This makes it easier to understand the cost of capital for a project, which is defined in Section I.B.

I.A. The Cost of Capital for a Firm

The way in which you define the cash flows of the firm will affect the definition of the weighted average cost of capital. For the rest of this section, here's the definition of the firm's cash flows: you should use the operating cash flows on an after-tax basis, before any interest payments or tax deductions because of the interest payments.[5] In other words, the relevant cash flow of the firm, CF_F, is equal to the after-tax cash flow of an otherwise identical firm with no debt.

---

[5] This is usually equal to the after-tax operating income plus noncash expenses, such as depreciation. It would also include any cash flows due to changes in working capital.

Let V denote the market value of the firm, E the market value of the equity, and D the market value of the debt; all these market values are observable. Since expected cash flows are constant and occur for an infinite number of periods, you can use the formula for a perpetuity to relate cash flows and value:

$$V = \frac{CF_F}{r_c} \qquad (2.4)$$

Remember that the value of the firm, V, and the cash flows of the firm, CF_F, are observable. Therefore, the cost of capital, r_c, is simply a number such that equation (2.4) is true. In other words, the cost of capital, r_c, is a consequence of the observable firm value and observable firm cash flows.

Equation (2.3) defines r_c as the weighted average cost of capital, but is this same as the cost of capital in equation (2.4)? The answer is yes. In fact, the only way equation (2.4) can be true is if equation (2.3) is true. To see this, you first must define the cost of equity.

Because interest payments are deductible for purposes of calculating tax liabilities, the cash flow available for shareholders is $CF_F - (1 - \tau)iD$.[6] This cash flow is also a perpetuity, so you can define the value of the equity as:

$$E = \frac{CF_F - (1 - \tau)iD}{r_E} \qquad (2.5)$$

where the cost of equity is r_E. Since you know the value of the equity, E, the value of the debt, D, the interest rate, i, the tax rate, τ, and the expected cash flows, you can define the cost of equity, r_E, such that equation (2.5) is true.

There are only two sources of financing in this example, so the total value of the firm must be equal to the sum of the market values of debt and equity:

$$V = E + D \qquad (2.6)$$

---

[6] This assumes that the market value of the debt is equal to the book value of the debt. Chapter 3 provides a detailed discussion of the issue of market versus book values.

You can rewrite equation (2.4) to solve for the cost of capital, r_c, and you can substitute equation (2.6) for the firm value. This gives you:

$$r_c = \frac{CF_F}{E + D} \tag{2.7}$$

You can rewrite equation (2.5):

$$CF_F = r_E E + (1 - \tau)iD \tag{2.8}$$

If you substitute equation (2.8) into equation (2.7), you will get:

$$r_c = \left(\frac{E}{E + D}\right) r_E + \left(\frac{D}{E + D}\right) (1 - \tau)i \tag{2.9}$$

Define w_E and w_D as the proportions of the firm financed with equity and debt, respectively. If you define the cost of debt, r_D, as $(1 - \tau)i$, and substitute these definitions into equation (2.9), you get the formula for r_c:

$$r_c = w_E r_E + w_D r_D \tag{2.10}$$

which is the weighted average cost of capital as defined by equation (2.3). This means that the weighted average cost of capital is in fact the discount rate you would use if you were going to find the present value of the firm's after-tax operating cash flows.[7] Using this weighted average cost of capital will result in a present value that is exactly equal to the actual value of the firm. An example illustrating this result is in Exhibit 2.1.

I.B. The Cost of Capital for a Project

Let's review the process that leads to the weighted average cost of capital for the firm. First, you need to know the expected cash flows and you need to observe the market values of the debt and equity. Given these variables, you can use equations (2.4) and (2.5) to define the overall cost of capital to the firm and the cost of equity, respectively.

---

[7] Section III of this chapter and Section II.B of Chapter 3 provide further discussion concerning the definition of cash flows.

Exhibit 2.1:   An Example of the Weighted Average Cost of Capital

Suppose the interest rate on the perpetual debt, i, is 10%. The market value of the debt is $100. The market value of the firm's equity is $300. The pre-tax cash flow of the firm is $100 per year; this will be constant forever. The firm is subject to a combined federal, state, and local tax rate of 40%.

The appropriate after-tax operating cash flow is:

$$CF_F = 100\,(1 - .4) = 60$$

The total value of the firm is just the sum of the debt and equity:

$$V = 100 + 300 = 400$$

Equation (2.4) states that the value of the firm is the discounted value of the after-tax operating cash flows:

$$400 = \frac{60}{r_c} \Rightarrow r_c = \frac{60}{400} = .15$$

This means that the present value of the after-tax operating cash flows will equal the market value of the firm if the discount rate is 15%. Is this equal to the weighted average cost of capital? To see if it is, you need the after-tax cost of debt and equity.

The after-tax cost of debt is:

$$r_D = .10\,(1 - .4) = .06$$

Equation (2.5) allows you to calculate the cost of equity:

$$300 = \frac{60 - (1 - .4)(.1)(100)}{r_E} \Rightarrow r_E = \frac{60 - 6}{300} = .18$$

Using these values and equation (2.10), the weighted average cost of capital is:

$$r_c = \left(\frac{300}{300 + 100}\right)(.18) + \left(\frac{100}{300 + 100}\right)(.06) = .15.$$

This example shows that the weighted average cost of capital is indeed the appropriate rate to use for discounting the after-tax operating cash flows of the firm.

In other words, you define the cost of equity and the cost of capital relative to specific streams of cash flows and observed market values. The result is r_c, the weighted average cost of capital, as defined in equation (2.9).[8] Here's the critical question: Will this definition of the weighted average cost of capital lead you to a correct accept–reject decision on proposed project? In fact, answering this question is the primary objective of this book, which is to help you find the required rate of return on new investments.

Suppose you are considering one of the company's proposed projects, one with perpetual constant cash flows equal to CF_P. The initial cost of the project is CF_0, and you intend to finance it with the same capital structure as the company, which contains a proportion of equity equal to w_E and a proportion of debt equal to w_D. According to the reasoning underlying equation (2.4), the value of this project is equal to the project's expected cash flows discounted at the weighted average cost of capital.

How do you estimate the weighted average cost of capital? This is where you use equation (2.10), which defines the weighted average cost of capital in terms of the cost of equity (r_E), the cost of debt (r_D), the proportion of equity financing (w_E), and the proportion of debt financing (w_D). You know the proportions of financing (w_E and w_D), for you know the project will have the same capital structure as the company. How do you find the costs of equity and debt (r_E and r_D)? Chapter 3 answers this question in considerable detail, but for the rest of this chapter, let's assume that if the capital structure and the risk of the project are identical to the capital structure and risk of the firm, you can use the firm's costs of equity and debt (r_E and r_D).[9]

With these estimates of r_E, r_D, w_E, and w_D, it's a simple matter for you to calculate the project's weighted average cost of capital, r_c, using equation (2.10).

Since you know the project's cash flows and the project's weighted average cost of capital, you can find the project value, V_P, by using equation (2.4), Exhibit 2.2 provides a numerical example to illustrate this procedure.

---

[8] Notice that this is different from a typical capital budgeting problem, where you estimate the cash flows and then determine whether the value of the project is greater than its cost.

[9] If the new investment has a different risk from the existing investments, then the cost of capital for the new investment should be different from the cost of capital for the existing investments. Chapter 4 explains in detail how you should accommodate this situation. Also, Arditti and Tysseland (1973) and Lewellen (1974) provide general discussions of this issue.

Exhibit 2.2: Valuing a Project

Suppose the firm in Exhibit 2.1 is considering a project that has the same risk as the firm itself. The project will be financed with a mixture of perpetual debt and equity in the same proportions as the firm. This project will last forever and generate a constant pre-tax cash flow of $20 each year. What is the value of the project?

The first data you need are the costs of equity and debt (r_E and r_D). Since the project is like the firm, the cost of equity is 18% and the after-tax cost of debt is 6% (see Exhibit 1 for these calculations). The firm is financed with 75% equity and 25% debt. Therefore, the weighted average cost of capital for the project is:

$$r_c = (.75)(.18) + (.25)(.06) = .15$$

As you might have expected, this cost of capital for the project is the same as the cost of capital for the firm as shown in Exhibit 2.1.

Remember that you discount the after-tax operating cash flows. This is equal to:

$$CF_P = 20 (1 - .4) = 12$$

Since these cash flows are a perpetuity, the value of the project, V_P, is:

$$V_P = \frac{12}{.15} = 80$$

You should accept the project if the initial cost of the project is less than the present value of the future cash flows. To see that this simple rule does in fact maximize the value to the shareholders, assume now that the value of the project, V_P, is greater than its initial cost, CF_0. From Exhibit 2.2, the project value is $80; suppose the initial cost is $60.

Define E_0 and D_0 as the respective market values of project equity and debt, given that you have accepted the project. Remember that the value of the project, V_P, is the total market value of the cash flows. Therefore, this market value of the project must equal the sum of the market values of the equity and debt (E_0 and D_0) that support the project. In other words, this is the amount that the shareholders and bondholders are willing to invest in the project, given the capital structure and the stream of cash flows. In this example, the shareholders and debtholders are willing to invest a total of $80.

If the firm is financed with 25% debt, then the bondholders are willing to invest \$20 (D_0 = .25 × 80). In return for this investment, they will receive a perpetual interest payment of \$2 per year (the interest rate is 10%). The shareholders will receive the cash flow of the project, less the interest payments (adjusted for taxes). Using equation (2.5) and the cost of equity of 18%, the value of E_0 is:

$$E_0 = \frac{20(1 - .4) - (1 - .4)(.1)(20)}{.18} = 60$$

As expected, the total of D_0 and E_0 equals the total value of the project as computed in Exhibit 2.2: 20 + 60 = 80.

Suppose you ask the equityholders to invest E_0 = 60 and the bondholders to invest D_0 = 20; each would be willing to do this, since these are the values that they each ascribe to their respective streams of cash flows. But the required initial investment is just CF_0 = 60, which is less than V_P = 80, the present value of the project; remember that the value of the project, V_P, is itself equal to the sum of the values of the equity and debt (E_0 and D_0) that support the project.

You raise 60 from the equityholders and 20 from the debtholders, respectively. You then accept the project, which has an initial cost of 60. You could then refund the amount $V_P - CF_0$ = 80 − 60 = 20 to the shareholders. If you did this, what would happen to the value of the debtholders' and shareholders' positions?

The expected cash flows of the project haven't changed, so the expected cash flows that accrue to each class of investor haven't changed. Therefore, the respective values of their stakes in the project would still be E_0 = 60 and D = 20. But the shareholders have just received an immediate cash flow of $V_P - CF_0$ = 20, so the total value of their position is equal to the value of their stake in the project plus the amount of the "rebate" ($E_0 + V_P - CF_0$ = 60 + 80 − 60 = 80).

This is somewhat simplified, since a portion of this refund would go to existing shareholders as well as to the new shareholders that financed the project. Yet accepting this project has clearly increased the value accruing to all the shareholders, both new and old. Notice that acceptance of the project and the subsequent rebate has not harmed the debtholders, because they are still receiving the portion of the project's cash flows that they expected.

Of course, you wouldn't actually have to go through this unrealistically complicated procedure of raising capital and then immediately rebating a portion to the shareholders; this just seems to be a simple way to understand the concept. A more realistic alternative is to raise only the amount CF_0. If you still raise D_0 from the debtholders, you need raise only $E_0 - (V_P - CF_0)$ from the shareholders. As in the previous case, the debtholders are compensated fairly for their investment. For the shareholders, their investment of $E_0 - (V_P - CF_0)$ entitles them to ownership of a position in the project with a value of E_0.

Keep in mind that the value of the equityholders' position has already been adjusted for risk and for the time value of money. So the net increase in the value of their investment, $V_P - CF_0$, truly represents additional value. The enhanced value of their position is directly related to how much the present value of the project (V_P) exceeds the cost of the project (CF_0).

Consider the opposite case where the value of the project is less than its cost, $V_P < CF_0$. Suppose the future cash flows are allocated so that the debtholders still receive enough to make the value of their position equal to D_0, and that the debtholders invest this amount in the project. The amount of investment required by the shareholders is $E_0 - (V_P - CF_0)$. But this is less than the value of their investment, E_0, as $(V_P - CF_0)$ is a negative number. In this case, the stockholders experience an erosion of value. The degree of erosion is directly related to how much the present value of the project (V_P) falls below the cost of the project (CF_0).

Therefore, if you find the present value of a project by discounting its after-tax operating cash flows by the weighted average cost of capital, you can maximize the value to the shareholders by using the simple rule: accept the project if the present value is greater than the cost, reject the project if the present value is less than the cost.[10]

II. The Cost of Capital Under More Realistic Assumptions

The assumptions needed in the previous section to justify the weighted average cost of capital model are obviously enormous simplifications of the much more complicated world in which we live. Given

---

[10] The net present value of a project is equal to the present value of the project less the initial cost of the project. If a project has a nonzero net present value, the market value of the equity changes. This causes the capital structure to change, which then changes the weighted average cost of capital. In other words, the project itself can affect the cost of capital. However, you can keep your capital structure constant by repaying capital in the appropriate amounts to the company's investors. This will keep your cost of capital constant. Section II.A examines this issue in more detail. Also, see Grinyer (1972, 1975) and Hemsted (1974) for a discussion of this issue.

these assumptions, it's only natural to wonder whether this model is wrong.

An engineering professor once said that all models are wrong, but that some models are useful. The model in the previous section has a basic conclusion: you should use the weighted average cost of capital to discount the cash flows of a project. The relevant question is whether this conclusion is useful. Section II shows that the weighted average cost of capital is indeed appropriate, even when the model is based on much more realistic assumptions.

The discussion has assumed a project with an infinite life. As Section II will show, the same conclusions apply to the more realistic case of a project with a finite life. But first, there's an important point to understand about the infinite life example.

Notice that immediately after investing in the project, the capital structure is such that the percentage financed with equity is w_E and the percentage financed with debt is w_D. The values of equity and debt immediately after adoption of the project are E_0 and D_0, respectively. Because of the infinite life of the project, the values of equity and debt at any point in the project's life are still equal to E_0 and D_0. This is because the value at any time is the discounted value of the future cash flows [see equations (2.4) and (2.5)]. But no matter how long the project has been in place, there is always an infinite future stream of cash flows. Therefore, the values of equity and debt never change during the infinite life of the project. The result is that the capital structure never changes. Keep this in mind during the discussion of a project with a finite life.

II.A. The Cost of Capital for a Project with a Finite Life

Consider a project with a finite life of T periods and a cash flow of CF_t in period t. As in the previous section, this cash flow is the after-tax cash flow from operations; it ignores any interest payments and tax implication of the interest payments.[11]

The overall cost of capital is the rate that makes the present value of the project's cash flows equal to the market value of the project. This is the finite period equivalent of equation (2.4), which is the same

---

[11] This assumes that the earnings before interest and taxes (EBIT) are actual cash flows. Section III provides a more detailed discussion on typical differences between EBIT and cash flows.

relationship for an infinite stream of cash flows. This finite period relationship is:

$$V_0 = \sum_{t=1}^{T} \frac{CF_t}{(1 + r_c)^t} \tag{2.11}$$

where V_0 is the current market value of the project and r_c is the cost of capital.

Let E_t denote the value of equity at time t. The debt has an original outstanding balance of B; no principal is repaid until the final period. The interest rate on the debt is denoted by i. The cash flow available for shareholders at time t is $CF_t - (1 - \tau)iB$. This implies that the value of equity at time 0, E_0, is:

$$E_0 = \sum_{t=1}^{T} \frac{CF_t - (1 - \tau)iB}{(1 + r_E)^t} - \frac{B}{(1 + r_E)^T} \tag{2.12}$$

where r_E is the cost of equity.

If the debt is issued at par, then the current value of the debt, D_0, is equal to the outstanding balance. It is also equal to the present value of the interest payments:

$$D_0 = B = \sum_{t=1}^{T} \frac{iB}{(1 + i)^t} + \frac{B}{(1 + i)^T} \tag{2.13}$$

$$= \sum_{t=1}^{T} \frac{(1 - \tau)iB}{(1 + r_D)^t} + \frac{B}{(1 + r_D)^T}$$

where $r_D = (1 - \tau) i$.

Notice that the overall cash flows [the cash flows that are discounted in equation (2.11)] are just the sum of the cash flows to the equityholders [the cash flows that are discounted in equation (2.12)] and the cash flows to the debt holders [the cash flows that are discounted in equation (2.13)]. Reilly and Wecker (1973), however, show that there does not generally exist a constant w (with w between 0 and 1) such that:

$$r_c = w\, r_E + w\, r_D \tag{2.14}$$

In other words, r_c cannot be a weighted average of r_E and r_D. This conclusion does not rest on finance theory, but is a simple consequence of algebra. The apparent implication does, however, affect finance theory: the weighted average cost of capital is not relevant, because it does not correctly value the total stream of income.[12]

Linke and Kim (1974) show that there is a solution to this apparent problem.[13] Consider the value of the project at time 1, which is just the discounted value of all cash flows that occur after the first period:

$$V_1 = \sum_{t=2}^{T} \frac{CF_t}{(1 + r_c)^{t-1}} \qquad (2.15)$$

Compare equations (2.11) and (2.15). As long as the cash flow at time 1 is positive, then V_0 is greater than V_1; i.e., the value of the project shrinks as time passes. This makes sense, because the project has a finite life. In fact, the project will be worth nothing immediately after time T, as the project has no cash flows beyond T.

The value of the equity and debt also shrink over time. But here's the catch: they don't necessarily shrink at the same rate. This means that the capital structure is changing over time. Since w_E and w_D are changing over time, the weighted average cost of capital is also changing over time. Therefore, you should not expect the single number derived from equation (2.15) to be a simple linear combination of r_E and r_D.

Suppose you go back to the stream of cash flows and specify that some of the cash flows are used as a repayment of capital to the shareholders and debtholders. What happens if you choose the size of the repayments in such a way that the capital structure remains constant over time: i.e., w_E and w_D don't change from period to period? If you do this and substitute the new cash flows into equations (2.11), (2.12), and (2.13), you will find that r_c is in fact the weighted average of r_E and r_D.

Here's the conclusion: if you hold the capital structure constant, the weighted average cost of capital is appropriate, even if the project has a finite life.[14]

---

[12] Ang (1973) extends the work of Reilly and Wecker (1973) to develop a cost of capital based on the Gordon dividend growth model.

[13] Reilly and Wecker (1975) confirm this result. Reilly, Brigham, Linke, Kim, and Ang (1974), Beranek (1975a, 1975b), and Findlay (1977) provide additional discussion on this issue.

[14] This result is shown in Shapiro (1979), Boudreaux and Long (1979), Ezzell and Porter (1979), Bloomfield and Ma (1975), Pettit (1975), McConnell and Sandberg (1975), Linke and Kim (1974), Nantell and Carlson (1975), and Henderson (1979). Arditti (1973) also confirms the result. See Findlay (1975) and Arditti (1975) for a discussion of the role of depreciation in definition of the weighted average cost of capital. Riener (1985) shows that the weighted average cost of capital is appropriate even for risky debt and risky tax shields. Taggart (1991) extends the analysis to include personal as well as corporate

II.B. Constant Capital Structure

You might think that the constant capital structure assumption is unrealistic, that no one goes through the effort of repaying capital from the cash flows of a project so as to maintain constant proportions of equity (w_E) and debt (w_D). You're probably right, but consider this episode that occurred on a college campus. The faculty members in a department felt a certain source of revenue should be dedicated solely to their department. In discussion of the departmental operating budget, however, a university administrator said that "all money is fungible." I don't know how Webster's dictionary would define "fungible," but I do know how this administrator would: "Once money gets into the pot, the original source doesn't matter."

The same is true for most companies with respect to project cash flows and project debt/equity ratios. Even if debt and/or equity are raised to fund a specific project, very rarely are the cash flows of the project explicitly linked to the debt and/or equity.[15] Instead, the cash flows of the entire firm usually support the obligations of the debt and/or equity. The implication of this is quite clear: the choice of capital structure typically is determined by the firm itself and not by individual projects.

Since most firms maintain a reasonably steady ratio of debt to equity, it is reasonable to assume that the ratio of debt to equity supporting a project is also held constant. Therefore, the weighted average cost of capital is appropriate, even for projects of finite duration.

III. Defining Cash Flows

Remember that the definition of the weighted average cost of capital depends on the definition of the cash flow stream. This book does not provide details about how to define project cash flows, since that's covered quite well in most good textbooks.[16] There are a few points, however, that are directly related to the traditional definition of cost

---

taxes. He concludes that the weighted average cost of capital is appropriate except for finite projects with fixed uneven debt shields.

[15] Revenue bonds are notable exceptions. For these situations, the alternative approach of Arditti, which is shown in the appendix, may be superior to the traditional weighted average cost of capital.

[16] See Shapiro (1989), Bierman (1986), or Brealey and Myers (1988) for excellent discussions on the estimation of cash flows.

of capital. If you aren't aware of these points, you might make some errors.

First, the basic rule of thumb is to define the project's cash flows as though the firm is financed only by equity. This has a very important implication: *do not deduct interest payments, the tax shields from interest payments, or principal payments when you estimate the cash flows for a project.*[17]

Second, there are several ways in which a project's cash flows differ from accounting after-tax earnings, defined by EBIT(1 − τ). EBIT typically incorporates noncash expenses, such as depreciation and amortization. The appropriate definition of cash flow does not include noncash expenses, except to the extent that they affect taxes. For example, depreciation reduces taxes, but otherwise has no effect on cash flow.

Third, many investments require staged capital expenditures. That is, additional capital costs are incurred in years subsequent to the initial installation. These costs should be included in the cash flows for the years in which they occur even though they do not appear in accounting earnings. The same is true for changes in working capital, which represent cash flows but do not appear in earnings.

Fourth, the acceptance of a project may affect cash flows of existing projects.[18] These incremental cash flows should be included in the cash flows of the proposed project. For example, widespread acceptance of O/S2 software by International Business Machines Corp. would probably increase sales of its PS/2 computers. Any projected cash flows for software development projects at IBM should also include cash flows because of increased computer sales. Projects may also reduce sales of existing products; e.g., the introduction of Diet Coke probably caused reduced sales of Tab. It's important to include the effect of a project on your existing product lines when estimating cash flows of the project.

Fifth, it is important to include in the cash flows any changes in working capital caused by acceptance of the project. Section II.B of Chapter 3 discusses this issue in detail.

---

[17] The appendix provides details of an alternative approach where the weighted average cost of capital and the cash flows are defined slightly differently.

[18] It's possible that the acceptance of a project might also affect the riskiness of other projects. See Partington (1981) for a discussion of this issue. It's also possible that the size of the project may affect the project's own riskiness; see Long and Racette (1974) and Booth (1980).

IV. Summary and Recommendations

First, you should use the weighted average cost of capital as the discount rate when you estimate the NPV of a project. This weighted average cost of capital is defined:[19]

$$r_c = \sum_{j=1}^{N} w_j \, r_j \qquad (2.16)$$

As this chapter shows, the weighted average cost of capital is indeed the appropriate rate to use in discounting projected cash flows. If the resulting NPV is positive, the project adds value to the shareholders; if it is negative, the project decreases value to the shareholders. This is true for projects with finite lives as well as for projects with infinite projects.

Second, you should use the after-tax cost of debt when you estimate the cost of capital. See Section I.C of Chapter 3 for more discussion of this issue. You should discount the after-tax cash flows, ignoring any financing expenses. The stream of cash flows should include all after-tax cash flows associated with the project, except those associated with financing expenses. In other words, the cash flows should be estimated as though the project is financed only with equity. The appendix discusses in detail the joint issues of how to define the cash flows and the cost of debt.

Third, you should use market values when you estimate the weights for the sources of financing. You should base the weights on the market values of the sources of financing. Section II.A of Chapter 3 provides a more detailed discussion of this issue.

---

[19] Chapter 3 explains in detail how to estimate the weights (w_j) and the costs (rj) of the components of capital structure.

Appendix

Defining Cash Flows for an Alternative Model: Using the Pre-Tax Costs of Debt and Equity

*T*he weighted average cost of capital in equation (2.10) is a direct result of the way in which you define cash flows. This may seem like a minor point, but overlooking it can lead to considerable confusion and potential errors in applying the discounted cash flow approach. This point is actually quite important, because it has significant implications with respect to the definitions of the cost of capital, the cost of equity, and the cost of debt (r_c, r_E, and r_D).

An alternative definition of cash flows leads to an alternative measure for the cost of capital. It also leads to alternative measures for the costs of equity and debt, ones that are based on pre-tax cash flows. These alternative definitions and measures are valid; that is, they lead to similar conclusions with respect to project acceptance or rejection. So the choice of definition is really one of convenience. In general, I recommend the traditional weighted average cost of capital, defined in equation (2.10), because it is usually easier to apply than the alternative measures, but this appendix provides a description of the alternative model so that you can make your own decision.[20]

A-I. An Alternative Model

In the text I define the relevant cash flows as the after-tax operating cash flows. For the purpose of discussion in this appendix, let's assume that the operating earnings of a firm are identical to actual cash flows. This is, of course, a tremendous simplification, but it leads to some valuable insights. In the traditional model, you define the relevant cash flows of the firm, CF_F, as the after-tax operating profit:

$$CF_F = EBIT\,(1 - \tau) \tag{A1}$$

where EBIT is earnings before interest and taxes. In this case, CF_F is defined as the operating earnings less the tax on these earnings. As

---

[20] A third choice is the adjusted net present value approach. See the appendix of Chapter 7 for a discussion of this approach.

recommended in the chapter, this definition of cash flows ignores any interest payments or taxes on interest payments.

The only changes to the analysis in the chapter are in equations (2.4) and (2.5), which are now expressed as:

$$V = \frac{EBIT\ (1 - \tau)}{r_c} \text{ and} \tag{A2}$$

$$E = \frac{EBIT\ (1 - \tau) - (1 - \tau)\ iD}{r_E} = \frac{(EBIT - iD)\ (1 - \tau)}{r_E} \tag{A3}$$

Arditti (1973, 1980) advocates a different approach that leads to a very different cost of capital, one that is based on pre-tax cash flows of debt and equity. This approach is different, but it's just as valid as the "traditional" approach. Both approaches work, but they aren't interchangeable; i.e., you can't use some of the definitions from one approach when you apply the other. To avoid this type of error, it's important that you understand the differences in the traditional approach and the Arditti approach.

Arditti defines the value of the firm, V, in terms of a different stream of cash flows. This alternative stream, CF_F^*, is defined:

$$CF_F^* = [(EBIT - iD)\ (1 - \tau)] + [iD] \tag{A4}$$

$$= EBIT\ (1 - \tau) + iD\tau$$

The rationale for this measure is a desire to base the analysis upon the same cash flows that accrue to investors. Notice that the first term in brackets, $(EBIT - iD)(1 - \tau)$, is the cash flow to shareholders, and the second term in brackets, iD, is the cash flow to debtholders.

Using this definition of cash flow, the total value of the company, V, can be expressed as:

$$V = \frac{[(EBIT - iD)\ (1 - \tau)] + [iD]}{r_c^*} \tag{A5}$$

$$= \frac{(EBIT)\ (1 - \tau) + iD\tau}{r_c^*}$$

where r_c^* is the alternative cost of capital.

Arditti defines the alternative cost of equity, r_E^*, as:

$$r_E^* = \frac{(\text{EBIT} - \text{iD})}{E} \tag{A6}$$

This is how you would calculate the cost of equity if there were no taxes. Notice that D and E are the same values as used in the previous model.

With a little algebra, you can rearrange equations (A5) and (A6) to get an expression for the alternative cost of capital:

$$r_c^* = r_E^* (1 - \tau) \left(\frac{E}{E + D} \right) + i \left(\frac{D}{D + E} \right) \tag{A7}$$

$$= r_E^* (1 - \tau) \, w_E + iw_D$$

where w_E and w_D are the proportions of equity and debt in the capital structure.

From equations (A2) and (A6), it's easy to show that the after-tax alternative cost of equity, $r_E^*(1 - t)$, is equal to the traditional cost of equity, r_E. Substituting this into equation (A7) yields:

$$r_c^* = r_E \, w_E + iw_D \tag{A8}$$

This alternative cost of capital, r_c^*, can be used to discount the alternatively defined cash flows of a project, CF_P^*. The result is the present value of the project, V_P^*. The same decision rule as in the traditional approach applies: accept the project if the present value, V_P^*, is greater than the cost, CF_0, and reject the project if its present value is less than its cost.

A-II. A Comparison of the Two Approaches

Exhibit A.1 presents the definitions of cash flows and costs of capital for two approaches.

Notice that the two costs of capital differ with respect to the treatment of debt. In the original case, the after-tax cost of debt is used. In the alternative model, the pre-tax cost of debt is used. The two approaches also specify different streams of cash flows, to be discounted. Since the two methods use different rates and specify different cash

Exhibit A.1: A Comparison of the Two Approaches

	Traditional Approach	Alternative Approach
Cash Flow	EBIT $(1 - \tau)$	EBIT $(1 - \tau) + iD\tau$
Weighted Average Cost of Capital	$r_E w_E + i(1 - \tau)w_D$	$r_E w_E + iw_D$

flows you might wonder if one method is superior to the other. In other words, do they lead to different decisions with respect to project evaluation? The answer is no: both methods give identical results.[21]

For example, using the numbers from Exhibits 2.1 and 2.2, the traditional cost of capital is 15%, and the traditional cash flow of the project is $12. Since the cash flow is a perpetuity, the value of the project is 12/0.15 = 80. Using the alternative approach, the alternative cost of capital is 16% ([.75 × .18] + [.25 × .10] = .16), and the alternative cash flow is 12.8 ([20(1 − .4)] + [.10 × 20 × .4] = 12.8). The value of the project is 12.8/.16 = 80. As you see, the two approaches give identical results.

In fact, the two approaches will always give the same results. The most straightforward and intuitive way to see this is to specify a particular cash flow and then compare the resulting present values that the two methods give. Suppose you choose to value all of the cash flows of the firm, using both approaches. In the traditional approach, the present value of the appropriately defined cash flows, when discounted by the traditional weighted average cost of capital, is exactly equal to the value of the firm. This is also true for the alternative method: if you define the cash flows appropriately and discount them by the alternative weighted average cost of capital, the present value is exactly equal to the value of the firm. The ways in which the appro-

---

[21] Arditti (1973) and Arditti and Levy (1977) show that this is true for a perpetuity with a zero net present value. Shapiro (1979), Ben-Horim (1979), Boudreaux and Long (1979), Ezzell and Porter (1979), Bloomfield and Ma (1975), Pettit (1975), McConnell and Sandberg (1975), Henderson (1979), and Nantell and Carlson (1975) show that this is also true for a perpetuity with a nonzero NPV. The conclusion is that both the traditional weighted average cost of capital and the alternative cost of capital are valid for any perpetuities. Miles and Ezzell (1980) show that the traditional weighted average cost of capital is appropriate for uneven cash flows, if there are no changes in the costs of equity and debt, the tax rate, or the capital structure. Keane (1976, 1979), Levacic and Rebmann-Huber (1979), and Partington (1979) also discuss the effect of differences in the timing of the tax deduction on interest payments.

priate cash flows and costs of capital are defined guarantee that the two methods will always agree.

You can't, however, mix the methods. For example, if you use the definition of cash flows from the traditional approach and the definition of the weighted average cost of capital from the alternative approach, you won't get the correct value for a project. Returning to the example, if you use the traditional cash flow of 12 and the alternative pre-tax cost of capital of 16%, you would mistakenly estimate a value of the project of 12/.16 = 75, when the true value is 80. Be alert, because it's easy to make this type of error.

In summary, there is more than one way to define the weighted average cost of capital, as long as you also use the appropriate definition for the cash flows. Since the traditional definition is the one that is most commonly used, that's the one used in the rest of this book.[22]

---

[22] There are certain cases where the alternative approach has some advantages. For example, subsidized debt, such as an industrial revenue bond, has a lower interest rate than does nonsubsidized debt. With the alternative approach, you can use the firm's marginal borrowing cost (i.e., the unsubsidized interest rate) when you estimate the cost of capital, and you can use the firm's actual interest expenses (which are based on the subsidized interest rate) when you estimate the project's cash flows. In most circumstances, however, it is easier to apply the traditional approach.

References

Ang, J.S. "Weighted Average Vs. True Cost of Capital." *Financial Management* 2(3) (Autumn 1973): 56–60.

Arditti, F.D. "The Weighted Average Cost of Capital: Some Questions on its Definition, Interpretation, and Use." *Journal of Finance* 28(4) (1973): 1001–1007.

————. "The Weighted Average Cost of Capital: Some Questions on its Definition, Interpretation, and Use: Reply." *Journal of Finance* 30(3) (1975): 889–892.

————. "A Survey of Valuation and the Cost of Capital." *Research in Finance* 2 (1980): 1–56.

Arditti, F.D., and H. Levy. "The Weighted Average Cost of Capital as a Cutoff Rate: A Critical Analysis of the Classical Textbook Weighted Average." *Financial Management* 6(3) (Autumn 1977): 24–34.

Arditti, F.D., and M.S. Tysseland. "Three Ways to Present the Marginal Cost of Capital." *Financial Management* 2(2) (Summer 1973): 63–67.

Ben-Horim, M. "Comment on 'The Weighted Average Cost of Capital as a Cutoff Rate'." *Financial Management* 8(2) (Summer 1979): 18–21.

Beranek, W. "The Cost of Capital, Capital Budgeting, and the Maximization of Shareholder Wealth." *Journal of Financial and Quantitative Analysis* 10(1) (1975a): 1–20.

————. "A Little More on the Weighted Average Cost of Capital." *Journal of Financial and Quantitative Analysis* 10(5) (1975b): 892–896.

Bierman, H., Jr. *Implementation of Capital Budgeting Techniques.* Tampa: Financial Management Association, 1986.

Bierman, H., Jr., and S. Smidt. *The Capital Budgeting Decision.* New York: Macmillan, 1960.

Bloomfield, T., and R. Ma. "The Weighted Average Cost of Capital: Some Questions on its Definition, Interpretation, and Use: Comment." *Journal of Finance* 30(3) (1975): 887–888.

Boness, A.J. "A Pedagogic Note on the Cost of Capital." *Journal of Finance* 19(1) (1964): 99–106.

Booth, L.D. "Stochastic Demand, Output and the Cost of Capital: A Clarification." *Journal of Finance* 35(3) (1980): 795–798.

Boudreaux, K.J., and H.W. Long. "The Weighted Average Cost of Capital as a Cutoff Rate: A Further Analysis." *Financial Management* 8(2) (Summer 1979): 7–14.

Brealey, R.A., and S.C. Myers. *Principles of Corporate Finance,* 3rd ed. New York: McGraw-Hill, 1988.

Durand, D. "The Cost of Capital, Corporation Finance, and the Theory of Investment: Comment." *American Economic Review* 49 (September 1959): 639–654.

Ezzell, J.R., and R.B. Porter. "Correct Specification of the Cost of Capital and Net Present Value." *Financial Management* 8(2) (Summer 1979): 15–17.

Findlay, M.C., III. "The Weighted Average Cost of Capital: Some Questions on its Definition, Interpretation, and Use: Comment." *Journal of Finance* 30(3) (1975): 879–880.

———. "The Weighted Average Cost of Capital and Finite Flows." *Journal of Business Finance and Accounting* 4(2) (1977): 217–227.

Grinyer, J.R. "Cost of Equity Capital." *Journal of Business Finance* 4(4) (1972): 44–52.

———. "The Cost of Equity Capital—A Reply." *Journal of Business Finance and Accounting* 2(3) (1975): 383–388.

Hemsted, J.R. "The Cost of Equity Capital—A Comment." *Journal of Business Finance and Accounting* 1(3) (1974): 445–448.

Henderson, G.V., Jr. "In Defense of the WACC." *Financial Management* 8(3) (Autumn 1979): 57–61.

Keane, S.M. "The Tax-Deductibility of Interest Payments and the Weighted Average Cost of Capital." *Journal of Business Finance and Accounting* 3(4) (1976): 53–61.

———. "The Tax-Deductibility of Interest Payments and the Weighted Average Cost of Capital—A Reply." *Journal of Business Finance and Accounting* 6(1) (1979): 111–114.

Levacic, R., and A. Rebmann-Huber. "The Tax-Deductibility of Interest Payments and the Weighted Average Cost of Capital Once Again." *Journal of Business Finance and Accounting* 6(1) (1979): 101–110.

Lewellen, W.G. "A Conceptual Reappraisal of Cost of Capital." *Financial Management* 3(4) (Winter 1974): 63–70.

Linke, C.M., and M.K. Kim. "More on the Weighted Average Cost of Capital: A Comment and Analysis." *Journal of Financial and Quantitative Analysis* 9(6) (1974): 1069–1080.

Long, M.S., and G.A. Racette. "Stochastic Demand, Output and the Cost of Capital." *Journal of Finance* 29(2) (1974): 499–506.

McConnell, J.J., and C.M. Sandberg. "The Weighted Average Cost of Capital: Some Questions on its Definition, Interpretation, and Use: Comment." *Journal of Finance* 30(3) (1975): 883–886.

Miles, J.A., and J.R. Ezzell. "The Weighted Average Cost of Capital, Perfect Capital Markets, and Project Life: A Clarification." *Journal of Financial and Quantitative Analysis* 15(3) (1980): 719–730.

Nantell, T.J., and C.R. Carlson. "The Cost of Capital as a Weighted Average." *Journal of Finance* 30(5) (1975): 1343–1355.

Partington, G.H. "The Tax-Deductibility of Interest Payments and the Weighted Average Cost of Capital: A Comment." *Journal of Business Finance and Accounting* 6(1) (1979): 95–100.

―――. "Financial Decisions, The Cost(s) of Capital and the Capital Asset Pricing Model." *Journal of Business Finance and Accounting* 8(1) (1981): 97–112.

Pettit, R.R. "The Weighted Average Cost of Capital: Some Questions on its Definition, Interpretation, and Use: Comment." *Journal of Finance* 30(3) (1975): 881–882.

Reilly, R.R., E.F. Brigham, C.M. Linke, M.H. Kim, and J.S. Ang. "Weighted Average Vs. True Cost of Capital: Reilly, Brigham, Linke, and Kim Versus Ang." *Financial Management* 3(1) (Spring 1974): 80–85.

Reilly, R.R., and W.E. Wecker. "On the Weighted Average Cost of Capital." *Journal of Financial and Quantitative Analysis* 8(1) (1973): 123–126.

―――. "On the Weighted Average Cost of Capital: Reply." *Journal of Financial and Quantitative Analysis* 10(2) (1975): 367.

Riener, K.D. "A Pedagogic Note on the Cost of Capital with Personal Taxes and Risky Debt." *Financial Review* 20(2) (1985): 229–235.

Shapiro, A.C. "In Defense of the Traditional Weighted Average Cost of Capital as a Cutoff Rate." *Financial Management* 8(2) (Summer 1979): 22–23.

―――. *Modern Corporate Finance.* New York: Macmillan, 1989.

Solomon, E. *The Theory of Financial Management.* New York: Columbia University Press, 1963.

Taggart, R.A., Jr. "Consistent Valuation and Cost of Capital Expressions with Corporate and Personal Taxes." *Financial Management* 20(3) (Autumn 1991): 8–20.

Chapter 3

How to Estimate Your Weighted Average Cost of Capital

*T*his chapter will show how to estimate your company's cost of capital, which is the weighted average cost of capital that you should use when discounting the cash flows of a proposed project.[1] There are two major steps in measuring a company's cost of capital. The first step is to estimate the cost of each separate component in the capital structure; Section I explains this process and provides numerous examples. The second step is to estimate the weights of each component in the capital structure; Section II discusses this in detail.

Keep in mind that estimating the cost of capital is not an exact science. By way of comparison, suppose you have to estimate the speed of light, which is a physical constant governed by the laws of nature. How is estimating the speed of light different from estimating the cost of capital? First, you begin the process by knowing that there is an exact measurement that equals the speed of light, and that your estimate will be increasingly accurate, the more digits you can estimate to the right of the decimal point. Second, you know that there is no place in the process for reasoned judgment when you estimate the speed of light. In other words, two rational scientists using perfectly accurate instruments would never reach different conclusions.

These two points are applicable for scientists who estimate the speed of light, but not to you when you estimate your company's cost

---

[1] As explained in Chapter 2, this is really a weighted average "marginal" cost of capital, as it is the cost of capital that your firm would incur if you undertake the additional marginal investment required by the proposed project.

of capital. As the next two sections show, you will have to exercise quite a bit of judgment when you estimate your cost of capital. Section III shows how to conduct a sensitivity analysis to measure how much your estimate of the cost of capital changes under different sets of reasonable assumptions.

Before plunging into the estimation techniques of Section I, you need to be aware of some limitations in this chapter. First, if the project in question is not an average project but is very different from your company's existing projects, you will have to modify the techniques used in this chapter.[2] Second, if your company doesn't have publicly traded stock, you will have to modify the techniques in this chapter, since they require that you have access to market prices for your company's stock. You run into this same problem if you want to estimate the cost of capital for a specific division within your company, even if your company's stock is publicly traded. Chapter 4 explains these issues in detail and shows how to make the necessary modifications.

It's also important to make a distinction between normal projects and strategic investments. Gallinger and Henderson (1985, p. 126) define a strategic investment as one that "will alter the basic character of the firm." If your proposed project has so much synergy with the rest of your firm that it changes the riskiness of your company's existing projects, your project is a strategic investment. If your proposed project has so much flexibility that managers can respond to future changes in the business environment in such a way as to alter the size or riskiness of the project's cash flows, your project is a strategic investment. The development of computer software by a computer hardware manufacturer, the introduction of a new product or product group, and the acquisition of a flexible manufacturing line are examples of strategic investments.

The discounted cash flow technique usually isn't appropriate for strategic investments. Chapter 8 discusses strategic investments in detail and describes some alternative valuation approaches to DCF that may be more appropriate for these investments.

I. Estimating Costs for the Separate Components of Capital Structure

The three major components in most capital structures are common equity, preferred equity, and debt. Section I.A shows how to

---

[2] This is also true if your project will not have the same capital structure as the rest of your firm. This is relatively unusual, but occasionally there are special financing

estimate the cost of common equity, Section I.B shows how to estimate the cost of preferred stock, and Section I.C shows how to estimate the costs of short- and long-term debt. Section I.D discusses costs of some of the other sources of financing in a capital structure. The estimation techniques of these sections implicitly assume that the components of the capital structure are measured according to their market values.[3] Section II discusses in detail the issue of market values versus book values.

I.A. The Cost of Common Equity

The two most commonly used methods for estimating the cost of common equity are the dividend growth model approach and the capital asset pricing model (CAPM) approach. Sections I.A.1 and I.A.2 describe these approaches in detail. These sections also include numerous examples that illustrate how to apply the two approaches. The appendix to this chapter describes several less commonly used approaches for estimating the cost of common equity.

I.A.1. Using Dividend Growth Models to Estimate the Cost of Common Equity

Although the principles underlying the dividend growth model approach have been known for over fifty years, it remains one of the most frequently used approaches used for estimating the cost of equity.[4] In a survey of *Fortune* 1000 firms, Gitman and Mercurio (1982) find that almost 30% of the respondents report using a dividend growth model.[5] Brigham (1975) surveyed 33 large corporations; although he does not report the exact percentage, he states that most of them use the dividend growth model.

---

arrangements specifically associated with a particular project. Examples are industrial revenue bonds or use of banking consortiums that finance offshore oil fields. Section II provides more discussion of the capital structure issue and how it affects the cost of capital.

[3] Williams and Findlay (1979) provide an interesting discussion of the relationship between market-based estimators of the cost of capital and static equilibrium conditions. They conclude that if markets are ex ante rational, then all projects must have a zero NPV.

[4] Williams (1938) is usually credited with the initial development of the concepts underlying the dividend growth model.

[5] Gitman and Mercurio (1982) report that another 35.6% of the respondents use the "return required by investors." This expression is somewhat ambiguous and could mean a number of different methods. It is likely, however, that at least some of these respondents are referring to a dividend growth model.

What is the dividend growth model? The basic idea is that the price of a stock is the present value of all future dividends.[6] P_0 denotes the price of the stock as it is observed at time 0, D_t denotes the dividend that is paid at time t, and r_E denotes the cost of equity.[7] Using these definitions, the dividend growth model is:

$$P_0 = \sum_{t=1}^{\infty} \frac{D_t}{(1 + r_E)^t} \tag{3.1}$$

You know the current price of the stock, P_0, since the stock in your company is publicly traded. If you could estimate the future dividends, you could simply solve equation (3.1) by finding the value for the cost of equity, r_E, that makes equation (3.1) true; this is equivalent to finding the internal rate of return on the stock. Of course, it would be a little difficult to implement the model in this form, since you would have to estimate an infinite stream of future dividends and store this infinite stream of numbers in a computer while the computer calculates the internal rate of return. Even with recent advances in computer technology, this is still an impossible task.

Gordon and Shapiro (1956) had a valuable insight that allowed them to evaluate this infinite stream of dividends: they assume that the future dividends are a function of time. In particular, they assume that the dividends will grow at a constant rate.[8] Let g denote this constant growth rate and let D_0 denote the current dividend. You can express the dividend at any time in the future as a function of time, the growth rate, and the current dividend:

$$D_t = D_0 (1 + g)^t \tag{3.2}$$

---

[6] See Shapiro (1989) or any other good finance textbook for other descriptions of this approach.

[7] The price, P_0, and the dividends, D_t, are nominal values; i.e., they are not "real" values that have been reduced to adjust for future inflation. This means that the cost of equity, r_E, is the nominal cost of equity and not the real cost of equity. Chapter 5 gives a more detailed description of inflation and its effects on the cost of capital.

[8] The assumption of a constant growth rate in dividends generally requires the assumptions of constant growth in earnings and a constant dividend payout rate; a consequence of these assumptions is that the stock price itself is expected to grow at a constant rate. Notice also that a constant growth rate of the dividend must be less than the long-term growth rate of the economy, or the firm would grow to be larger than the entire economy.

If you substitute this equation into equation (3.1), you will get the infinite geometric series:

$$P_0 = \sum_{t=1}^{\infty} D_0 \left[\frac{1 + g}{1 + r_E} \right]^t \tag{3.3}$$

Suppose the growth rate, g, is greater than or equal to the cost of equity, r_E. This means that the term in brackets is greater than or equal to one. But if you add an infinite number of values that are all greater than or equal to one, you're going to get an infinite value. This would imply that the stock has an infinite price. Therefore, the growth rate must be less than the cost of equity. Notice that as the growth rate approaches the cost of equity, the price of the stock gets larger and larger.

If the growth rate is less than the cost of equity, which it must be to make the bracketed term less than one, the infinite series in equation (3.3) converges to a finite value. In fact, the infinite summation can be replaced with a closed form solution:[9]

$$P_0 = D_0 \frac{(1 + g)}{(r_E - g)} = \frac{D_1}{r_E - g} \tag{3.4}$$

This simple formula is commonly known as the dividend growth model.[10] If you take the estimate of the growth rate, g, and the most recently observed dividend, D_0, you can estimate the next dividend, D_1. Using the observed value of the current price, P_0, you can solve equation (3.4) for the cost of equity:

$$r_E = \frac{D_1}{P_0} + g \tag{3.5}$$

The result in equation (3.5) implies that the cost of equity is equal to the expected dividend yield plus the expected growth rate.

Suppose your company has a current price of $26.25 per share, a current dividend of $2 per share, and an expected growth rate in

---

[9] Suppose that $x = \sum_{n=1}^{\infty} a^n$. This infinite series converges to $x = a/(1 - a)$. If you substitute $(1 + g)/(1 + r_E)$ for a, you will get equation (3.4).

[10] Sometimes it is referred to as the Gordon Growth Model.

dividends of 5% per year. Exhibit 3.1 shows the estimated cost of equity.[11] Exhibit 3.1 also shows how sensitive this estimate is to different assumptions about the growth rate.

The rest of this section will show you how to apply the dividend growth model to your company. Section I.A.1.a describes techniques for estimating the growth rate; this section also has several numerical examples to illustrate the techniques. Section I.A.1.b shows how to

Exhibit 3.1: Estimating the Cost of Equity Using the Constant Dividend Growth Model

---

Baseline Scenario

The current stock price is $26.25 per share, and the most recent dividend is $2.00 per share. The assumed constant growth rate in dividends is 5% per year. Using equation (3.5), the estimated cost of equity is found to be:

$$r_E = \frac{2(1 + .05)}{26.25} + .05 = .08 + .05 = .13$$

The estimated cost of equity is 13%. Notice that this is the sum of the expected dividend yield (8%) and the expected growth rate in dividends (5%).

Sensitivity Analysis

Suppose you are uncertain about the exact growth rate in dividends, but you think it will be somewhere between 3% and 7%. A table shows the estimated cost of equity under different assumptions about the dividend growth rate.

Growth Rate	3.00%	3.50%	4.00%	4.50%	5.00%	5.50%	6.00%	6.50%	7.00%
Cost of Equity	10.85%	11.39%	11.92%	12.46%	13.00%	13.54%	14.08%	14.61%	15.15%

As you can see, the estimated cost of equity is very sensitive to the estimated growth rate. Notice that the cost of equity is approximately equal to the baseline expected dividend yield of 8% plus the growth rate. The reason that this relationship is approximate is because the expected dividend yield changes as the expected growth rate changes.

---

[11] The examples in this section assume annual dividends because this makes the numerical examples easier to understand. The same concepts apply to the more realistic case of quarterly dividends.

apply the constant dividend growth model, and Section I.A.1.c explains how to relax the assumption of a constant growth rate by allowing the growth rate to change over time. Section I.A.1.d describes several refinements and modifications of the basic approach such as the accommodation of quarterly rather than annual dividends.[12]

I.A.1.a. Estimating the Dividend Growth Rate

There are two primary approaches to choosing the dividend growth rate. The first uses forecasts from analysts, and the second uses historical and current financial data.

Analysts' Forecasts

Since your objective is to find the expected dividend growth rate, you could use a forecast of the future growth rates from financial analysts. There are many different organizations that report forecasted growth rates. For example, IBES (Institutional Brokers' Estimates System) collects expected growth rates from numerous financial analysts and reports an average growth rate based on the analyst forecasts.[13] The Value Line Investment Survey also provides estimates of future dividend growth. For example, Value Line reports in the July 31, 1992, volume that IBM had a 3.5% growth in dividends during the past ten years and a 2.0% growth rate during the past five years. Value Line projects a 5.0% growth rate in dividends from 1992 through 1997.[14]

There are many studies showing that analysts' forecasts are better predictors of actual growth rates than are predictors based solely on historical information. Also, the results of valuation models, such as the dividend growth model, are typically more accurate when the growth rate comes from analyst forecasts.[15] Therefore, you should use analyst forecasts as an estimate of your company's expected dividend growth rate, if such forecasts are available.

---

[12] See Farrell (1985) for a description of the dividend growth model within the context of portfolio management.

[13] IBES, Inc. is a subsidiary of Citibank.

[14] There are other methods for estimating the growth rate. One particularly promising method is that of Ben-Horim and Callen (1989), who use Tobin's q to estimate the growth rate in dividends.

[15] For example, see Chatfield, Hein, and Moyer (1990), Vander Weide and Carleton (1987–1988), and Brown and Rozeff (1978, 1979–1980).

If analyst forecasts are not available for your company, you must use historical financial data. There are two approaches that use such data. The first is the time series method, which uses the historical time series of dividends to estimate the growth rate. The second is the sustainable growth method, which estimates the dividend growth rate by using the relationship between the amount that the company reinvests in itself and the rate of return on those reinvestments.

The Historical Time Series Approach

Exhibit 3.2 presents selected data for a hypothetical company, UTF, Inc. Using data for the past ten years, we find the average growth rate in dividends for UTF has been approximately 4.4%, using an arithmetic average of each annual growth rate.[16]

Another way to estimate the growth rate is to calculate the geometric average growth rate; this is sometimes called a "compound

Exhibit 3.2: Selected Data for UTF, Inc. (net income, shareholders equity, and dividends reported in $ million)

Year	Net Income	Shareholders' Equity	Annual Dividends	Annual Growth Rate in Dividends	Plowback Ratio	Return on Equity
1981	100	821	44		.56	12.2%
1982	76	866	46	4.2%	.40	8.8%
1983	118	891	47	2.1%	.60	13.2%
1984	117	945	49	4.1%	.58	12.4%
1985	101	983	51	3.9%	.50	10.3%
1986	73	1,042	53	3.8%	.27	7.0%
1987	100	1,094	57	7.0%	.43	9.1%
1988	141	1,154	60	5.0%	.57	12.2%
1989	159	1,206	63	4.8%	.60	13.2%
1990	155	1,272	66	4.5%	.57	12.2%
Average				4.4%	.50	10.9%

---

[16] Let g_t denote the growth rate in dividends during the year t. If there are T years, the arithmetic average is: $\sum_{t=1}^{T} g_t / T$.

growth rate."[17] You can estimate growth this way by solving the equation:

$$44 (1 + g)^{10} = 66 \qquad (3.6)$$

Solving this equation for g gives an estimated geometric growth rate of approximately 4.1%.[18]

The Sustainable Growth Method

The sustainable growth method states that the growth rate in dividends is:[19]

$$g = (\text{plowback ratio}) (\text{return on equity}) \qquad (3.7)$$

If you use the average values of the plowback ratio and return on equity of .50 and 10.9%, respectively, you get a sustainable dividend growth rate of approximately 5.4%.

Comparing the Approaches

The historical arithmetic average growth rate is 4.4%, the historical geometric average growth rate is 4.1%, and the historical sustainable growth rate is 5.4%. Which of these is "correct"? The answer is "None!" Which of these is a reasonable estimate? The answer is "All of them."

There are several reasons for this apparent contradiction. Keep in mind that you are trying to estimate the future growth rate, not the past growth rate. Using the past to estimate the future is reasonable, but it's certainly not going to produce a perfect predictor of the future growth rate.[20] Notice that these estimated growth rates used ten years of data; maybe you would want to use fewer years if you think your growth rate has changed during the ten-year interval. You might want to use an estimation procedure that gives more weight to the most recent observations if you believe these observations most accurately

---

[17] Let D_0 denote the dividend at time 0, D_T the dividend at time T, and g the geometric, or compounded, growth rate. The compound growth rate is found by solving the equation for g: $D_0 (1 + g)^T = D_T$.

[18] The geometric average is always less than the arithmetic average.

[19] See Shapiro (1989) or any financial management textbook for an explanation of why this formula is appropriate.

[20] If you believe that the future will be exactly like the past, the geometric growth rate might be most appropriate, since the dividend growth model assumes that dividends will grow at a compounded growth rate.

reflect the current state of your company.[21] The most important point is to realize that there are many reasonable approaches that will give different, but reasonable, estimates.

The two previous approaches share a common trait: they rely on historical data. But what you really need is an estimate of future growth. Consider that there are many companies that had high dividend growth during a fairly long period but, for various reasons, you might expect these companies to have much lower growth in subsequent periods. While there is not explicit formula for adjusting the historical growth rate, it would obviously be wrong to use an unadjusted historical rate for such a company. You and your company's management team probably have pretty good insight with respect to your company's growth prospects. Therefore, you might want to take the historical estimate and use your own judgment to adjust it so that it better reflects your expected growth.

I.A.1.b. *Applying the Dividend Growth Model*

What is the cost of common equity for UTF? UTF has 10 million shares of stock, which means that the 1990 dividend per share is $6.60. The stock price at the beginning of 1990 is $98 per share; during 1989 the price ranged from a low of $92 to a high of $115. The dividend growth model of equation (3.5) assumes that you will use the current price, which is $98. In utility rate case hearings it's a common practice to use an average price during a recent period. Your best bet is to see how sensitive the estimated cost of equity is to your choice of price.

The same logic applies to your choice of growth rate. Looking at historical growth rates, you might judge the future growth rate of UTF to be somewhere between 4.1% and 5.1%, with 4.6% representing a reasonable choice. Exhibit 3.3 shows the estimated cost of common equity using these assumptions.

The "most likely" estimate of the cost of equity is for a growth rate of 4.6% and a stock price of $98. The cost of equity result is shown in bold in Exhibit 3.3 and is approximately 11.3%. Notice that the other "reasonable" estimates for the cost of equity in Exhibit 3.3 range from a low of 9.8% to a high of 12.3%. As you can see, small changes in the inputs to the model produce fairly large changes in the estimated cost of equity.

---

[21] For example, you might want to use a moving weighted average or exponential smoothing.

Exhibit 3.3: Estimating the Cost of Common Equity for UTF (the dividend growth model)

Estimate of Stock Price	Estimate of Growth Rate		
	4.1%	4.6%	5.1%
92	11.3%	11.8%	12.3%
98	10.8%	**11.3%**	11.8%
115	9.8%	10.3%	10.8%

Note: The current dividend is $6.60.

I.A.1.c. *Multistage Growth Models*

For many companies, it may not be reasonable to assume constant growth. For example, Microsoft Corporation and Phar-mor Incorporated almost certainly grew more rapidly during the 1980s than they will grow in the 1990s. Since a company's growth rate in dividends may not be constant, how can you modify the dividend growth model to estimate the cost of equity? That's the question this section answers.

The key to modifying the growth model is recognizing the long-term impact of economic competition. For example, high growth will attract other firms into the industry. At some point the extra competition will cause the growth rates for all the firms to decrease to a steady state rate that is profitable enough to keep firms in business but is not so profitable that additional firms are attracted to the industry. Therefore, the presence of economic competition means that it's reasonable to assume a constant long-term growth rate.

The multistage growth model incorporates nonconstant short-term growth rates with the more realistic condition of a constant long-term growth rate. Let's assume your firm is having exceptional growth now, but that you expect it to level off at a steady state long-term rate within the next six years. This means there are five years before the growth rate becomes constant. You can rewrite the basic stock valuation model in equation (3.1) to reflect this new condition:[22]

$$P_0 = \sum_{t=1}^{5} \frac{D_t}{(1 + r_E)^t} + \sum_{t=6}^{\infty} \frac{D_5 (1 + g)^{t-5}}{(1 + r_E)^t} \tag{3.8}$$

Equation (3.8) states that the price of the stock is equal to the discounted present value of all future dividends. The only difference

---

[22] This example assumes annual dividend payments, but the approach can easily be extended to accommodate the case of quarterly dividends.

between this and equation (3.1) is that the dividends from the sixth year on are expressed in the second summation as the product of the dividend in fifth year, D_5, and the compounded constant growth rate that occurs after the fifth year, $(1 + g)^{t-5}$.

With a little algebra, you can rewrite equation (3.8) as:

$$P_0 = \sum_{t=1}^{5} \frac{D_t}{(1 + r_E)^t} + \frac{\sum_{t=1}^{\infty} D_5 \left[\dfrac{1 + g}{1 + r_E} \right]^t}{(1 + r_E)^5} \qquad (3.9)$$

Notice that the numerator of the fraction in the second term of equation (3.9) is an infinite geometric series. Using the same substitution for this infinite series as you did to get equation (3.3), equation (3.9) becomes:

$$P_0 = \sum_{t=1}^{5} \frac{D_t}{(1 + r_E)^t} + \frac{D_5 \left[\dfrac{1 + g}{r_E - g} \right]}{(1 + r_E)^5} \qquad (3.10)$$

Equation (3.3) implies that the expected price of the stock at time 5, P_5, is:

$$P_5 = D_5 \left[\frac{1 + g}{r_E - g} \right] \qquad (3.11)$$

If you substitute this into equation (3.10), you get:

$$P_0 = \sum_{t=1}^{5} \frac{D_t}{(1 + r_E)^t} + \frac{P_5}{(1 + r_E)^5} \qquad (3.12)$$

$$= \sum_{t=1}^{4} \frac{D_t}{(1 + r_E)^t} + \frac{D_5 + P_5}{(1 + r_E)^5}$$

You can observe the current stock price, P_0, since the stock is publicly traded. If you forecast the dividends through the fifth year (D_1 through D_5) and estimate the long-term growth rate (g), then the only unknown in equation (3.12) is the cost of equity, r_E. There is no simple closed-form solution to this equation for the cost of equity, r_E. However, through trial and error, you can quickly find the cost of equity that makes equation (3.10) true.

Here's an example that illustrates the multistage growth model. Suppose a company has a current dividend of $1 and current price of $50. Recent dividend growth has been about 15% per year. From your analysis of this industry, you conclude that after five more years of high growth the long-term growth rate for dividends will drop to about 8% per year. Exhibit 3.4 is a worksheet that finds the cost of equity.

The second column of Exhibit 3.4 shows estimates of the dividend growth rates for each of the next five years. There is no single best way to estimate these rates. You should do sensitivity analysis using several reasonable patterns.

To find the internal rate of return of equation (3.12), which is the cost of equity, you need to know the current price, the dividends in years 1 through 5, and the expected price at year 5. Of these required

Exhibit 3.4: A Multistage Growth Model

Year	Dividend Growth Rate	Forecasted Dividend	Total Expected Cash Flows (Including payment of the current value and receipt of the year 5 price)	
0			($50.00)	
1	15%	$1.15	$1.15	
2	13%	$1.30	$1.30	
3	11%	$1.44	$1.44	
4	10%	$1.59	$1.59	
5	9%	$1.73	$75.50	
Current Price =	$50		IRR of Expected Cash Flows =	**10.53%**
Current Dividend =	$1			
Long-Term Growth Rate =	8%			
Expected Price at Year 5 =	$73.77			
Cost of Equity =	**10.53%**			

inputs, only the price at year 5 is unknown. Unfortunately, equation (3.11) shows that you need to know the cost of equity in order to determine the price at year 5. In other words, you need to know the cost of equity in order to estimate the cost of equity.

There is a simple way to resolve this problem of circularity. At the lower left in the spreadsheet you make an initial guess for the cost of equity. Using this guess, the dividend at year 5, and the long-term growth rate, you can estimate the expected price at year 5; this is shown in the cell above the cost of equity. You add this expected price to the dividend at year 5 to find the cash flow at year 5; the fourth column shows the cash flows for each period, including the initial estimated "cost" of the stock.

The spreadsheet calculates the internal rate of return for the cash flows; this is shown below the column of cash flows. If this is not the same as your initial guess for the cost of equity, you should try another value for your guess. After just a few iterations, you will find a guess for the cost of equity so that your guess equals the internal rate of return for the cash flows. In this example, the cost of equity is 10.53%.

In this example, the growth rate becomes constant after five years. You could just as easily model this with the growth rate becoming constant at any time.[23] If you use a multistage growth model, you should always perform sensitivity analysis with respect to the assumed time at which the growth rate becomes constant. You should also check the sensitivity of the results with respect to the inputs, which are the estimated growth rates in each period and the estimated long-term growth rate. For example, a change in the long-term growth rate from 8% to 6% changes the estimated cost of equity from 10.53% to 8.72%. If you leave the long-term constant growth rate at 8% but let the growth rate decline faster, the cost of equity changes from 10.53% to 10.04%.[24]

This type of sensitivity analysis is very easy if you construct a spreadsheet similar to the one in Exhibit 3.4. Given the sensitivity of the model to your choice of inputs and the relative ease of the sensitivity analysis, you should always do some sensitivity analysis to determine the most likely range for your estimated cost of capital.

---

[23] See Holt (1962) for a suggested approach for finding the time at which growth rates become constant in a multistage model.

[24] The new growth rates are 15%, 11%, 9%, 8.5%, and 8.2%.

I.A.1.d. Refinements in the Basic Dividend Growth Model

Finally, there are two potential problems to recognize. The first is the assumption of a constant dividend growth rate, and the second is the assumption that there is a full period between the current date and the date of the first dividend. There are ways to handle these problems.

Keep in mind that these are refinements of the basic model. Therefore, the change in the estimated cost of equity usually is very small.

Adjusting for Quarterly Dividend Payments

Even if the annual rate is constant, most firms change dividends only once a year. This means that instead of growing smoothly, dividends actually grow in a step fashion, with constant quarterly dividend payments during the year.

Siegel (1985) provides an approximation of the constant growth model in equation (3.4) that corrects for the case of constant quarterly dividend payments with annual changes in the dividend. Let D^* denote the most recently paid quarterly dividend, and let N denote the number of quarters since the firm last changed the dividend. If g^* is the quarterly growth rate, you can redefine the adjusted current dividend as:

$$D_0^* = D^* [1 + g^* (N - 1.5)] \qquad (3.13)$$

To apply Siegel's correction, all you have to do is to use this adjusted value of D_0^* in the quarterly version of equation (3.4).

For example, suppose you want to adjust the cost of equity for UTF, the company in Exhibit 3.3. UTF pays quarterly dividends on the last day of March, June, September, and December. The current date is January 1.

Your first step is to find the quarterly growth rate. Your most likely estimate of annual growth is 4.6%; you must convert it to a quarterly basis. Siegel suggests the conversion:

$$g^* = (1 + g)^{.25} - 1 \qquad (3.14)$$

If you apply this formula to UTF's annual growth rate of 4.6%, you will get a quarterly growth rate of 1.131%.

It has been four quarters since UTF has changed the dividend; therefore, $N = 4$. The most recently paid dividend is $6.60/4$, which is $1.65. Using equation (3.13), the adjusted current dividend is:

$$D_0^* = 1.65\,[1 + .01131\,(4 - 1.5)] = 1.697 \qquad (3.15)$$

You can find the quarterly cost of equity by using equation (3.4):

$$r_E^* = \frac{1.697}{98} + 0.0113 = 2.86\% \qquad (3.16)$$

You can convert this to an annual cost of equity:

$$r_E = (1 + 0.0286)^4 - 1 = 11.94\% \qquad (3.17)$$

Notice that this corrected value of differs from the 11.3% shown in Exhibit 3.3, which ignores the quarterly aspect of dividend payments.

Notice that it also is different from the rate you get if you simply find the quarterly cost of equity using the unadjusted quarterly dividend. For example, if you replace the adjusted quarterly dividend of 1.697 with the unadjusted value of 1.65 in equation (3.16), you would get a quarterly cost of equity equal to 2.81%. This is equivalent to an annual rate of 11.72%.

The correction produces a relatively small change in the cost of equity. Even though the corrected rate of 11.94% is similar to the uncorrected rates, the amount of effort required to make the adjustment is small.

Linke and Zumwalt (1984) show another method for accommodating quarterly dividends. They show that the annual cost of equity can be found by solving the equation:

$$r_E = \frac{\left[\begin{array}{c} D_{1,Q1}\,(1 + r_E)^{.75} + D_{1,Q2}\,(1 + r_E)^{.5} \\ + D_{1,Q3}\,(1 + r_E)^{.25} + D_{1,Q4} \end{array}\right]}{P_0} + g \qquad (3.18)$$

where $D_{1,Qi}$ is the expected dividend in the next year during the ith quarter. It is defined as:

$$D_{1,Qi} = D_{0,Qi} (1 + g) \qquad (3.19)$$

where $D_{0,Qi}$ is the most recently observed dividend during the ith quarter.

The spreadsheet in Exhibit 3.5 applies the Linke-Zumwalt correction to UTF. Notice that you must use trial and error to find the value of the cost of equity, r_E, that makes equation (3.18) true, as there is no way to algebraically solve for r_E.

If you knew the cost of equity, you could evaluate the right-hand side of equation (3.18). The lower left corner of the spreadsheet shows an initial trial value for the cost of equity. The spreadsheet in Exhibit 3.5 uses this trial value to calculate the right-hand side of equation (3.18); this value is shown in the spreadsheet just above the initial trial value (the right-hand side of equation (3.18) should equal the cost of equity). If the calculated right-hand side of equation (3.18) is different from the trial value for the cost of equity, you need to try a different value for the cost of equity. Using the spreadsheet in Exhibit 3.5, it only takes a few iterations to find the correct cost of equity.

Exhibit 3.5: Linke-Zumwalt Adjustment for Quarterly Dividends

Annual Growth Rate =	4.60%			
Current Stock Price =	$98			
	Quarter 1	Quarter 2	Quarter 3	Quarter 4
Last Year's Dividend	1.65	1.65	1.65	1.65
Expected Dividend for Next Year	1.73	1.73	1.73	1.73
Numerator in Bracket of Equation (3.18)	1.88	1.83	1.78	1.73
Calculated Right-hand Side of Equation (3.18) =	11.95%			
Trial Value for Cost of Equity =	11.95%			

Notice that the Linke-Zumwalt value of 11.95% is slightly different from the Siegel value of 11.94%. This is because Siegel uses an approximation, while Linke uses an exact formula. There is a small cost associated with the increased accuracy of the Linke-Zumwalt approach: Linke-Zumwalt requires an iterative search for the cost of equity, something that Siegel does not require, although this iterative search is easy to perform using a spreadsheet on a microcomputer.

The Time Until the First Dividend Payment

A second potential problem is caused by the date on which you are estimating the cost of equity. The previous models assume that there is exactly one period between the date on which you are using the model and the date on which the first dividend payment occurs. Siegel (1985) provides a correction when there is not a full quarter between the current date and the next dividend payment date.

Suppose the current date (the date on which you are using the model) is between dividend payment dates. Let p denote the proportion of the period that has elapsed since the last payment. For example, if your company makes quarterly dividend payments, and it has been one month since the last payment, p would be equal to one-third. Let P_p denote the current price (the price that is p periods after the last dividend payment) and D_1^* denote the next quarterly dividend [after making Siegel's adjustment from equation (3.13)]. You can adjust the price that you use in the model by making the correction:

$$P_0^* = (P_p - pD_1^*) (1 - g^*p) \qquad (3.20)$$

To apply this correction, you would simply use this value of price, P_0^*, in the model of equation (3.4).

For example, suppose it is November 15, and you want to estimate the cost of equity for UTF. The last dividend payment was on September 30, and the next will be on December 31; therefore, the proportion of elapsed time, p, is equal to .5. Suppose the observed price on November 15 is $98. If you use the same quarterly dividend growth rate of 1.13%, the adjusted price, based on equation (3.20), is:

$$P_0^* = [98 - (1.697) (.5)] [1 - .01131) (.5)] = 96.602 \qquad (3.21)$$

Using the quarterly version of equation (3.4), this gives a quarterly cost of equity equal to:

$$r_E = \frac{1.697}{96.602} + .0113 = 2.888\% \tag{3.22}$$

Therefore, the annualized cost of equity for UTF, as estimated on November 15, is 12.06%.

I.A.2. Using the Capital Asset Pricing Model to Estimate the Cost of Equity

A second major approach for estimating the cost of equity is the capital asset pricing model approach.[25] CAPM specifies an explicit relationship between the expected return on an asset and the risk of that asset. The expected return is the return required by investors, which means that the expected return for a stock is equal to the company's cost of equity. This implies a conceptually straightforward process for estimating the cost of equity: you measure the risk of your company's stock and then use CAPM to "translate" that risk into the cost of equity.

The primary objective of this section is to provide an intuitive explanation for CAPM and show how to use it to estimate your company's cost of equity. Section I.A.2.a defines the basic CAPM. Section I.A.2.b shows how to estimate beta, one of the parameters in CAPM. Section I.A.2.c shows how to estimate the risk-free rate and the market premium, which are the other parameters required by CAPM. Section I.A.2.d demonstrates how to apply these parameters when you estimate the cost of equity; the section also shows you how sensitive your estimated cost of capital is to the different choices you make with respect to CAPM's parameters.

I.A.2.a. *CAPM and its Relationship to the Cost of Equity*

CAPM is a simple model that relates risk and return. Let R_i denote the return on an asset, R_f the return on a risk-free asset and R_m the return on the entire market of assets (don't worry right now about how

---

[25] See Sharpe (1964), Lintner (1965), Mossin (1966), and Black (1972) for the development of the CAPM.

to measure these returns, because the rest of this section explains that in detail).[26]

CAPM states that the expected return on the asset is:

$$E[R_i] = R_f + \beta_i (E[R_m - R_f])$$ (3.23)

The beta of the security, denoted by β_i in equation (3.23), is the relevant measure of risk for security i. Beta is the covariance between the security's return and the market's return, divided by the variance of the market's return. In other words, beta measures a company's volatility relative to the entire market. If a company has a beta exactly equal to one, the company has the same risk as the market itself. If the market goes up, the company's stock will probably go up; if the market goes down, the company's stock will probably go down. If a company has a beta that is greater than one, its stock will probably go up higher than the market, if the market is going up; it also will go down farther than the market, if the market is falling. The reverse is true for a company with a beta less than one. A low beta firm is less sensitive to swings in the market.

If you want to use the CAPM to measure your company's cost of equity, you need an estimate of your company's beta, an estimate of the risk-free rate, and an estimate of the expected market premium, $E[R_m - R_f]$. The next three sections show you how to choose estimates for these parameters.

I.A.2.b. *Estimating Beta*

There are several ways to find an estimate of your company's beta. The easiest is to simply look it up in one of the many published sources. One such source is the Value Line Investment Survey, which reports the betas and other financial information for many companies. For example, the July 31, 1992, volume of the Value Line Investment Survey reports a beta of .95 for IBM.[27]

An alternative is to estimate beta yourself. The most commonly used method is with a simple regression, with the return on your

---

[26] These returns are holding-period returns. For example, suppose the price of the asset at time $t - 1$ is P_{t-1}, the price at time t is P_t, and the asset paid dividends of D_t during the period from $t - 1$ to t. The return is defined as: $(P_t - P_{t-1} + D_t)/P_{t-1}$.

[27] Value Line estimates the return on a stock by calculating its weekly percentage price change. The return on the market is estimated by calculating the weekly percentage change in the New York Stock Exchange Composite Index. Five years of weekly data are used. Value Line adjusts the historical beta to reflect a regression to the mean.

company as the dependent variable and the return on the market as the independent variable.[28] The slope of the regression is an estimate of beta.

Although this approach sounds quite simple, there are a number of issues to be resolved before you can actually apply the approach. A discussion of these issues and a comprehensive example using actual data follow.

Choosing the Market Index

The first choice is the index you will use for the return on the market. Theory makes three suggestions: (1) the market portfolio should include as many securities as possible, (2) the returns for the securities should include any dividend payments as well as price changes, and (3) the securities in the market portfolio should not be an equally weighted average, but market value-weighted. An index like the Dow Jones Industrial Average falls short on all three counts: (1) it includes only 30 securities, (2) it doesn't include dividends, and (3) it isn't value-weighted.[29] Most researchers use the Chicago Center for Research in Security Prices (CRSP) value-weighted index, which includes dividends. If you don't have access to such an index, a reasonable alternative would be the NYSE composite index or the Wilshire 5000 Equity Index, although these indexes don't include dividends.

The inability to specify the true market portfolio introduces an econometric problem called "errors in variables." If the market index you choose is highly correlated with the true market index, the resulting bias in your estimated beta will be fairly small. Since most large, well-diversified indexes are highly correlated with one another, they are probably also highly correlated with the true market index.[30]

---

[28] Most textbooks also show an approach in which you specify future states of nature; e.g., you might divide the next year into three possibilities: pessimistic, most likely, and optimistic. For each state you would estimate the probability of the state occurring, the return on your stock, and the return for the stock market. Using these values, you can easily estimate the variance of the market return and the covariance between your company stock and the market. For an example, see Shapiro (1989, pp. 118–120). This approach is conceptually appealing, but is very difficult to implement in practice.

[29] The Dow Jones Industrial Average (DJIA) is a "price-weighted" index. The level of the DJIA is found by summing the prices of the 30 stocks and then dividing by an adjustment factor that takes into account stock splits and other changes. See Reilly (1985) for more details about the construction of market indexes.

[30] There is debate as to whether any index is adequate. Roll (1977) suggests that it is impossible either to test the CAPM or to use it for evaluating the performance of portfolio managers. This is because of the nature of the efficient set mathematics, compounded by the inability to specify the true market index.

The Choice of Return Interval

The second major choice is the interval over which you measure return. The two most frequent choices are daily returns and monthly returns. If you use monthly returns, you should estimate the regression using returns in excess of the risk-free rate. Since you are measuring the stock returns on a monthly basis, it makes sense to proxy the risk-free rate with the yield on a T-bill that has a maturity close to one month. In this case, your regression equation would be:

$$(R_{it} - R_{ft}) = a_i + b_i (R_{mt} - R_{ft}) + \varepsilon_{it} \qquad (3.24)$$

where R_{it} is the return on your company in period t, R_{ft} is the risk-free rate in period t, R_{mt} is the return on the market in period t, ε_{it} is the regression residual for period t, and a_i and b_i are the regression intercept and slope, respectively. The slope of the regression, b_i, is the estimate of your company's beta.[31]

If you use daily returns, you probably will be unable to find a suitable proxy for a daily risk-free rate. In this case, your regression would be the market model:

$$R_{it} = a_i + b_i R_{mt} + \varepsilon_{it} \qquad (3.25)$$

Assuming that the CAPM is the correct model, does ignoring the risk-free rate in equation (3.25) bias your estimates of beta? This depends on whether or not the risk-free rate is correlated with the market return. For low degrees of correlation, which seems to be the case, your estimated slope will have only a slight bias. In other words, you can use the estimated slope from equation (3.25), b_i, as your estimate of beta.

The Choice of Estimation Period

Your next decision is how long to make your estimation period. For example, one year of monthly data provides only 12 observations, while a year of daily data provides about 250 observations. All else equal, it's better to have more observations in your regression than to have fewer observations; this is because the confidence interval around the estimated coefficient will be smaller.

---

[31] If CAPM is the correct model, you would not expect your intercept, a_i, to be significantly different from zero.

But all things are not equal. First, monthly returns are less noisy than daily returns, so you might expect to get a tighter confidence interval using monthly returns if you have the same number of observations as with daily returns. But as your estimation period spans a longer period of calendar time, there is a greater chance that your company's beta may have shifted over the period.

Daves, Ehrhardt, and Kunkel (1992) examine a large sample of stocks and find that using two to three years of daily returns is a reasonable choice. This combination of return interval (daily) and estimation period (two to three years) provides a large number of observations without incurring a high risk of a change in beta. If you decide to use monthly returns, you should use three to four years of data.

Sensitivity of the Estimated Beta

Here are your choices: (1) equal-weighted versus value-weighted index; (2) include or omit dividends in index; (3) daily or monthly data; (4) market model or CAPM if you use monthly data; and (5) number of years' worth of data (one year, two years, three years, or four years). Exhibit 3.6 shows the results of estimating the beta of IBM using different combinations of these choices.

Each cell in Exhibit 3.6 reports the estimated beta (shown in bold) and the 95% confidence interval around the estimated beta (shown in parentheses). The results in Panel A are based on daily data using the market model equation (3.25). The results in Panels B and C are based on monthly data, with the market model used in Panel B and the excess returns model equation (3.24) used in Panel C. The first and second columns in each panel report the results based on the CRSP value-weighted index; the index of the first column includes dividends, and the index in the second column excludes dividends. The third and fourth columns are similar to the first two columns, except the index is the CRSP equally weighted index.

Although Exhibit 3.6 is only one example, it illustrates six general principles.

1. It doesn't make much difference whether you include dividends in the market index. The first row of data in Panel A is based on the daily returns during 1990. The estimated beta for the value-weighted index with dividends is 1.02, with a 95% confidence interval of .90 to 1.14. Comparing this with the results in the next column, which is for the value-weighted index without dividends, you can see there is no change. In general, the values in the columns with dividends

Exhibit 3.6: What Is IBM's Beta?

Panel A: Daily Data Using the Market Model Equation (3.25)

Time Period	Value-Wtd w/Div	Value-Wtd w/o Div	Equal-Wtd w/Div	Equal-Wtd w/o Div
1990 only	**1.02**	**1.02**	**1.09**	**1.08**
95% Confidence	(.90,1.14)	(.90,1,14)	(.90,1.27)	(.90,1.27)
1989–1990	**.96**	**.96**	**1.10**	**1.09**
95% Confidence	(.86,1.05)	(.86,1.05)	(.95,1.24)	(.95,1.24)
1988–1990	**1.03**	**1.03**	**1.20**	**1.20**
95% Confidence	(.96,1.10)	(.96,1.10)	(1.08,1.32)	(1.08,1.31)
1987–1990	**1.05**	**1.05**	**.99**	**.99**
95% Confidence	(1.00,1.11)	(1.00,1.11)	(.91,1.08)	(.91,1.07)

Panel B: Monthly Data Using the Market Model Equation (3.25)

Time Period	Value-Wtd w/Div	Value-Wtd w/o Div	Equal-Wtd w/Div	Equal-Wtd w/o Div
1990 only	**.83**	**.83**	**.77**	**.77**
95% Confidence	(.44,1.22)	(.44,1.22)	(.39,1.14)	(.39,1.14)
1989–1990	**.92**	**.92**	**.79**	**.79**
95% Confidence	(.59,1.26)	(.59,1.26)	(.45,1.12)	(.45,1.12)
1988–1990	**.91**	**.91**	**.82**	**.82**
95% Confidence	(.61,1.22)	(.61,1.21)	(.52,1.12)	(.52,1.12)
1987–1990	**.82**	**.82**	**.72**	**.72**
95% Confidence	(.54,1.09)	(.54,1.09)	(.46,.99)	(.46,.99)

Monthly Data Using the Excess Returns Model Equation (3.24)

Time Period	Value-Wtd w/Div	Value-Wtd w/o Div	Equal-Wtd w/Div	Equal-Wtd w/o Div
1990 only	**.83**	**.83**	**.77**	**.77**
95% Confidence	(.45,1.22)	(.44,1.22)	(.39,1.14)	(.40,1.14)
1989–1990	**.92**	**.92**	**.79**	**.77**
95% Confidence	(.59,1.26)	(.59,1.25)	(.45,1.12)	(.45,1.12)
1988–1990	**.92**	**.92**	**.82**	**.82**
95% Confidence	(.61,1.22)	(.61,1.22)	(.52,1.12)	(.53,1.12)
1987–1990	**.82**	**.82**	**.72**	**.72**
95% Confidence	(.54,1.09)	(.54,1.09)	(.46,.99)	(.46,.99)

are almost identical to those in the columns without dividends (first column versus second column and third column versus fourth column). In other words, it doesn't make much difference whether you include dividends in the market index.

2. **It doesn't make much difference whether you adjust for the risk-free rate.** In the case of monthly data, the beta estimate is virtually unchanged whether you use the market model equation (3.25) or the excess returns model equation (3.24); i.e., there are virtually no differences between Panels B and C.

3. **It does matter whether you use a value-weighted index or an equal-weighted index.** The choice of a value-weighted index versus an equal-weighted index does make a difference. For example, the one-year daily beta with a value-weighted index is 1.02, and the one-year daily beta with the equal-weighted index is 1.09. For daily returns, the beta that is estimated from the equal-weighted index is typically bigger than the beta for the value-weighted index; the reverse is true for the monthly data in Panels B and C. Keep in mind, however, that these differences generally are not statistically significant for IBM. You can see this by looking at the confidence intervals. The confidence intervals for the value-weighted betas typically include the estimate of beta by the equal-weighted index; the reverse is also true.[32]

4. **You get tighter confidence intervals around estimates when you have more observations.** Notice that the confidence intervals tend to shrink as the estimation period increases. For example, when using four years of daily data and a value-weighted index, the confidence interval is from 1.00 to 1.11, which is about half the size of the confidence interval for the one-year beta. Notice also that the confidence intervals are much tighter for daily data than for monthly data. Even with four years of monthly data, the confidence interval for the value-weighted index is from .54 to 1.09.[33]

5. **The estimate of beta changes as more years of observations are added to the regression.** Notice that the estimate of beta does

---

[32] Daves, Ehrhardt, Kuhlmeyer, and Kunkel (1993) show there is a positive relationship between beta and firm size. This implies that betas estimated with a value-weighted index will in fact be different from betas estimated with an equal-weighted index.

[33] There is an adjustment you might consider if you decide to use monthly data. With the small number of observations in monthly regressions, a statistical phenomenon called "regression to the mean" could affect your estimated beta. See Blume (1975) and Vasicek (1973) for details. Litzenberger, Ramaswamy, and Sosin (1980) provide an interesting comparison of adjustment techniques.

change as more years of data are added to the regression. For example, the one-year daily beta with a value-weighted index is 1.02 while the two-year beta is .96. There is similar variation for the monthly betas. This could be the result of noise in the return-generating process; notice that the confidence intervals are so large that changes in beta might not be statistically significant. Still, there may be actual shifts in beta. Daves, Ehrhardt, and Kunkel (1992) find that 59% of the stocks in their sample have significant shifts in beta during a four-year period. In other words, estimated betas are not particularly stable from period to period.

6. Betas estimated using daily returns differ from betas estimated using monthly returns. Notice that the betas in Panel A, which are estimated using daily data, are different from the betas in Panels B and C, which are estimated using monthly data. This may be because of noise in the data; the confidence intervals are so large that IBM's daily betas may not be statistically significantly different from IBM's monthly betas. However, the differences may in fact be because of the "intervaling effect," which can be caused by nonsynchronous trading.[34]

Nonsynchronous trading occurs when the time of a company's reported return differs from the time of the market's reported return. Are there days when your company's stock does not trade at all, or trades only a few times during the day? If this is the case, your estimate of beta using equation (3.25) will probably be lower than the true beta. Although this is especially a problem for thinly traded companies, it can also indirectly affect larger companies. This is because the market index itself is affected by the nonsynchronous trading of any companies included in the index. Even though one company may trade frequently, the market index you use may be "tainted" by other companies that trade infrequently. This imperfection in the market index can affect the betas of frequently traded companies.

If you use daily data, Dimson (1979) and Scholes and Williams (1977) provide simple corrections that will allow you to estimate the true beta. Instead of regressing the company's return against only the contemporaneous market return, as in equation (3.25), Dimson would add some market returns that lead and lag the company's return. For example, suppose you choose to add two days of leading returns and two days of lagging returns; let $R_{m, t-2}$ and $R_{m, t-1}$ denote the two lagging returns. In other words, if R_{mt} is the return on the market for

---

[34] See Smith (1978) and Levhari and Levy (1977) for further discussion of the intervaling effect.

Wednesday, then $R_{m,t-2}$ and $R_{m,t-1}$ are the returns for Monday and Tuesday, respectively. Let $R_{m,t+1}$ and $R_{m,t+2}$ denote the leading returns (which would be the market returns on Thursday and Friday, if it is Wednesday). The regression equation is:

$$R_{it} = a_i + b_{i,-2} R_{m,t-2} + b_{i,-1} R_{m,t-1} + b_{i,0} R_{mt} \qquad (3.26)$$
$$+ b_{i,+1} R_{m,t+1} + b_{i,+2} R_{m,t+2} + \varepsilon_{it}$$

where $b_{i,-2}$ and $b_{i,-1}$ are the coefficients for the lagged market returns of $R_{m,t-2}$ and $R_{m,t-1}$, respectively; and $b_{i,+1}$ and $b_{i,+2}$ are the coefficients for the leading market returns of $R_{m,t+1}$ and $R_{m,t+2}$, respectively. Your adjusted estimate of beta is the sum of all the coefficients:

$$\hat{\beta}_i = b_{i,t-2} + b_{i,t-1} + b_{i,0} + b_{i,+1} + b_{i,+2} \qquad (3.27)$$

When applied to the IBM data, the Dimson adjustment changes the two-year (1990–1989) beta of IBM (daily returns, value-weighted index with dividends) from .96 to .88. Large firms probably are heavily traded, and IBM is a large firm.[35] Therefore, the change in IBM's beta is consistent with the expectation that the adjusted beta probably will increase for thinly traded firms and might decrease slightly for heavily traded firms.

Recommendations

You should try to find several published sources for your beta. If these are similar to one another, you should use them as an estimate of your beta. If they are very different from one another, or if you have reason to believe that they don't accurately measure your company's beta, you should estimate beta.

If you do estimate your company's beta, you should use a value-weighted index; it won't make too much difference whether or not this includes dividends. Using two to three years of daily data is a reasonable choice. You probably should use an adjustment for nonsynchro-

---

[35] There may be other factors affecting the relationship between beta and firm size. Alberts and Archer (1973) use a sample of stocks taken from the 1961–1969 period to test the hypothesis that larger firms have less risk than smaller firms. Their tests support this hypothesis, consistent with anecdotal evidence and conventional wisdom that states that big firms generally have smaller betas than do small firms. Daves, Ehrhardt, Kuhlmeyer, and Kunkel (1993) find that this relationship has changed during the decade of the 1980s. For this decade, larger firms actually have larger betas than do small firms.

nous trading, such as the one by Dimson (1979). If you decide to use monthly data, you should use three to four years of data.

I.A.2.c. Estimating the Risk-Free Rate and the Market Premium

In addition to your estimate of beta, you also need an estimate of the risk-free rate and the market premium.

Estimating the Risk-Free Rate

There are many different securities that could be candidates for a proxy of the risk-free rate. What characteristics should a "good" candidate have? First, it should have no default risk. For all practical purposes, this limits your choice to U.S. Treasury securities. Which Treasury security should you choose?

To answer this question, you need to think about the CAPM. There are many assumptions underlying it, and one of these assumptions states that CAPM is a one-period model. When you choose a risk-free rate, it seems reasonable that the period over which the risk-free rate is measured ought to correspond to the length of the CAPM period. But what is the appropriate CAPM period? Is it a day, a week, a month, a quarter, a year, or some longer period? Unfortunately, there is no definitive answer to this question. If you use daily or monthly data to estimate CAPM, which is reasonable, you are implicitly assuming that the CAPM period is fairly short. Therefore, it is reasonable to use a short-term risk-free rate.

Keep in mind that your resulting cost of equity will correspond to the implicit length of the CAPM period. If you're trying to find the rate at which you should discount cash flows of a long-term project, you should adjust the cost of equity to reflect this difference between the length of your project's cash flows and the length of the implied CAPM period. This is an important issue, and Chapter 5 provides a detailed discussion. For now, I assume you are finding a cost of equity that corresponds to the length of the implied CAPM period, which is short.

The most commonly used estimate of the short-term risk-free rate is the yield on a short-term Treasury bill. But which bill should you use? In the absence of any other compelling reasons, you should use the rate on the Treasury bill whose maturity is closest to one month. There also are reasonable arguments for using the yield on the most recently auctioned 13-week bill; the trading is usually heavy for this bill, which might give you more confidence in the reported yield.

Yields on Treasury bills are reported in a number of sources, such as *The Wall Street Journal*. For example, *The Wall Street Journal* reported that for 10/23/92 the yield on the bill maturing in 31 days was 2.50%, and the yield on the most recently auctioned 13-week bill (maturing in 86 days) was 2.98%.[36]

Estimating the Market Premium

The final input you need for the CAPM is the expected return on the market. More precisely, you need the expected market premium, which is the amount that the market return is expected to exceed the risk-free rate. There are two commonly used methods for estimating the market premium: (1) the historical average approach, and (2) the growth model approach.[37]

1. The historical average approach. The most commonly used approach relies on historical data. Even this simple recommendation presents several choices. Do you use all available years or just data from a recent sample? Do you use a geometric average (i.e., a compound average) or an arithmetic average? There are no definitive answers to these questions, although there are some guidelines that can help you make your decision.

With respect to the number of observations that you should use, most textbooks recommend using an historical average based on a

---

[36] *The Wall Street Journal* actually reports the bid and ask "discount yields." You can use a relationship to convert the discount yield into a yield to maturity: Y = [365 D] [360 − (Dt)], where Y is the yield to maturity, D is the discount yield, and t is the number of days until the bill matures. The mean of the bid and ask discount yields for the 31-day T-bill cited was 2.46%, and the similar mean for the 13-week T-bill was 2.92%.

[37] Three less commonly used methods are the survey approach, the conditional variance approach, and the econometric approach. Many institutional brokerage firms regularly survey their clients and other institutional investors in an effort to determine the "expected market premium." The concept underlying surveys is appealing, since it is a direct attempt to measure investor attitudes. As with all surveys, however, there exists potential bias with respect to the sample selection and with respect to the truthfulness of the respondents. It's easy to profess a bull-like attitude, but it's another thing when it actually comes to plunging into the market.

Merton (1980) suggests modeling the expected return on the market as a function of the current variance of the market. He applies several different functional forms to data spanning 1926–1978. His results suggest that the realized market premiums do vary over time and that the premiums are related to the changing variance in the market.

A third approach is that of Glenn and Litzenberger (1979), who infer the market premium using a pooled time series and cross section of stock returns. Litzenberger, Ramaswamy, and Sosin (1980) also infer the premium by using cross-sectional regressions.

large number of observations.[38] This recommendation is based on the assumption that past historical events and prior investor attitudes toward risk are representative of the future.

Which should you use, a geometric average or an arithmetic average? An example may be instructive.[39] Suppose you start off with $50 and invest it. The investment is worth $100 after one year, which is a 100% rate of return. You are not so fortunate during the second year, and the value of the investment falls to $50, which is a return of -50%. Your geometric average return for the two-year period is 0% (recall that you compute the geometric rate of return by solving this equation for g: $50 (1 + g)^2 = 50$). Your arithmetic average return is 25% (this is $[100 - 50]/2$). Which of these is "correct"?

If you engage in a buy-and-hold strategy, then the geometric average is correct. After all, you began with $50 and ended up with $50, so your return was 0%. Suppose, however, that you engaged in a rebalancing strategy. After the first year, you cashed in the one-year gain of $50 and left your original $50 in the investment. At the end of two years, you would have your one-year gain of $50 (ignoring any interest you might have earned during the year), and you would have $25 resulting from your loss during the second year (this is a 50% loss on your rebalanced investment of $50). Therefore, your value at the end of two years would be $75, which represents a simple two-year rate of return equal to 50%. Your simple average annual rate of return would be half of this, which is exactly equal to the previously calculated arithmetic average of 25%.

Therefore, if you believe that stockholders in your company engage in a buy-and-hold strategy, you should use a geometric average. If you believe that stockholders rebalance their portfolios monthly, however, you should use an arithmetic average.[40]

There is something else to consider when choosing between the geometric average and the arithmetic average. Suppose that in the example you have an equal chance of a 100% return or a 50% loss. In this simple two-period example, there are only three possible outcomes.

---

[38] For example, Shapiro (1989) reports the mean premium of stock market returns relative to short-term Treasury yields and long-term bond yields for the period 1926–1988. See Chapter 9 in Ibbotson and Sinquefield (1989) for another recommendation for using a long time period.

[39] This example is in Chapter 6 of Copeland, Koller, and Murrin (1990).

[40] See Carleton and Lakonishok (1985) for further discussion of this issue. They also suggest that if your company is small, then you should consider using an equally weighted market return rather than a value-weighted return, since the equally weighted return more closely approximates the returns received by investors in small firms.

First, you could get two 100% returns, giving you a final value of $200; the probability that this occurs is one in four. Second, you could get one 100% return and one 50% loss, giving you a final value of $50; the probability of this is two in four (you could get a 100% return and a 50% loss, or you could get a 50% loss and a 100% return). Third, you could get two 50% losses, giving you a final value of $12.5; the probability of this is one in four. Your expected ending value is:

$$\left(\frac{1}{4}\right) 200 + \left(\frac{2}{4}\right) 50 + \left(\frac{1}{4}\right) 12.5 = 78.125$$

If you start with $50, what expected rate of return gives you the expected payoff of $78.125? The answer is 25%: $50 (1 + .25)^2 = 78.125$. This means that in order for you to get your expected payoff, you must have an expected return equal to the arithmetic average return.

Since you are really interested in the expected market return, I recommend you use the arithmetic average.[41]

Ibbotson Associates (1990) reports the average returns on stocks and T-bills during the 1926–1989 period. The geometric average returns on stocks and T-bills were 10.3% and 3.6%, respectively, which implies a geometric risk premium of 6.7%.[42] The arithmetic average returns on stocks and T-bills were 12.4% and 3.7%, respectively, which implies an arithmetic risk premium of 8.7%.[43] Keep in mind that this is the risk premium that would be appropriate for a short-term project, which is why the T-bill return is used. Chapter 5 describes the adjustments that would be required for longer-term projects.

2. The growth model approach. The growth model approach uses either the constant dividend growth model, shown in equation (3.4), or a multistage growth model such as the one shown in equation (3.10).

---

[41] This is also the recommendation of several textbooks, such as Shapiro (1989) and Ross, Westerfield, and Jaffe (1990). See Chapter 9 in Ibbotson and Sinquefield (1989) for another recommendation to use the arithmetic average. For a different recommendation, see Chapter 6 in Copeland, Koller, and Murrin (1990), where the geometric average is recommended.

[42] This is slightly different from calculating the risk premium each month and then calculating the geometric average of this monthly premium.

[43] Interestingly, the market premium has been much smaller during recent decades. Although stock returns have been roughly the same during this century, interest rates have been much higher during the past couple of decades. In fact, the mean market premium for the period July 1963 through December 1990 is only 4.25%. According to conventional statistical t-tests, this number is not significantly different from zero. See Daves and Ehrhardt (1992) for further details.

In either case, you first obtain estimates for the expected growth rate in dividends for a number of companies. You then average these individual estimates to obtain an estimate of the expected growth rate for the market. With the observed price level for some market index, you can apply the same methods described in Section I.A to find the "cost of equity" for the market.

There are several appealing features to this approach. First, the approach incorporates market data and investor expectations, something that is probably preferable to an approach that uses only investors' predictions of the market premium. The approach also allows the expected market premium to vary over time as market conditions change.

Harris and Marston (1992) use this approach to estimate the expected market return for each year between 1982 and 1991; they find that the estimated return varied from a high of 20.08% in 1982 to a low of 14.71% in 1987. Their most recent estimate was an expected return of 15.61% for 1991.[44] With an average T-bill rate during 1991 of approximately 5.2%, this implies a market premium of 10.41%.

I.A.2.d. *Applying the CAPM in Estimating the Cost of Equity*

Given the many choices you have to make in estimating beta, the risk-free rate, and the market premium, it's generally a good idea to do some sensitivity analysis. Following is an example of a sensitivity analysis for UTF's cost of equity.

Using three years of monthly data, a value-weighted index, a risk-free rate taken from a T-bill whose maturity is closest to 30 days, and the CAPM model of equation (3.24), the estimated beta of UTF is 1.05, with a 95% confidence interval ranging from .57 to 1.53. This means that you are 95% certain that the true beta is somewhere between .57 and 1.53. Notice that the confidence interval is quite large.[45] Using three years of daily data, the value-weighted index, and the market model of equation (3.25), the estimate of beta is 1.0, with a 95% confidence interval ranging from .89 to 1.11.

The differences in the size of the confidence intervals for the daily data and the monthly data are probably due to the different number

---

[44] For other examples of this approach, see Malkiel (1979), Brigham, Shome, and Vinson (1985), and Harris (1988).

[45] The size of this confidence interval is typical of most companies; see Daves, Ehrhardt, and Kunkel (1992) for recent evidence.

of observations used in the regression. The monthly regression uses only 36 observations, while the daily sample has 751 observations. Because the estimates of UTF's beta are fairly close for the daily data and the monthly data, only the results from the daily regression are used in the sensitivity analysis. These are the estimated beta of 1.0, the lowest end of the 95% confidence interval (.89), and the highest end of the 95% confidence interval (1.11).

The sensitivity analysis uses the 30-day and 13-week T-bill rates, which are 2.50% and 2.98%.[46] The analysis also uses the historical geometric market premium (6.7%), the historical average market premium (8.7%), and the Harris and Marston (1992) growth model value (10.41%).

I recommend you use the estimated value of beta, the 30-day T-bill rate, and the historical arithmetic risk premium. Using equation (3.23), the estimated cost of equity is:

$$r_E = .025 + 1.0 \,(.087) = 11.2\% \qquad (3.28)$$

Exhibit 3.7 reports the estimated cost of equity for each of the eighteen combinations of beta, risk-free rate, and risk premiums. Notice that the values range from a low of 8.5% to a high of 14.7% when using the growth model risk premium. As this indicates, the decisions you make with respect to the inputs of the CAPM can make a very big difference in your estimate of the cost of equity. Even though 11.2% is the recommended cost of capital for UTF (based on the actual estimate of beta, the 30-day T-bill rate, and the arithmetic average risk premium), it would be wise to find a range of likely values and to use this range when doing sensitivity analysis in a capital budgeting study.

I.B. The Cost of Preferred Stock

In contrast to estimating the cost of common equity, it is relatively easy to estimate the cost of preferred stock. Let P_{P0} denote the current market price of the preferred stock, and let D_P denote the fixed dividend payment. Since the dividend is fixed, the growth rate in dividends is

---

[46] These are the rates taken from *The Wall Street Journal* for October 23, 1992.

Exhibit 3.7: Sensitivity Analysis for the Cost of Equity

		Estimates of Beta		
		Low End of 95% Confidence Interval	Estimate from Regression	High End of 95% Confidence Interval
		.89	1.00	1.11
Historical Geometric Market Premium =	6.70%			
30-day T-bill =	2.50%	8.5%	9.2%	9.9%
13-week T-bill =	2.98%	8.9%	9.7%	10.4%
Historical Arithmetic Market Premium =	8.70%			
30-day T-bill =	2.50%	10.2%	**11.2%**	12.2%
13-week T-bill =	2.98%	10.7%	11.7%	12.6%
Growth Model Market Premium =	10.41%			
30-day T-bill =	2.50%	11.8%	12.9%	14.1%
13-week T-bill =	2.98%	12.2%	13.4%	14.5%

Note: Estimated costs of equity are shown in the boxes.

equal to zero.[47] If you apply the growth model of equation (3.5) and substitute the growth rate of zero, the cost of the preferred stock is:

$$r_P = \frac{D_P}{P_{P0}} \qquad (3.29)$$

---

[47] This assumes that the dividend payments are current.

Consider a hypothetical company that has preferred stock with a fixed quarterly dividend payment of $1.50 per share. The market price of the preferred stock is $66. Using equation (3.29), the quarterly cost of the preferred stock is:

$$r_P = \frac{1.50}{66} = 2.27\% \tag{3.30}$$

This is equivalent to a 9.4% annualized cost of preferred stock. Keep in mind your objective is to find the cost of any new capital you would have to raise if you undertook new projects. The approach of equation (3.30) provides a good estimate of the cost that you would incur if you issued new preferred stock.

What about finite-maturity preferred stock or convertible preferred stock? Finding the cost of finite-maturity preferred stock is similar to finding the cost of debt, which is discussed in the next section. Section I.D discusses the cost of capital of convertible preferred stock.

I.C. The Cost of Debt

There are several choices to make when you estimate the cost of debt. Should you use the average coupon rate on your existing debt, or should you use the coupon rate you would have to pay if you issued debt today? Should you use the pre-tax cost of debt or the after-tax cost? Should you try to adjust the cost of debt for expected bankruptcy costs?

Let i denote the coupon rate you would pay if you issued debt today, and let i_h denote the average coupon rate that you are paying on existing debt. Which of these rates should you use when you estimate your cost of debt?

Keep in mind that you're trying to estimate the cost of capital you will use to discount the cash flows of a proposed project. If you can no longer borrow at the historical rate, it doesn't seem appropriate to use the historical cost of debt when you estimate your weighted average cost of capital. For this reason, virtually no textbooks recommend using the historical cost of debt.[48] Instead, you should use the current coupon rate.

---

[48] Despite this rare example of unanimity from within the academic profession, Gitman and Mercurio (1982) report that approximately one-third of the companies they surveyed do in fact use the historical cost of debt.

How should you estimate this current coupon rate? One approach is to calculate the yield to maturity of your existing debt, if it is publicly traded.[49] A second approach is to look at the yields on similar bonds. If you know the bond rating of your company, you could find the average current yield of seasoned bonds with that rating. For example, Moody's Bond Record reports that the average yield on seasoned Aaa bonds during September 1992 was 7.92%. An alternative to these two approaches is to find the average new-issue yield for bonds in your company's risk class.

In general, the average seasoned yield differs from the average new-issue yield. One potential reason for the difference is the treatment of taxes. Often the portfolio of seasoned bonds will contain discount and premium bonds, while the portfolio of new issues contains only bonds that are very close to par. Since the tax liability is a function of the bond's tax basis, investors subject to taxes face different after-tax cash flows for discount and premium bonds and for par bonds. Shiller and Modigliani (1979) find that much of the difference in yield occurs because of this differential treatment of taxes. They conclude that the "new issue yield averages should provide a more reliable measure of the cost of debt capital than is provided by seasoned yield averages."[50]

Even if two companies with the same bond rating issue "identical" bonds on the same date, the two bonds often will have different coupon rates. This means that even if you follow Shiller and Modigliani's suggestion and use the average new-issue yield for bonds with the same rating as your company, you may not get the true cost of debt for the company. What should you do?

This problem reminds me of a recent exchange when I was presenting a paper in a workshop. One of my colleagues asked a question about an institutional feature in the market for government bonds. I started to answer, "I think that . . . ," when another colleague interrupted me. He said, "Don't think. Ask someone who knows."

This also is good advice for you, at least the part about asking. When you want to find the current coupon rate at which your firm could issue debt, ask someone who knows such as an investment banker or bond trader. Asking an informed professional for an estimate of the coupon rate at which your company could currently issue debt

---

[49] The yield to maturity is simply the discount rate that makes the present value of all future contractual cash flows of the bond equal to the bond's current price. In other words, it is the internal rate of return on the bond.

[50] Shiller and Modigliani (1979, p. 297).

is probably the best way to estimate your company's pre-tax cost of debt.

These comments also apply to finite preferred stock. If its market price is available, you could calculate the "yield" on the finite preferred stock in the same manner that you would calculate the yield on debt. You also could find the rates at which other companies with similar risk as yours are currently offering finite preferred stock. Best yet, you could ask an investment banker.

To estimate your company's cost of debt, should you use the pre-tax coupon rate, i, or should you adjust it to an after-tax basis? Remember the reason that you're estimating your cost of capital: you want to discount the cash flows of a proposed project. The answer to the pre-tax/after-tax question depends on how you define the cash flows of your project. As Chapter 2 demonstrates, if you use the traditional definition of cash flows, which is the after-tax cash flows of the project ignoring any interest expenses or tax ramifications of those interest expenses, then you should use the after-tax cost of debt.[51] Equation (3.31) defines this after-tax cost:

$$r_D = (1 - \tau)\,i \qquad\qquad (3.31)$$

where τ is your corporate tax rate.[52] In the absence of any other compelling reasons, you should use your marginal tax rate. The federal corporate tax rate is currently approximately 34%. Typical state and local taxes are in the range of 5% to 7%. Examples in the remainder of this book will use a combined tax rate of 40%.[53]

---

[51] An alternative is to account for the tax shield of debt explicitly by adding this tax shield to the other after-tax cash flows of the project. In this case, you would use the pre-tax interest rate on debt as your cost of debt. See Keane (1976) for details. Notice that this approach is easier to implement if the tax system imposes a lag between the timing of the interest expense and the recognition of the tax shield. Even in such a tax system, you could still use the traditional definition of cash flows, but you would have to use a much more complicated adjustment than in equation (3.31) to find the appropriate after-tax cost of debt. It is much easier simply to adjust the cash flows to reflect the tax shield of debt and then use the pre-tax interest rate as the cost of debt.

[52] Haley (1971) provides an interesting discussion of the impact of changes in tax rates on the overall cost of capital and the value of the project.

[53] Somewhat surprisingly, Gitman and Mercurio (1982) report that 60% of the firms they surveyed did not adjust the cost of debt to reflect taxes. This might be because these firms use a definition of cash flows that is different from the one in Chapter 2. For example, many utilities adjust the cash flows instead of the cost of debt. It's also possible that these firms are simply making a mistake or that the respondents didn't understand the question.

If your firm has a permanent level of short-term debt, then you should include short-term debt as another component in your capital structure. This means you should estimate the cost of the short-term debt separately from the cost of the long-term debt, since the interest rate on short-term debt is likely to differ from that of long-term debt.[54]

Should you try to adjust the cost of debt to reflect any bankruptcy risk? To understand this issue, consider the cost of debt at its time of issue. If the debt is issued at par, the coupon rate on the debt is also equal to the debt's promised yield to maturity. Keep in mind that this promised yield to maturity is based on the promised contractual cash flows of the bond. But if there is any bankruptcy risk, the expected cash flows are less than the promised contractual cash flows, which means that the expected yield on this bond is less than the promised yield. Should you use this expected yield or should you use the promised yield?

If the bond is of investment-grade quality and is issued at par, which is typical of most bonds, you should use the promised yield, which is the same as the coupon rate.[55] The proofs in Chapter 2 are based upon the assumption that the coupon rate equals the promised yield, and these proofs state quite clearly that you should use the coupon rate.[56] (Section I.D discusses bonds that are below investment-grade quality.)

How frequently should you update your company's cost of debt? For example, suppose your company issues some debt at a coupon rate of 10%. You estimate your cost of debt using the after-tax cost of this rate, you find your cost of capital, you discount the cash flows of a project, and you accept that project. After the project has been implemented, the yield on your bond changes to 8%. Maybe this is because the market interest rates fall, and the market price of the debt increases, or maybe it is because your company gets an improved bond rating. Or maybe the pre-tax yield on your bond stays at 8%, but a change in the tax code increases your company's marginal tax rate. Do such changes affect your cost of capital, and should you try to anticipate such occurrences when you estimate your cost of capital?

---

[54] An alternative is to have a single category of debt in your capital structure and define this as the sum of the short- and long-term debt. If you do this, you should define the cost of debt as the weighted average of the costs of short- and long-term debt.

[55] There is no universally accepted answer for the case of original-issue discount bonds. One approach is to use the imputed interest rate, which is just the yield (i.e., the IRR) of the bond.

[56] See Brennan (1973) and Keane (1975) for further discussion of this issue.

The answers are "yes" and "no." The first answer is "yes," because it does affect your current cost of debt, which has changed. In other words, the cost of capital you will use to discount subsequent projects is now different from your previous cost of capital. The second answer is "no," because the uncertainty of such future occurrences was reflected in the bond's price (and coupon rate) at the time you issued the bond. Therefore, you used the correct cost of debt when you estimated your cost of equity and when you discounted the cash flows of the project. The project may turn out to have more or less value than you expected, but your decision-making process was correct.[57]

I.D. The Cost of Other Elements in the Capital Structure

Common stock, straight debt, and straight preferred stock are the three most commonly used sources of financing. Other sources of financing used to a lesser degree include convertible debt, callable debt, variable-rate debt (perhaps with "floors," "caps," "collars," or other interest-rate sensitive features), below investment-grade quality bonds (commonly called "junk" bonds), extendible debt, retractable debt, puttable debt, foreign-denominated debt, interest rate swaps, currency swaps, yield curve notes, leases, convertible preferred stock, warrants, executive stock options, and minority interests. This list will continue to expand, as the number of new types of securities is limited only by the creativity of financial engineers.

There is bad news, and there is good news. The bad news is that establishing the value and cost of capital for most of these instruments is extremely difficult. The good news is that these instruments usually constitute a small percentage of most firms' financing and have a relatively small impact on most firms' cost of capital. It is beyond the scope of this book to assign a cost of capital to these instruments, but there are a few general guidelines that can help you avoid some common mistakes.

Warrants and executive stock options do have a cost of capital. You are making a mistake if you simply assign a zero cost to these instruments. Although not easy to apply, option pricing techniques can provide you an estimate of the cost of capital for these instruments.

---

[57] If the project value and the value of the securities change enough, you may have to make adjustments in your capital structure to return the capital structure to its desired level. Section II discusses the issue of capital structure in more detail.

See Copeland and Weston (1988, pp. 268–276) for a description of these option pricing techniques; you can find further discussion in Chapter 6 of Copeland, Koller, and Murrin (1990).

Convertible preferred stock carries a lower dividend payment than otherwise identical nonconvertible preferred, but that doesn't mean that convertible preferred stock has a lower cost of capital. Recall the previous example in which UTF had preferred stock with a fixed quarterly dividend of $1.50 per share and a current price of $66. As shown by equation (3.29), the annualized cost of this preferred is 9.4%. Consider now a company that is otherwise identical to UTF, but that has convertible preferred stock with a dividend of $1.20 per quarter and a current price of $66. It is incorrect to estimate the cost of the convertible preferred by equation (3.29), which produces an annualized cost of 7.5%.

If you naively used equation (3.29), you might incorrectly conclude that the cost of convertible preferred is about 190 basis points less than that of the nonconvertible preferred. This would imply the financial equivalent of a free lunch, but, as you know, there are no free lunches. Where is the hidden cost of this lunch? It appears in two places.

First, you can consider the convertible preferred to be equivalent to a package consisting of a nonconvertible preferred and a warrant. A ballpark estimate of the value of this nonconvertible proportion of the package can be found by discounting the quarterly dividend by the quarterly cost of the otherwise identical nonconvertible preferred. This cost is the same as for UTF, since the two companies are otherwise identical. Therefore, the value of the nonconvertible portion is equal to 1.25/.027, which is about $46.30. The difference between this and the price of $66 is the value of the "warrant," which is $19.70.

As noted earlier in this section, the warrant clearly has a "cost of capital," even though it may be very difficult to estimate. If the cost of the warrant is between zero and 9.4%, the combined cost of the package is between the naive 7.5% and 9.4%, the cost of the nonconvertible. If the cost of the warrant is greater than 9.4%, then the combined cost of the package is greater than 9.4%.

The second hidden cost occurs because of "spillover" effects. Even though having convertible preferred instead of nonconvertible preferred may not change the overall value of the firm, it will almost certainly change the riskiness, and therefore the cost, of the existing common equity. See Chapter 4 for further discussion of this issue.

Just as in the case of convertible preferred stock, the cost of convertible debt is not equal to its coupon rate. You can apply the same basic approach; i.e., divide the convertible debt into two components, one a straight bond and the other a warrant.

Bonds that are of below investment-grade, junk bonds, have a higher probability of bankruptcy than do bonds of investment-grade quality. If a junk bond is issued at par, its coupon rate (which is its promised yield to maturity) is greater than the bond's expected yield (which is based on the expected payments, given the probability of bankruptcy). This means that the coupon rate on the junk bond is not the appropriate measure for its cost of capital. As an approximation, Copeland, Koller, and Murrin (1990) suggest that you use the yield to maturity on BBB-rated debt as the cost of debt for a junk bond.

In comparison to these instruments, usually it's a little easier to find the cost of a lease. Most textbooks recommend using the after-tax cost of debt as the cost of a lease.

Chapter 7 discusses the cost of debt that is denominated in a foreign currency.

II. Estimating Weights for the Components of the Capital Structure

After you have estimated the costs of the components of capital structure, you need to estimate the weights. The weights used in the weighted average cost of capital are defined by:

$$w_j = \frac{M_j}{\displaystyle\sum_{j=1}^{N} M_j} \tag{3.32}$$

where there are N different components in the capital structure, and M_j is the market value of the jth component.

Section II.A. explains the use of weights based on market values versus the use of weights based on book values. Section II.B. describes some common mistakes associated with the effects of working capital and deferred taxes.

II.A. Market Weights versus Book Weights

Suppose there is a firm with the capital structure shown in the simple balance sheet of Exhibit 3.8. The market value of debt for this company is $3.2 million, and the market value of equity is $12 million. Should you use book values to compute the weights, or should you

Exhibit 3.8: A Simple Balance Sheet

Assets		Liabilities and Shareholders' Equity	
Cash	300,000	Accounts Payable	300,000
Inventory	400,000		
Accounts Receivable	300,000	Deferred Taxes	300,000
		Long-Term Debt	3,000,000
Net Plant, Property, & Equipment	7,000,000		
		Common Stock at Par	200,000
		Paid-In Capital	1,700,000
		Retained Earnings	2,500,000
Total	$8,000,000	Total	$8,000,000

use market values? Should you use current values, or should you use target values?

Remember from Chapter 2 that the justification for using the weighted average cost of capital is based on the assumption that the weights are market values. In fact, the mathematics of Chapter 2 clearly indicate that market values are the correct choice. Intuitively, this is because the cost of capital is going to be used in evaluating a proposed project. Therefore, the relevant concern is how much the project will earn with respect to the costs of the new capital, not the old capital. Most textbooks recognize this and recommend using market values.[58] It may be tempting to use the balance sheet in Exhibit 3.8 to estimate the weights for the weighted average cost of capital, but it can lead to substantial mistakes, as an example shows.

Consider the book value of the common equity, which is $4.4 million. Given total liabilities and shareholders' equity of $8 million, the book weight for the equity is 4.4 divided by 8, which is 55%. This implies a debt ratio of 45%. You might also calculate a book weight for equity based only on the equity and long-term debt. To do this, you divide the book value of equity by the sum of the book values of equity and long-term debt, which is 4.4/(4.4 + 3); this book weight

---

[58] See Brennan (1973) for an example from the finance literature in support of using market weights. Counterarguments are made by Elliot (1980) and Beranek (1977), who favor using book weights.

for equity is 59.46%. This implies a debt ratio of 40.54%. You should use neither of these book weight approaches.

For this particular company, the market value of equity is $12 million, and the total market value of sources of financing is $15.2 million (the sum of market equity and market debt), which gives a correct weight of 78.95% for equity. The correct debt ratio is 21.05%.

In this example, the market value of equity and the book value of equity are very different. Such differences in the value of market equity and book equity are typical, rather than an exception. For example, the Financial Accounting Standards Board ruling concerning accounting for unfunded pension liabilities (SFAS No. 106) has had an enormous impact on the reported book equity of many companies. Any impact on market values, however, is very much smaller. In fact, there may be no change in market values if financial analysts were already aware of the companies' pension situation.

Market values of debt sometimes are different from book values of debt, although not usually to the extent that market equity differs from book equity. When market interest rates are relatively stable, the coupon rate on newly issued debt often will be similar to the rate on previously issued debt. Unless the creditworthiness of the firm has changed, the market and book values of debt will be very close. When there are large changes in market rates, the book values and market values will differ by quite a bit. For example, interest rates were extremely high in 1980; the market value of existing debt was substantially lower than the book value for many firms during this year.

As this simple example indicates, using book values instead of market values can lead to substantial errors in estimating the weights.

There is also the issue of whether to use weights based on the actual market values of debt and equity or whether to use weights based on the target market capital structure. Since firms usually raise capital in large increments, the target ratios and the actual ratios often differ. Even if actual and target ratios initially are equal, changes in the business environment can affect the firm's debt and equity differently, causing the actual and the target ratio to differ. Given that the target ratio is the ratio that the firm is trying to maintain, the target market ratio is probably the best predictor of the firm's future capital structure.[59] So if your current market values differ from your target values,

---

[59] Petry (1975) reports that approximately two-thirds of the firms in his sample state that they try to keep constant book weights when they raise additional capital. In other words, they have a target book ratio. Petry examined the behavior of 84 firms during periods in which they issued capital. You would expect a firm to issue equity if its actual

and you believe your firm will try to reach this target, you should use the target ratio when you estimate the weights.[60]

Which weights do companies actually use? In a survey of large firms, Brigham (1975) finds that 29 of 31 respondents used book values; they did not indicate whether these were actual values or target values. Petry (1975) reports that approximately one-half of a sample of 284 firms stated that they used market weights when they computed the weighted average cost of capital. According to Gitman and Mercurio (1982), about 16.4% of the firms they surveyed reported using book weights. It's not clear whether these firms in the Gitman–Mercurio sample used their book values out of convenience or whether they used their book values because their book weights were close to their target weights. Another 28.8% of the Gitman–Mercurio respondents reported using current market values; once again, it's not clear how close these are to their target ratios. Over 41% specifically stated that they used weights based on their target capital structure, but they didn't explain whether the target was based on book or market values.[61]

In summary, you should use market values when you estimate the weights for the components of your capital structure. The most common components are common stock, preferred stock, short-term debt, and long-term debt.

II.B. The Rest of the Balance Sheet

You might think something is missing, because the list of components does not include deferred taxes or accounts payable.[62] After all, accounts payable represent a short-term "loan" from the suppliers; some argue that deferred taxes are a "loan" from the IRS. You are right in that you should not ignore these accounts. But they affect the project's cash flows, not the weighted average cost of capital. The following sections explain this in detail.

---

leverage were greater than its target leverage; you would expect the firm to issue debt if its actual leverage were less than its target leverage. Despite the firms' avowed concern with the target ratio, Petry found virtually no relationship between the choice between issuing debt or equity and the difference between the actual ratio and the target ratio. This was true whether the ratio is defined using book weights or market weights.

[60] Zanker (1977) goes even further. Suppose there is an optimal capital structure for your firm, but your firm does not have this capital structure. Zanker argues that you should use the weights based on the optimal capital structure.

[61] The limited evidence of these surveys appears to indicate a trend away from using book weights and toward using market weights.

[62] The list also does not include retained earnings. As discussed in Chapter 2, retained earnings are simply a substitute for common equity, if taxes and flotation costs are ignored. See Chapter 5 for further discussion of this issue.

II.B.1. Working Capital

Some companies define working capital as the difference between current assets and current liabilities; other companies exclude cash and short-term loans from the definition. No matter which definition your company uses, the acceptance of a project is almost always associated with changes in the working capital accounts. For example, there are usually increases in raw materials and work-in-process inventories as production begins. There may also be buildups of finished goods inventory if the product is not being built to order. Accounts receivable will also typically increase as sales increase. Notice that these increases in the assets portion of working capital require additional cash from the firm.

There are also typically buildups in current liabilities, such as accounts payable and wages payable. In contrast to the working capital assets, increases in these liability accounts slow down the cash outflows of the firm.

The net effects of these working capital requirements should be incorporated into the cash flow stream of the project. Exhibit 3.9 gives a simple example that illustrates this point.

Suppose that the hypothetical project of Exhibit 3.9 will last seven years. Sales start at $1 million in the first year, increase to $3 million, and then taper off as the project winds down. Analysis for this hypothetical company shows that for every dollar of sales, current assets will have an average increase of $.30; i.e., the extra activity due to additional sales causes cash, inventory, and accounts receivable to increase. Current

Exhibit 3.9: Cash Flows Due to Working Capital Requirements

Year	Sales	Working Capital	Incremental Cash Flow	Cumulative Cash Flow
1	1,000,000	100,000	−100,000	−100,000
2	1,800,000	180,000	−80,000	−180,000
3	2,500,000	250,000	−70,000	−250,000
4	3,000,000	300,000	−50,000	−300,000
5	3,000,000	300,000	0	−300,000
6	2,300,000	230,000	70,000	−230,000
7	1,300,000	130,000	100,000	−130,000
8	0	0	130,000	0

Note: Sales, working capital, and all cash flows are reported in dollars.

liabilities will have an average increase of $.20 for every extra dollar of sales. The net result is an increase in working capital of $.10 for each additional dollar of sales. Exhibit 3.9 shows the sales profile over time and the extra working capital.

Notice that as sales grow, so does the "investment" in working capital. The sales of the first year cause an increase in working capital (relative to not accepting the project) of $100,000. This buildup is in fact a cash cost to the company of $100,000; therefore, the cash flow for the first year is a negative $100,000. Sales in the second year are higher, which causes the working capital for the second year to be higher, up to $180,000. Keep in mind that the company has already invested $100,000 in working capital during the previous year. Therefore, the net cost of working capital in the second year is just $80,000, which is a negative cash flow of $80,000.

As sales begin to decrease, the required investment in working capital also decreases. For example, working capital drops from $300,000 to $230,000 between years five and six. This decrease in working capital causes a positive cash flow of $70,000 in year six. In other words, the company is selling inventory faster than it is producing inventory, and it is collecting on accounts receivable faster than it is adding to accounts receivable. The net effect is positive cash flow.

Even though the cash flows associated with changing levels of working capital are not a part of earnings and have no impact on taxes, they should be included in the cash flow stream of the project.

II.B.2. Deferred Taxes

The same applies to deferred taxes. Deferred taxes typically are created when a company uses different accounting procedures for the financial statements that it reports to the public and the financial statements that it reports to the IRS. A common source of difference is the treatment of depreciation. Companies often use accelerated depreciation for the IRS and straight-line depreciation for the public. The effect of this is to lower reported earnings for the IRS during the initial life of the project. This difference causes the publicly reported taxes to overstate the actual taxes in the early years of the project. The difference between reported and actual taxes is accounted for by the deferred tax account. The situation is reversed during the latter years of the project, when the accelerated depreciation charges are actually lower than they would have been under straight-line depreciation. During these latter years, the actual taxes are greater than the reported taxes, and the deferred tax account decreases. By the end of the project's life, the net effect of any deferred taxes associated with the project is zero.

The simplest way to treat deferred taxes is to compute the cash flows for the project using the same accounting conventions that are used to compute the actual taxes. If this is not the case, if you are constrained to using the same procedures as in the publicly reported financial statements, you should treat deferred taxes in much the same way that you handle working capital. There would be a positive adjustment to reported cash flow during the early life of the project, since your reported cash flow overstates the actual taxes. There would be a commensurate negative adjustment to reported cash flows during the latter years of the project. As mentioned earlier, it is much easier to simply use the same accounting treatments for the project as for the IRS.

In either case, you do not treat deferred taxes as a source of financing when estimating the weighted average cost of capital.

II.B.3. Recommendations

Chapter 2 provides a well-founded theory that validates your use of the weighted average cost of capital. To be consistent with this theory, you should use target market values for each source of financing. If you don't have access to market prices for the securities in your capital structure, your only choice is to use book values. Even in this case, however, you do not treat accounts such as accounts payable and deferred taxes as sources of financing.

When in doubt about whether an item is a source of financing, look at the direction of causality. Sources of financing are the funds required in order to accept the project; these sources typically include equity and debt. In other words, the sources cause (or allow) the project to exist. Items such as accounts payable are not sources of financing, but are consequences of the project, i.e., they are caused by the project.

Finally, retained earnings are not a distinct source of financing. Retained earnings exist only because a firm does not distribute all net income to shareholders. The decision to use retained earnings to finance a project is equivalent to the joint decision of distributing net income to shareholders and simultaneously raising new capital. If a firm maintains a constant capital structure, and if the value of a firm is independent of its dividend policy, the only relevant sources of financing are the external sources.[63]

---

[63] See Chapter 5 for further discussion of flotation costs.

III. Sensitivity Analysis

As shown earlier in this chapter, you should always perform sensitivity analysis when you estimate the costs of each component. Many companies also conduct sensitivity analysis with respect to the valuation methods they choose. For example, you could use either the CAPM or the dividend growth model to find the cost of equity. You could also use the historical cost of your company's debt, the average seasoned yield of equivalent-rated debt, or the average new-issue yield. You could use actual book weights, current market weights, or target rates.

An example uses data for the hypothetical company UTF to illustrate this type of sensitivity analysis. UTF's cost of equity is approximately 12.0%, according to the Linke correction to the dividend growth model; see Exhibit 3.5. Exhibit 3.7 shows that the cost of equity, based on the CAPM, is about 11.2%. The average rate on existing debt for UTF is approximately 9.5%; the book value of this debt is $420 million. Using the book value of equity from Exhibit 3.2, which is $1,272 million, the book weight of equity is 1272/(1272 + 420) = 75.2%. The book weight of debt is 420/(1272 + 420) = 24.8%.

UTF's debt is rated Aaa; the current average seasoned yield for similarly rated debt is 7.1%; the average new-issue yield for such debt is 6.9%.[64] The market value of UTF's debt is $445 million, and the market value for UTF's equity is $1,644 million. Therefore, the market weight for equity is 1644/(1644 + 445) = 78.7%; the market weight for debt is 21.3%. UTF has a target of 80% equity and 20% debt.

Exhibit 3.10 reports the cost of capital for the 18 possible combinations of choices. My recommendation is to use CAPM, the new-issue yield, and target ratios for the weights. This combination produces a weighted average cost of capital of 9.8%. The other choices of inputs result in a range from 9.4% to 10.7%.

It's probably well worth your time to conduct such a sensitivity analysis, which can be done very quickly using spreadsheet software. The analysis will provide two primary benefits. First, you can be reasonably confident that your cost of capital does in fact lie in the range indicated by the sensitivity analysis. Second, it should help dispel any notions that others in your company may have about the precision with which the cost of capital can be measured. There may exist a unique value for the cost of capital, but the existing tools of financial

---

[64] These are the values reported for September 1992 in *Moody's Bond Record*.

Exhibit 3.10: Sensitivity Analysis for the Cost of Capital

			Weights for Debt		
			Target Market	Actual Market	Book
Tax Rate =	40%		20.0%	21.3%	24.8%
CAPM Cost of Equity =	11.2%				
	New-Issue Yield =	6.9%	9.8%	9.7%	9.4%
	Seasoned Yield =	7.1%	9.8%	9.7%	9.5%
	Historical Yield =	9.5%	10.1%	10.0%	9.8%
Growth Model Cost of Equity =	12.0%				
	New-Issue Yield =	6.9%	10.4%	10.3%	10.1%
	Seasoned Yield =	7.1%	10.5%	10.4%	10.1%
	Historical Yield =	9.5%	10.7%	10.7%	10.4%

analysis are not refined enough to identify any such unique value. The best you can ask for is a reasonable range of values.

IV. Summary and Recommendations

I recommend that you use the CAPM to find your cost of equity because it does not require you to make assumptions about the growth rate in dividends. If you estimate your own beta rather than getting your beta from a published source, I recommend that you use daily returns for a two- to three-year period. I think a value-weighted market index that includes dividends is the most reasonable choice. If your company has stable growth in dividends, you also should use the dividend growth model. You should use this in conjunction with the CAPM, not as a replacement. I strongly recommend doing a sensitivity analysis, such as the one in Exhibit 3.7.

To estimate your cost of debt, I recommend that you use the after-tax new-issue yield for bonds in your risk class. It would be better still if you can get an investment banker to provide an estimate of the rate at which you can issue new debt. You should base your weights upon your target market leverage ratios. I also recommend you do a sensitivity analysis for your cost of capital, such as the one in Exhibit 3.10.

Appendix

Alternative Methods for Estimating the Cost of Equity

The body of the chapter describes only two methods for estimating the cost of equity, the dividend growth model approach and the CAPM approach. These two approaches are by far the most widely used, perhaps because they are appropriate for the vast majority of companies, although there are several less commonly used alternative approaches, some of which may be appropriate in special situations. They include: the earnings/price approach, the option-based approach, and approaches based on multifactor models of expected return.[65]

A-I. The Earnings/Price Approach

In the earnings/price approach, the cost of equity is defined as:

$$r_{E, E/P} = \frac{EPS_0}{P_0} \qquad (A1)$$

where $r_{E,E/P}$ is the earnings/price definition of the cost of equity, P_0 is the current stock price, and EPS_0 is the current earnings per share.[66] This cost of equity, $r_{E,E/P}$, is often called the "capitalization rate," since it is the rate that "capitalizes" the current earnings into the value of the firm. Notice that this is the inverse of the price/earnings ratio (P/E).

This method is certainly easy to implement, but it has a number of shortcomings. One difficulty has to do with the definition of earnings.

---

[65] There is virtually no support in the academic literature for using accounting information, such as the return on equity (ROE) or return on assets (ROA), to estimate the cost of capital; for discussion of this issue, see Gordon (1976). Yet surveys consistently find that corporations still use measures based on accounting information when conducting capital budgeting studies. Brigham (1975) found that 48% of his sample used the accounting rate of return (ARR). He also found that 94% used a discounted cash flow approach, so it appears that the firms using ARR also use a discounted cash flow approach. Kim, Crick, and Kim (1986) found that 19% of their sample used ARR, but that only 8% used ARR as the primary measure.

[66] Usually EPS_0 is defined as the current earnings, although sometimes it is defined as expected future earnings. See Solomon (1955) for a discussion.

For example, it is possible for changes in accounting conventions to affect the reported earnings without having any impact on the cash flows of the firm.

There is another major problem with this approach. To see this, compare this model with the dividend growth model:

$$r_E = \frac{D_1}{P_0} + g \tag{A2}$$

where D_1 is the dividend at time 1, and g is the growth rate in dividends. Let b denote the dividend payout rate. This allows you to express the earnings per share at time 0 as a function of the dividend at time 1:

$$EPS_0 = \frac{D_1}{(1 + g)b} \tag{A3}$$

If you substitute this into equation (A1) and do some algebra, you can express the earnings/price cost of equity as a function of the growth model cost of equity, the growth rate, and the payout ratio:

$$r_{E, E/P} = \frac{r_E - g}{(1 + g)b} \tag{A4}$$

Reasonable values for the growth model cost of equity, the payout ratio, and the growth rate are 12%, 40%, and 5%, respectively. If you substitute these values into equation (A4), you will get an earnings/price cost of equity equal to 16.67%. Notice that this is quite different from the 12% cost of equity implied by the dividend growth model. If the growth rate is 10% (the growth model cost of equity and the payout ratio are unchanged from 12% and 40%), the earnings/price cost of equity is 4.5%. In fact, the two models will rarely agree.[67] There may be some reasonable uses for the capitalization rate of equation (A1), but an estimate for the cost of equity is not one of those uses.[68]

---

[67] The two approaches give the same results if there is no growth and there is no reinvestment ($g = 0$ and $b = 1$). There are other fortuitous combinations of the growth rate, payout ratio, and dividend growth model cost of equity that produce no difference between the earnings/price cost of equity and the dividend growth model cost of equity, but these combinations are rare.

[68] Despite the shortcomings of the E/P ratio, Gitman and Mercurio (1982) report that 15.8% of the firms they surveyed used this measure. Many of their respondents reported using multiple measures, so it is not clear whether they used the E/P ratio exclusively or whether they used it in conjunction with other measures.

A-II. The Option-Based Approach

Black and Scholes (1973) have developed a widely used model for pricing options. They show as well how the stock in a firm is analogous to a call option. If the firm has outstanding zero-coupon debt that is payable in full on a particular date, stock in the firm is like an option to buy the firm's assets. This option has an expiration date equal to the maturity date of the zero-coupon debt and an exercise price equal to the face value of the debt.[69]

Let R_f denote the risk free rate; r_c the cost of capital for the entire firm; V the current total market value of the firm; E the current market value of the equity; D the face value of the debt at maturity (the debt is assumed to have no coupon payments of principal payments until its maturity); T the time until the debt matures; and σ the standard deviation of the value of the firm's assets. Copeland and Weston (1988, pp. 468–471) show that the cost of equity for the firm can be expressed as a function of these variables:

$$r_E = R_f + N(d_1)(r_c - R_f)\frac{V}{E} \qquad (A5)$$

where d_1 is defined:

$$d_1 \frac{\ln(V/D) + R_f T}{\sigma\sqrt{T}} + \frac{1}{2}\sigma\sqrt{T} \qquad (A6)$$

and $N(d_1)$ is the cumulative probability of the standard normal distribution with d_1 as the upper limit.[70] Although equation (A5) provides useful insights into the effects of leverage and firm volatility on the cost of equity, the stylized assumptions underlying equation (A5) make it difficult to apply. In other words, you cannot use equation (A5) to estimate your company's cost of equity directly.

Hsia (1991) suggests an approximation that will allow you to use equation (A5). Let A denote the annual interest payments and B denote the current market value of the firm's debt. If the capital structure is constant over time, then the debt will always be "rolled over" when

---

[69] See Galai and Masulis (1976) for a more detailed discussion.

[70] Suppose there is an urn containing numbers that are generated by a normal probability distribution that has a mean of zero and a variance of one. You reach into the urn and pull out a number. $N(d_1)$ is the probability that the number you pull out is less than or equal to d_1.

it matures. Therefore, Hsia assumes that you can approximate the actual debt as a perpetuity with current value B equal to the current market value of the existing debt and an annual payment A equal to the actual annual coupon payments of the existing debt. Hsia then assumes that the perpetuity can be approximated with a zero-coupon bond of the same duration as the perpetuity.[71] Since the duration of a zero-coupon bond is its maturity, this provides an input for the expiration date of the debt in equation (A5). As Hsia shows, this is just the ratio of the current value of debt to the annual interest payment, which is B/A.

If the current value of this substitute zero-coupon bond is B, and if the zero-coupon bond appreciates in price at a rate equal to the yield of the actual debt, then the face value of the zero-coupon bond at its maturity date is B_e, where e is defined such that $\ln(e) = 1$.[72]

After estimating the volatility of the firm, σ, you can substitute the values of the zero-coupon bond into equations (A5) and (A6) to get a usable formula for the cost of equity.[73] Following considerable algebraic manipulations, Hsia shows that the cost of equity is:

$$r_E = R_f + \left[\frac{A}{B} - R_f \right] \left[\frac{B}{E} \right] \left[\frac{N(d_1)}{N(-d_1)} \right] \qquad (A7)$$

where d_1 is defined:

$$d_1 = \frac{\ln(1 + E/B) + (1/A)(R_f B - A)}{\sigma \sqrt{B/A}} + \frac{1}{2} \sigma \sqrt{B/A} \qquad (A8)$$

Although Hsia (1991) makes a number of assumptions without rigorous justification, his suggested approach does provide a practical way to use option pricing in finding the cost of equity. Following is an example using the hypothetical firm UTF.

The average coupon rate for UTF is 9.5%; see Exhibit 3.10. With a book value of debt equal to $420 million, the annual interest payment, denoted by A, is A = (.095)(420) = $39.9 million. The market value of debt, B, is $445 million. As Hsia shows, a perpetuity that pays $39.9

---

[71] See Bierwag (1977) for a more detailed discussion of duration.

[72] The value of e is approximately 2.71828.

[73] Hsia (1991) suggests you estimate σ using option pricing theory. You can directly observe the value of the equity, which is itself a function of σ and the observable variables A, B, and R_f. It is straightforward to find the value of σ that make the relationship between equity and the observed variables true. See Hsia (1991) for further details.

million per year and that has a current value of $445 million would have a duration of 445/39.9, which is 11.15 years. A zero-coupon bond with a current market value of $445 million and a current yield equal to the yield on the perpetuity would grow to (445)(e) = $1209.63 million in 11.15 years. In other words, Hsia suggests that you can model the coupon-paying fixed-maturity debt of UTF as though the debt is a zero-coupon bond that matures in 11.15 years with a face value of $1209.63 million; the current market value of this hypothetical zero-coupon bond is $445 million.

UTF has a market value of equity, E, equal to $1644 million. The only missing variable in equation (A8) is σ, the standard deviation of the market value of the firm. The value of σ for UTF is .575.[74]

Using these values in equation (A8), the value of d_1 is:

Computation of d1	
E =	1644
B =	445
A =	39.9
Rf =	.025
σ	.575
d1 =	.93430352

The standard normal cumulative density function evaluated at d_1, $N(d_1)$, is:

$$N(.934) = .8249 \text{ and } N(-.934) = .1751.$$

---

[74] The Black–Scholes option pricing formula expresses the value of a call option in terms of the current price of the stock, the risk-free interest rate, the time until the option matures, the exercise price of the option, and the standard deviation of the rate of return on the stock. The equity in a firm can be modeled as a call option, with the market value of the equity equivalent to the value of the call option. The exercise price of the "option" is the face value of the debt in the firm, and the time until the "option" expires is the maturity date of the debt. All these variables, with the exception of σ, the standard deviation of the rate of return on the firm's value, are known for UTF. Therefore, you can simply "solve" the Black–Scholes formula to find an estimate of σ. A value of .575 for σ "solves" the Black–Scholes formula when you use the data for UTF.

Using equation (A7), the cost of equity is:

Computation of Cost of Equity	
E =	1644
B =	445
A =	39.9
Rf =	.025
N(d1) =	.8249
N(−d1) =	.1751
Cost of Equity =	10.7%

Hsia's option pricing approach produces a cost of equity for UTF equal to 10.7%. This is similar to UTF's cost of equity using the dividend growth model (12.0%) and UTF's cost of equity using the CAPM (11.2%).

A-III. Multifactor Models

A number of studies suggest that the CAPM may not correctly specify the expected returns of stocks.[75] The arbitrage pricing theory (APT) of Ross (1974, 1976) provides a sound theoretical justification for the existence of multifactor models. Space constraints prohibit an in-depth discussion of APT or a complete description of all the possible multifactor models. Instead, this section focuses upon several specific models and shows how they can be used to estimate the cost of equity.

Think about a firm that produces steel and another firm that makes children's clothing. The stock returns for both companies will probably react to unexpected changes in energy costs and unexpected changes in labor costs. It is likely, however, that the producer of steel will react more sharply to changes in energy costs than will the maker of children's clothing. The reverse will probably be true for changes in labor costs. The unexpected changes in energy costs and the unexpected changes in labor costs are factors that are common to both companies,

---

[75] For example, it appears as though small stocks and low P/E ratio stocks receive a greater return than that predicted by the CAPM. See Reilly (1985) or any other textbook in investments for further discussion of these anomalies.

although each company has a different sensitivity to the factors. If you compare two steel producers, their stock returns would undoubtedly be different even if they each had the same sensitivity to energy and labor costs, since each company has other unique attributes. This suggests that there is also a unique component to stock returns, in addition to the common factors.

APT assumes that the difference between the actual return on a security and its expected return is a function of several common factors and an error that is specific to the particular security. Let δ_{kt} denote the unexpected change in the kth common factor at time t, b_{ik} denote the sensitivity of the ith company to this kth source of risk, and ε_{it} denote an error term that is specific to the ith firm. If there are K sources of risk, then:

$$R_{it} - E[R_{it}] = \sum_{k=1}^{K} b_{ik}\, \delta_{kt} + \varepsilon_{it} \tag{A9}$$

In his derivation of APT, Ross (1974, 1976) shows that the expected return must be a function of the security's sensitivities:

$$E[R_{it}] = \lambda_{0t} + \sum_{k=1}^{K} \lambda_{kt}\, b_{ik} \tag{A10}$$

where λ_{0t} is the risk-free rate on date t, and λ_{kt} is the risk premium for bearing the kth source of risk on date t.

A-III.A. The "Unspecified" APT Approach

If you have a sample of historical returns for a group of companies, you could apply a statistical technique called factor analysis to estimate the sensitivities, b_{ik}. You can estimate the risk premiums by using a procedure similar to that of Fama and MacBeth (1973). In this approach, you pick a particular sample date, t, and regress the returns on that date for all the companies in your sample against the companies' sensitivities:

$$R_{i\tau} - R_{f\tau} = a_0 + \sum_{k=1}^{K} a_{k\tau}\, b_{ik} + w_{i\tau} \tag{A11}$$

where the a's are the estimated regression coefficients. These regression coefficients are the estimates of the risk premiums ($\lambda_{k\tau}$) for that particular date, τ. If you do this for each date in your sample period, you will have estimates of the risk premiums, $\lambda_k \tau$, for each date. Although the description in this appendix is brief, this actually is a fairly complicated process. See Roll and Ross (1980) for a detailed example of this approach.

Your next step is to find the expected risk premium for each source of risk. In the absence of any other compelling reasons, you could estimate this as the average risk premium during your sample period:

$$\overline{\lambda}_k = \sum_{t=1}^{T} \lambda_{kt} \qquad \text{(A12)}$$

when there are T periods in your sample.

To find the cost of equity, you can take equation (A10) and substitute the risk-free rate for λ_{0t}; you should also substitute the average risk premium that you found in equation (A12). The result is:

$$r_E = R_f + \sum_{k=1}^{K} b_{ik} \overline{\lambda}_k \qquad \text{(A13)}$$

There is one important advantage to this approach. The way in which you define the factors is designed to provide high explanatory power with the common factors. In other words, you will be unlikely to overlook any sources of systematic risk with this model. At the same time, the computational procedures are relatively complex, and the resulting factors are defined somewhat arbitrarily. It is also difficult to link the estimated factors with any macroeconomic factors, which reduces the intuitive appeal of the model.

A-III.B. A Priori Multifactor Models

To avoid the problems with the unspecified factors in the previous section, you might instead specify the factors a priori. A good example of this is the multifactor model of Chen, Roll, and Ross (1986). They hypothesize that stock returns are a function of several macroeconomic variables: industrial production (IP), unexpected inflation (UI), the change in expected inflation (DEI), the risk premium between long-term government bonds and low-quality corporate bonds (UPR), and the steepness of the term structure (UTS).[76] In contrast to the "unspeci-

---

[76] They also try several other variables, including the growth rate in real per capita consumption and an oil price inflation term.

fied" APT model, this approach has considerable intuitive appeal; there are logical reasons why the hypothesized factors should affect stock returns.

Using a time series of historical returns for your company, you could find the sensitivities to the factors by the regression:

$$R_i = a + b_{IP} IP + b_{UI} UI + b_{DEI} DEI + b_{UPR} UPR \quad (A14)$$
$$+ b_{UTS} UTS + \varepsilon$$

The expected return on equity is:

$$r_E = R_f + b_{IP} \lambda_{IP} + b_{UI} \lambda_{UI} + b_{DEI} \lambda_{DEI} + b_{UPR} \lambda_{UPR} \quad (A15)$$
$$+ b_{UTS} \lambda_{UTS}$$

where the λ's are the risk premiums for the hypothesized factors. You can estimate the risk premiums in exactly the same way as in the previous example of an "unspecified" APT model; i.e., conduct a cross-sectional regression like that of equation (A11) for each date in your sample period, and then average the estimated risk premiums as in equation (A12).

A variation on this type of multifactor model is to specify a priori the sensitivities (b_{ik}) instead of the factors. For example, Fama and French (1992) find that size (b_S) and the book–equity/market–equity ratio ($b_{B/M}$) are significantly related to stock returns. Since these variables are directly observable, you don't need to conduct a time series regression, such as equation (A14). The cost of equity is:

$$r_E = R_f + b_S \overline{\lambda}_S + b_{B/M} \overline{\lambda}_{B/M} \quad (A16)$$

where the risk premiums (the average λ's) are estimated using cross-sectional regression similar to those in the previous example.

A-III.C. Industry Index Models

Another alternative multifactor model is to retain the market index but also to add an industry index. Let R_I denote the return on an industry index, which is usually a portfolio of stocks from the same industry. Some define the industry by either the two-digit or three-digit Standard Industrial Classification (SIC) code; see Langetieg (1978) and Fertuck (1975), for example. Others such as Sharpe (1982) define the industry as broader set of SIC codes. The time series regression for your company is:

$$R_i = b_0 + b_m R_m + b_I R_I + \varepsilon \qquad (A17)$$

where the b's are the estimated regression coefficients.[77]

The cost of equity is:

$$r_E = R_f + b_m \overline{\lambda}_m + b_I \overline{\lambda}_I \qquad (A18)$$

where the λ's are the risk premiums. You can estimate these premiums with cross-sectional regressions such as in the previous examples.

A-III.D. Using Interest Rate Indexes

Since stocks represent a claim to a future stream of income, it is certainly reasonable that changes in interest rates may affect stock returns.[78] This suggests a multifactor model, with at least one factor representing interest rate effects. There are many different ways to model this interest rate factor. Fogler, John, and Tipton (1981) use two interest rate factors, the excess return on a three-month U.S. Treasury bond and the excess return on a long-term Aaa utility bond. Flannery and James (1984) use the return on a Government National Mortgage Association (GNMA) certificate, the percentage change in yields of an index of seven-year U.S. Treasury bonds, and the return on a one-year U.S. Treasury bond. Oldfield and Rogalski (1981) use five factors that they extract from U.S. Treasury bills using factor analysis. Ehrhardt (1991) estimates the term structure of interest rates using U.S. Treasury bonds; he then constructs three measures of interest rate risk (short-term, medium-term, and long-term) using the estimated term structures.

As you can see, there are many reasonable ways to model interest rate risk. After you have defined the measure of interest rate risk, however, the approach for estimating the cost of equity is identical to that of the previous multifactor model with an industry factor.

---

[77] A variation on this approach is to express all returns as the returns in excess of the risk-free rate. Also, you could orthogonalize the industry index with respect to the market index. See Langetieg (1978) for an example.

[78] Merton (1973) develops an intertemporal CAPM. Under certain simplifying assumptions, his model implies that stock returns are a function of bond portfolios as well as the stock market portfolio.

A-IV. Miscellaneous Approaches

There are a number of other possible approaches. For example, Gitman and Mercurio (1982) find in their survey that 13% of the respondents estimate the cost of equity by adding a risk premium to their cost of debt. There are problems with this approach, because it is not clear how you should compute that risk premium.[79] Notice that this approach is consistent with the underlying concept of the CAPM, but it places particular restrictions on the CAPM. For example, adding a premium to the cost of debt is like applying the CAPM to a company that has a beta equal to one; it also assumes that the premium is defined as the risk premium on the market portfolio and that the risk-free rate is the yield on the bond.

Elliott (1980, p. 17) suggests using "the average return on stockholders' equity achieved by all industries" as an estimate of the cost of equity. This is equivalent to the CAPM, except that it implies that the beta is equal to one. In other words, this method does not differentiate between the riskiness of individual companies.

Finally, Kalotay (1982) suggests finessing the entire issue by not estimating the cost of equity. He suggests instead that you directly estimate the cost of capital rather than the costs of the components of capital structure. In several examples, Kalotay finds the discount rate that equates the current price with the combined stream of coupon payments and dividend payments.

A-V. Summary and Recommendations

When should you use one of the more complicated models in this appendix instead of the simpler approaches of the CAPM or the dividend growth model? The answer depends on the nature of your company. If you don't have very predictable dividends, then you shouldn't use the dividend growth model. Suppose that you try to use the CAPM, and you estimate your beta using a regression (such as equation [3.24] in the body of the chapter). If you don't get a statistically significant beta or if the R^2 of your regression is less than about .05 for daily data or .15 for monthly data, then you should try one of the multifactor models described in this appendix. If your company is very sensitive to certain commodity prices (a candy manufacturer would be sensitive to sugar and cocoa prices), you might want to include such factors in a multifactor model. If your industry is subject to cyclicity,

---

[79] Keane (1976) even suggests that the cost of debt should be used as the cost of capital.

you might want to add an industry index to your model. In other words, there is no single answer that fits all firms. You'll have to use your own judgment as to which model is right for your company.

References

Alberts, W.W., and S.H. Archer. "Some Evidence on the Effect of Company Size on the Cost of Equity Capital." *Journal of Financial and Quantitative Analysis*, 8(2) (1973): 229–242.

Ben-Horim, M., and J.L. Callen. "The Cost of Capital, Macaulay's Duration, and Tobin's q." *Journal of Financial Research* 12(2) (1989): 143–156.

Beranek, W. "The Weighted Average Cost of Capital and Shareholder Wealth Maximization." *Journal of Financial and Quantitative Analysis*, 1977, 12(1), 17–31.

Bierwag, G.O. "Immunization, Duration, and the Term Structure of Interest Rates." *Journal of Financial and Quantitative Analysis* 12 (December 1977): 725–744.

Black, F. "Capital Market Equilibrium with Restricted Borrowing." *Journal of Business* 45 (1972): 444–455.

Black, F., and M. Scholes. "The Pricing of Options and Corporate Liabilities." *Journal of Political Economy* 81 (May/June 1973): 637–654.

Blume, M.E. "Betas and their Regression Tendencies." *Journal of Finance* 30(3) (1975): 785–795.

Brennan, M.J. "A New Look at the Weighted Average Cost of Capital." *Journal of Business Finance* (Spring 1973): 24–30.

Brigham, E.F. "Hurdle Rates for Screening Capital Expenditure Proposals." *Financial Management* 4(3) (1975): 17–26.

Brigham, E.F., D. Shome, and S. Vinson. "The Risk Premium Approach to Measuring Utility's Cost of Equity." *Financial Management* (Spring 1985): 33–45.

Brown, L.D., and M.S. Rozeff. "The Superiority of Analysts' Forecasts as Measures of Expectations: Evidence from Earnings." *Journal of Finance* 33(1) (1978): 1–16.

———. "Analysts Can Forecast Accurately!" *Journal of Portfolio Management* 6(3) (1979–1980): 31–34.

Carleton, W.T., and J. Lakonishok. "Risk and Return on Equity: The Use and Misuse of Historical Estimates." *Financial Analysts Journal* (January-February 1985): 38–47.

Chatfield, R.E., S.E. Hein, and R.C. Moyer. "Long-Term Earnings Forecasts in the Electric Utility Industry: Accuracy and Valuation Implications." *Financial Review* 25(3) (1990): 421–440.

Chen, N., R. Roll, and S.A. Ross. "Economic Forces and the Stock Market." *Journal of Business* (July 1986): 383–403.

Copeland, T., T. Koller, and J. Murrin. *Valuation: Measuring and Managing the Value of Companies*. New York: Wiley, 1990.

Copeland, T.E., and J.F. Weston. *Financial Theory and Corporate Policy* 3d ed. Reading, Mass.: Addison-Wesley, 1988.

Daves, P., and M.C. Ehrhardt. "The Disappearing Market Premium." Working Paper, University of Tennessee, 1992.

Daves, P.R., M.C. Ehrhardt, G. Kuhlmeyer, and R.A. Kunkel. "Changes in the Relationship Between Firm Size and Systematic Risk." Working Paper, University of Tennessee, 1993.

Daves, P.R., M.C. Ehrhardt, and R.A. Kunkel. "Estimating Systematic Risk: The Choice of Return Interval and the Number of Observations." Working Paper, University of Tennessee, 1992.

Dimson, E. "Risk Measurement When Shares Are Subject to Infrequent Trading." *Journal of Financial Economics* 7 (1979): 197–226.

Ehrhardt, M. "Diversification and Interest Rate Risk." *Journal of Business Finance and Accounting* 18(1) (January 1991): 43–59.

Elliott, G.S. "Analyzing the Cost of Capital." *Management Accounting* 62(6) (1980): 13–18.

Fama, E.F., and K.R. French. "The Cross-Section of Expected Stock Returns." *Journal of Finance* 47(2) (1992): 427–466.

Fama, E.F., and J. MacBeth. "Risk, Return, and Equilibrium: Empirical Tests." *Journal of Political Economy* 81 (May–June 1973): 607–636.

Farrell, J., Jr. "The Dividend Discount Model: A Primer." *Financial Analysts Journal* (November–December 1985): 16–25.

Fertuck, L. "A Test of Industry Indices Based on S.I.C. Codes." *Journal of Financial and Quantitative Analysis* (December 1975): 837–848.

Flannery, M.J., and C.M. James. "The Effect of Interest Rate Changes on the Common Stock Returns of Financial Institutions." *Journal of Finance* 39(4) (September 1984): 1141–1153.

Fogler, H.R., K. John, and J. Tipton. "Three Factors, Interest Rate Differentials and Stock Groups." *Journal of Finance* 36(2) (May 1981): 323–335.

Galai, D., and R.W. Masulis. "The Option Pricing Model and the Risk Factor of Stock." *Journal of Financial Economics* (1976): 53–81.

Gallinger, W., and G.V. Henderson, Jr. "Hurdle Rates For Strategic Investments." *Advances in Financial Planning and Forecasting* 1 (1985): 125–144.

Gitman, L.J., and V.A. Mercurio. "Cost of Capital Techniques used by Major U.S. Firms: Survey and Analysis of Fortune's 1000." *Financial Management* 11(4) (1982): 21–29.

Glenn, D.W., and R.H. Litzenberger. "An Interindustry Approach to Econometric Cost of Capital Estimation." *Research in Finance* 1 (1979): 53–76.

Gordon, L.A. "The Return on Investment and the Cost of Capital." *Management Accounting* 57(8) (1976): 37–40.

Gordon, M.J., and E. Shapiro. "Capital Equipment Analysis: The Required Rate of Profit." *Management Science* 3 (October 1956): 102–110.

Haley, C.W. "Taxes, the Cost of Capital, and the Firm's Investment Decisions." *Journal of Finance* 26(4) (1971): 901–917.

Harris, R.S. "Using Analysts' Growth Forecasts to Estimate Shareholder Required Rates of Return." *Financial Management* (Spring 1988): 58–67.

Harris, R.S., and F.C. Marston. "Estimating Shareholder Risk Premia Using Analysts' Growth Forecasts." *Financial Management* (Summer 1992): 63–70.

Holt, C.C. "The Influence of Growth Duration on Share Prices." *Journal of Finance* 17(3) (1962): 465–475.

Hsia, C. "Estimating a Firm's Cost of Capital: An Option Pricing Approach." *Journal of Business Finance and Accounting* 18(2) (1991): 281–287.

Ibbotson Associates, Inc. *1990 Stocks, Bonds, Bills, and Inflation.* Charlottesville, Va.: 1990 Yearbook.

Ibbotson, R.G., and R.A. Sinquefield. *Stocks, Bonds, Bills and Inflation: Historical Returns (1926–1987).* Charlottesville, Va.: The Financial Analysts Research Foundation, 1989.

Kalotay, A.J. "Notes on the Definition of the Cost of Capital." *Journal of Financial Education* 11 (1982): 76–78.

Keane, S.M. "Some Aspects of the Cost of Debt." *Accounting and Business Research* (Autumn 1975): 298–304.

———. "The Investment Discount Rate—In Defence of the Market Rate of Interest." *Accounting and Business Research* (Summer 1976): 228–236.

Kim, S.H., T. Crick, and S.H. Kim. "Do Executives Practice What Academics Preach?" *Management Accounting* (November 1986): 49–52.

Langetieg, T.C. "An Application of a Three-Factor Performance Index to Measure Stockholder Gain from Merger." *Journal of Financial Economics* 6 (1978): 365–383.

Levhari, D., and H. Levy. "The Capital Asset Pricing Model and the Investment Horizon." *The Review of Economics and Statistics* 59 (1977): 92–104.

Linke, C.M., and J.K. Zumwalt. "Estimation Biases in Discounted Cash Flow Analyses of Equity Capital Cost in Rate Regulation." *Financial Management* 13(3) (1984): 15–21.

Lintner, J. "The Valuation of Risk Assets and the Selection of Risky Investments." *The Review of Economics and Statistics* (February 1965): 13–37.

Litzenbeger, R., K. Ramaswamy, and H. Sosin. "On the CAPM Approach to the Estimation of a Public Utility's Cost of Equity Capital." *Journal of Finance* 35(2) (1980): 369–383.

Malkiel, B. "The Capital Formation Problem in the United States." *Journal of Finance* (May 1979): 291–306.

Merton, R. "An Intertemporal Capital Asset Pricing Model." *Econometrica* (September 1973): 867–888.

———. "On Estimating the Expected Return on the Market." *Journal of Financial Economics* 8 (1980): 323–361.

Mossin, J. "Equilibrium in a Capital Asset Market." *Econometrica* (October 1966): 768–783.

Oldfield, G., Jr., and R. Rogalski. "Treasury Bill Factors and Common Stock Returns." *Journal of Finance* (May 1981): 337–350.

Petry, Glenn H. "Empirical Evidence on Cost of Capital Weights." *Financial Management* 4(4) (1975): 58–65.

Reilly, F.K. *Investment Analysis and Portfolio Analysis* 2d ed. New York: CBS College Publishing, 1985.

Roll, R. "A Critique of the Asset Pricing Theory's Tests." *Journal of Financial Economics* (March 1977): 129–176.

Roll, R., and S. Ross. "An Empirical Investigation of the Arbitrage Pricing Theory." *Journal of Finance* (December 1980): 1073–1103.

Ross, S.A. "Return, Risk, and Arbitrage." In *Risk and Return in Finance,* Irwin Friend and James Bicksler, eds. New York: Heath Lexington, 1974.

———. "The Arbitrage Theory of Capital Asset Pricing." *Journal of Economic Theory* (December 1976): 343–362.

Ross, S.A., R.W. Westerfield, and J.E. Jaffe. *Corporate Finance* 2d ed. Homewood, Il.: Richard D. Irwin, 1990.

Scholes, M., and J. Williams. "Estimating Betas From Nonsynchronous Data." *Journal of Financial Economics* 5 (1977): 309–327.

Shapiro, A.C. *Modern Corporate Finance.* New York: Macmillan, 1989.

Sharpe, W.F. "Capital Asset Prices: A Theory of Market Equilibrium under Conditions of Risk." *Journal of Finance* (September 1964): 425–442.

———. "Factors in New York Stock Exchange Security Returns, 1931–1979." *Journal of Portfolio Management* (Summer 1982): 5–19.

Shiller, R.J., and F. Modigliani. "Coupon and Tax Effects on New and Seasoned Bond Yields and the Measurement of the Cost of Debt Capital." *Journal of Financial Economics* 7(3) (1979): 297–318.

Siegel, J.J. "The Application of the DCF Methodology for Determining the Cost of Equity Capital." *Financial Management* 14(1) (1985): 46–53.

Smith, K.V. "The Effect of Intervaling on Estimating Parameters of the Capital Asset Pricing Model." *Journal of Financial and Quantitative Analysis* 13 (1978): 313–332.

Solomon, E. "Measuring a Company's Cost of Capital." *Journal of Business* 28(4) (1955): 240–252.

Vander Weide, J.H., and W.T. Carleton. "Investor Growth Expectations: Analysts vs. History." *Journal of Portfolio Management* 14(3) (1987–1988): 78–83.

Vasicek, O.A. "A Note on Using Cross-Sectional Information in Bayesian Estimation of Security Betas." *Journal of Finance* 28(5) (1973): 1233–1239.

Williams, E.E., and M.C. Findlay, III. "Capital Budgeting, Cost of Capital and Ex Ante Static Equilibrium." *Journal of Business Finance and Accounting* 6(4) (1979): 455–474.

Williams, J.B. *Theory of Investment Value.* Cambridge, Mass.: Harvard University Press, 1938.

Zanker, F.W.A. "The Cost of Capital for Debt-Financed Investments." *Journal of Business Finance and Accounting* 4(3) (1977): 277–284.

Chapter 4

The Cost of Capital for a Division, a Project, or a Private Company

Chapter 3 shows you how to estimate the cost of capital for a typical project in a company with publicly traded stock. But what if your company is privately held? Or maybe your company is pursuing a conglomerate acquisition of a privately held company (or division) in a completely different line of business? In neither case can you estimate the cost of equity using the methods in Chapter 3, because those methods require observations of market prices for the company's stock.

You can run into the same problem even if your company has publicly traded stock. For example, suppose your company owns and operates a chain of fast food restaurants. Among the items you serve is a sandwich made with a croissant. You purchase the croissants from another company, which delivers them to your restaurants, but you are considering a change. You will open your own bakery to supply your restaurants with croissants. The bakery will also sell baked goods to external customers. What cost of capital should you use for this project?

You could always punt, and use your company's overall cost of capital, but this solution isn't very satisfying, and it probably won't maximize the value of your company. Perhaps bakeries are riskier than restaurants. This means that your company's overall cost of capital is too low for the proposed bakery project. If you use your company's cost of capital to discount the cash flows of the project, your estimate of the project's NPV will be greater than the project's true NPV. This could lead you to accept the project even though it has a negative NPV.

The reverse is true if bakeries are not as risky as restaurants: you might reject a project that has a positive NPV.

This problem is even more severe if you have a large number of projects with differing risks. Suppose your company has only two divisions, one that manufactures electronic circuit boards, and one that assembles small electronic appliances such as portable televisions. Let's assume that virtually all projects in the circuit board division are similar to one another, and that projects in the television assembly division are similar to one another. Projects in the circuit board division are riskier than the projects in the television assembly division, however.

The overall cost of capital for your company is an average of the higher cost of capital for the circuit board division and the lower cost of capital for the television assembly division. If you use the overall cost of capital for your company to evaluate projects in both divisions, you will systematically accept poor projects from the circuit board division and systematically reject value-adding projects in the television assembly division.[1]

In a rare show of unity, the academic literature is virtually unanimous in recommending adjustments when evaluating projects with different levels of risk.[2] Rarer still, most corporations agree with academicians on this point. Surveys consistently indicate that many companies make adjustments for projects or divisions with differing risks.[3] More recent surveys also show that more and more companies are now adjusting for divisional and/or project risk.

Given that you should make an adjustment, how do you actually estimate the divisional or project cost of capital? Section I shows how

---

[1] See Taggart (1987) for an interesting discussion on the way companies allocate capital to their divisions and the role that the divisional cost of capital plays.

[2] See, for example, Bower and Lessard (1973), Shapiro (1989), or any corporate finance textbook.

[3] In a survey of 33 large companies, Brigham (1975) finds that about one-half of the companies adjust the cost of capital to reflect differences in risk. Approximately 45% of the respondents adjust for different divisions, 35% for different types of projects (replacement, expansion, new product, and so forth), and 23% for individual projects. In a later survey with a much larger sample, Gitman and Mercurio (1982) find that about two-thirds of their respondents adjust for risk, with 59.9% adjusting individual projects. Of those that adjust for risk, about 39% adjust the cash flows, 32.2% adjust the cost of capital, and 19.5% adjust both. Kim, Crick, and Kim (1986) survey companies in the *Fortune* 1000, and find that 44% make some adjustment for projects of differing risk. Weaver, Clemmens, Gunn, and Dannenburg (1989) conducted a panel discussion of executives at the 1988 Financial Management Association. Three of the four executives indicated that their firms adjust the cost of capital for divisional and/or project risk, with the fourth stating that his company was interested in implementing an adjustment for risk.

to estimate the systematic risk of an individual line of business using the pure-play approach and the multiple regression approach. With an estimate of systematic risk, you can use the capital asset pricing model of Chapter 3 to estimate the cost of equity. If your capital structure is different from that of the typical firm engaged in that line of business, you must make an adjustment; Section II describes these adjustments. The appendix describes several types of changes that may affect your company's systematic risk: leasing, unfunded pension liabilities, accounting procedures, exchange listings, and liquidity.

The focus in this chapter is on estimating risk when you do not have access to market stock prices and on making adjustments in the cost of capital both when the project is in a different line of business and when the capital structure of your firm is different from the capital structure of the line of business. There are many other differences between projects that are unrelated to differences in lines of business or capital structures. For example, the addition of a new product within a single line of business probably has a different type of risk from the replacement of worn equipment used to produce an existing product within that line of business. Chapter 8 addresses these types of risk.

I. Estimating Systematic Risk When Stock Prices Are Not Observable

If you knew the systematic risk of your division or project, you could apply the CAPM approach of Chapter 3 to determine your cost of equity. But how can you estimate the systematic risk of an asset when you can't observe the asset's market prices? There are two schools of thought on estimating systematic risk lacking access to market prices. One is based primarily on accounting data, and the other is based primarily on market data. The accounting-based approaches are used much less frequently than the market-based approaches; therefore, this chapter describes only the market-based approaches.[4]

The market-based approaches assume that the systematic risk for a particular line of business is constant for all firms that compete in

---

[4] Some of the accounting-based approaches describe the estimation of "accounting betas"; see Beaver, Kettler, and Scholes (1970); Gonedes (1973); Beaver and Manegold (1975); Hill and Stone (1980); and Bartley (1982). Kulkarni, Powers, and Shannon (1989) describe a variation that can be used to estimate the accounting beta of a product line. There are several approaches that blend accounting and market data; see Rosenberg and McKibben (1973); Gordon and Halpern (1974, 1977); Weston and Lee (1977); Maus (1980); and Gup and Norwood (1982).

the line of business.[5] For example, if two different firms each have a division that competes in the retail clothing industry, the divisional beta for the retail clothing division will be the same for both firms.

There are two different market-based approaches: (1) the pure-play approach, and (2) the multiple regression approach.

I.A. The Pure-Play Approach

The idea behind the pure-play approach is straightforward. First, you find a sample of publicly traded firms that compete in a single line of business similar to the line of business of your division. This is where the pure-play approach gets its name: the firms in the comparison group are "pure-plays" in the sense that they compete in a single line of business. Second, you use the stock returns to determine the beta of each pure-play firm. Third, you use these market-determined betas to estimate the beta for your division.

Fuller and Kerr (1981) provide a good example of this approach. Suppose you are interested in finding the beta for a papermaking division. If you follow the Fuller and Kerr approach, you would find a pure-play firm that competes in only the papermaking line of business. This pure-play firm should also be similar to your division with respect to size of revenues.[6] Since the pure-play firm is publicly traded, you can estimate its market beta and use this as an estimate of your division's beta.

If you find more than one firm that is a matching pure play, you can use either the average beta or the median beta of these pure-play firms. There is no clear-cut guide as to whether you should use the average beta or the median beta. Usually the average and the median will be similar, but if they are not, you should view both of them with some caution. The only reason that the average and median would differ significantly is that the sample contains some outliers whose betas are very different from the betas of the other firms in the sample. If this is the case, you might consider deleting the outliers from your sample.

For example, suppose you have ten pure-play firms in your sample. Exhibit 4.1 reports the betas for each company in the sample; it also shows the average beta and the median beta.

---

[5] Findlay, Gooding, and Weaver (1976) suggest an alternative market-based approach. Instead of estimating a divisional beta relative to market returns, they suggest estimating a firm's divisional beta relative to the firm's own returns.

[6] Fuller and Kerr (1981) also tried to find pure plays that competed in the same geographical area.

Exhibit 4.1: Average Beta vs. Median Beta in the Pure-Play Approach

Company	Beta		
1	.91		
2	.93		
3	.95		
4	.97		
5	.99		
6	1.01		
7	1.03		
8	1.05		
9	1.07		
10	2.50		
Average of all Betas =	1.14	Average Beta (excluding Company 10) =	.99
Median of all Betas =	1.00	Median Beta (excluding Company 10) =	.99

Notice that the average beta of 1.14 is quite a bit different from the median beta of 1.00. As you can see, this difference is attributable to the beta of company 10, which is different from the betas of the other nine companies. Excluding company 10 produces approximately equal average and median betas.

You should always check the average beta and median beta for differences, although you can have problems even if the average and the median are similar. For example, suppose you have a different sample of ten pure plays. Exhibit 4.2 reports their betas.

Notice that the average beta and the median beta are both equal to 1.00. In this case, however, you shouldn't be very confident in 1.00 as an estimate of the line of business beta for your division. After all, the pure-play betas vary from .10 all the way to 1.90. The standard deviation provides a measure for this dispersion. With such a large standard deviation, you can be only 95% confident that your divisional beta lies between .62 and 1.38. Therefore, you should

Exhibit 4.2: The Pure-Play Approach Confidence Interval

Company	Beta			
1	.1			
2	.3	Median Beta =	1.00	
3	.5			
4	.7	Average Beta =	1.00	
5	.9			
6	1.1	Standard Deviation of Beta =	.61	
7	1.3			
8	1.5		Low End	High End
9	1.7	95% Confidence Interval =	.62	1.38
10	1.9			

always check the 95% confidence interval as well as comparing the average and median.[7]

You probably have two questions in mind. First, is it reasonable to assume that the beta of a division is constant no matter which company owns the division? Second, can you actually find a pure-play firm that matches your division?

Fuller and Kerr (1981) provide a fairly convincing answer to the first question. They collected a sample of 60 multidivisional firms, with a total of 142 divisions. For each of these divisions, they found a matching pure play. Occasionally they found more than one pure-play firm that matched. In these cases, they estimated the market betas for all these matching pure plays and selected the pure-play firm with the median beta.

Keep in mind that the overall beta for a multidivisional firm should be the weighted average of the divisional betas:

$$\beta_{Mj} = \sum_{s=1}^{N} w_{js}\, \beta_{js} \tag{4.1}$$

where β_{Mj} denotes the overall beta for multidivisional firm j, w_{js} denotes the percentage of market value of multidivisional firm j in segment s,

---

[7] Roughly speaking, the 95% confidence interval is from AVERAGE + 1.96 $(\sigma/\sqrt{n})$ to AVERAGE − 1.96 $(\sigma/\sqrt{n})$, where AVERAGE is the beta, σ is the estimate of the standard deviation of the betas, and n is the number of betas in the sample. The 1.96 is based on the normal distribution; strictly speaking, you should use the appropriate value from the student −t distribution for the number of observations in your sample.

and β_{js} denotes the beta for the pure-play firm in business segment s; there are a total of N possible segments.

Fuller and Kerr (1981) proxied the market value weights, w_{js}, with the percentage of sales in the division. With these weights and the matching pure-play betas, they used equation (4.1) to estimate the overall beta for the multidivisional firms. Comparison of these estimated overall betas with the actual market betas indicates a very close fit. In a regression of actual market beta against the pure-play estimate, the intercept is −.055, and the slope coefficient is 1.067; the R^2 for the regression is .78. These results indicate that the weighted average of the pure-play betas quite closely approximates the market beta. This implies that a particular divisional beta is not significantly different for any of the firms that operate in that line of business.

So the answer to your first question is "yes, it's reasonable to assume that divisional betas are pretty much the same for all firms." Unfortunately, the answer to your second question is often "no." There are many lines of business for which it is very difficult to find a matching pure play. In this case you use the multiple regression approach.

I.B. The Multiple Regression Approach

The regression approach assumes that the overall market beta of a firm is the weighted average of the divisional betas. The approach also assumes that the beta for a division is constant, no matter which firm owns the division. Finally, the regression approach assumes that you have access to a sample that has more companies than total number of divisions.[8] I explain the approach in a simple way and give an example to illustrate ways you can implement the approach for your company.

Suppose you collect a sample of M firms. For each firm in the sample, you must estimate the overall market beta, β_{Mj}. You must also define the business segments for each firm in your sample. Suppose you do this, and it results in N different business segments, where N, the number of business segments, is less than M, the number of companies. Your next step is to define the market weight for each segment in each company, w_{js}. Given these inputs, you run the regression:

$$\beta_{Mj} = \sum_{s=1}^{N} w_{js}\, \beta_s + \varepsilon_j \qquad (4.2)$$

---

[8] If this is not the case, you can't use the regression approach. An alternative that you can use in this situation is the goal-programming approach. See Boquist and Moore (1983) and Crum and Bi (1988).

where ε_j is the error term. The market betas for your firms are the dependent variables in a regression, and the weights for the divisions are the explanatory variables in the regression. The estimated coefficients, β_s, are the divisional betas. Ehrhardt and Bhagwat (1991) and Wood, McInish, and Lawrence (1992) show that this approach provides excellent estimates of divisional betas.[9]

How do you actually implement this approach for your company? What criteria should you use to select your sample? How do you define your business segments? How do you measure the weights? I explain how two different research studies answer these questions.

Ehrhardt and Bhagwat (1991) defined business segments by the two-digit SIC code using the COMPUSTAT business segment data base. Taking all firms with valid data, this resulted in a sample of 4,287 firms with a total of 70 different business segments. They also divided several selected two-digit segments into three-digit segments, which resulted in a total of 110 different business segments. They used the percentage of segment sales to total firm sales to define the weights; they also replicated their study using weights based on net operating income instead of sales.[10]

Wood, McInish, and Lawrence (1992) defined business segments by the product line designation of the Value Line Data Base II. This resulted in a sample of 299 firms with a total of 42 different business segments. They used sales to define segment weights.

Keep in mind that these researchers were interested in testing a methodology, not in estimating the beta for a particular division. As a result, they used extremely large samples, and found betas for many different divisions. You are probably interested primarily in finding the betas for the divisions of your company. An illustration shows how you can apply this method to your company.

Suppose your company has two divisions, and that you can define a distinct SIC code or Value Line product line designation for each

---

[9] Ehrhardt and Bhagwat (1991) show that the confidence intervals around the resulting estimates of divisional betas are typically smaller than the confidence intervals around the mean betas obtained by the pure-play approach. Wood, McInish, and Lawrence (1992) show that their estimates of the divisional betas are significantly different from the comparable pure-play estimates. As an explanation, they suggest that synergy and debt capacity differences for multidivisional firms may cause a divisional beta for multidivisional firms to differ from the same divisional beta for a single-division firm. If this is the case, using pure-play betas to proxy the divisional betas of multidivisional firms may lead to errors. The regression approach partially accommodates this phenomenon by finding divisional betas that reflect an "average" degree of synergy/debt capacity effects.

[10] An alternative would be to use the reported book assets of the division when you proxy the weights, although these book values might not be highly correlated with the market weights.

division; for the rest of this example, let's assume you are going to use the Value Line product line designation.[11] You could limit the firms in your sample to only those companies that compete in any of the two product lines of your company's divisions. Suppose you do this, and the result is a sample containing your firm and 60 other firms. Exhibit 4.3 shows the reported sales in each business segment for the first 25 firms in your sample.

The first row of Exhibit 4.3 reports the sales for your company. Notice that your company has sales in business segments A and B, but not in any of the other eight segments. Even though there are ten different segments with sales for some company, no company competes in all ten different segments. The last column of Exhibit 4.3 reports the number of segments in which each company competes. As the column shows, each individual company in the sample competes in one to four different segments. For example, company 1 competes in only segment A, while company 22 competes in four different segments (A, C, D, and E). Notice that you could use companies 1 through 15 to estimate a pure-play beta for segment A, as this is the only segment in which they have sales. Similarly, you could use companies 16 through 18 to estimate a pure-play beta for segment B.

The last row in Exhibit 4.3 reports the number of companies with any sales at all in each particular segment. Notice that segments A and B report the greatest number of companies. This is not surprising, as your sampling criteria required that any company in the sample have sales in either segment A or B.

After you estimate the betas for each of the companies in your sample, you must estimate the weights for each product line for each company. Most research indicates that using the ratio of product line sales to total firm sales is a reasonable proxy for the weight.[12] Exhibit 4.4 reports the observed market betas and the weights, based on sales, for the first 25 companies in your sample.

Your regression has 61 observations, one for each company (your company and the other 60 companies). The regression has 10 explanatory variables, one for each product line (segments A through J). Notice

---

[11] For most data sources, the sum of the segment sales will equal the total company sales. If your data source doesn't adjust for intradivisional sales, however, the sum of segment sales may not equal the reported sales for the company.

[12] Fuller and Kerr (1981) use sales weights and find a close fit between actual overall betas and the "portfolio" of weighted segment betas. Ehrhardt and Bhagwat (1991) use sales weights and net operating income weights; they find no noticeable differences in results. Wood, McInish, and Lawrence (1992) conduct simulations to determine whether using sales weights introduces an errors-in-variables problem; they find no evidence of such a problem.

Exhibit 4.3: Segment Sales for Each Company

| Company | Segment Sales for Segments A through J | | | | | | | | | | Total Segments |
	A	B	C	D	E	F	G	H	I	J	
Your Company	4	6	0	0	0	0	0	0	0	0	2
1	4	0	0	0	0	0	0	0	0	0	1
2	2	0	0	0	0	0	0	0	0	0	1
3	5	0	0	0	0	0	0	0	0	0	1
4	6	0	0	0	0	0	0	0	0	0	1
5	2	0	0	0	0	0	0	0	0	0	1
6	4	0	0	0	0	0	0	0	0	0	1
7	3	0	0	0	0	0	0	0	0	0	1
8	7	0	0	0	0	0	0	0	0	0	1
9	9	0	0	0	0	0	0	0	0	0	1
10	2	0	0	0	0	0	0	0	0	0	1
11	6	0	0	0	0	0	0	0	0	0	1
12	4	0	0	0	0	0	0	0	0	0	1
13	6	0	0	0	0	0	0	0	0	0	1
14	2	0	0	0	0	0	0	0	0	0	1
15	8	0	0	0	0	0	0	0	0	0	1
16	0	3	0	0	0	0	0	0	0	0	1
17	0	9	0	0	0	0	0	0	0	0	1
18	0	2	0	0	0	0	0	0	0	0	1
19	2	2	0	0	3	0	0	0	0	0	3
20	0	3	0	0	0	4	0	0	0	3	3
21	0	3	0	4	0	0	0	4	0	0	3
22	1	0	4	6	7	0	0	0	0	0	4
23	2	0	0	0	0	2	0	0	4	0	3
24	0	3	0	2	0	0	5	0	0	0	3
25	0	2	0	0	0	0	0	4	0	0	2
Number in Segment	30	35	9	13	13	11	9	8	7	7	

Note: To conserve space, only 25 of the total 60 companies are shown.

Exhibit 4.4: Company Betas and Segment Weights

Company	Company Beta	Segment Weights									
		A	B	C	D	E	F	G	H	I	J
Your Company	1.10	.400	.600	.000	.000	.000	.000	.000	.000	.000	.000
1	.80	1.000	.000	.000	.000	.000	.000	.000	.000	.000	.000
2	.86	1.000	.000	.000	.000	.000	.000	.000	.000	.000	.000
3	.69	1.000	.000	.000	.000	.000	.000	.000	.000	.000	.000
4	.80	1.000	.000	.000	.000	.000	.000	.000	.000	.000	.000
5	.83	1.000	.000	.000	.000	.000	.000	.000	.000	.000	.000
6	.84	1.000	.000	.000	.000	.000	.000	.000	.000	.000	.000
7	.87	1.000	.000	.000	.000	.000	.000	.000	.000	.000	.000
8	1.00	1.000	.000	.000	.000	.000	.000	.000	.000	.000	.000
9	.76	1.000	.000	.000	.000	.000	.000	.000	.000	.000	.000
10	.73	1.000	.000	.000	.000	.000	.000	.000	.000	.000	.000
11	1.04	1.000	.000	.000	.000	.000	.000	.000	.000	.000	.000
12	.73	1.000	.000	.000	.000	.000	.000	.000	.000	.000	.000
13	.88	1.000	.000	.000	.000	.000	.000	.000	.000	.000	.000
14	.86	1.000	.000	.000	.000	.000	.000	.000	.000	.000	.000
15	.84	1.000	.000	.000	.000	.000	.000	.000	.000	.000	.000
16	1.04	.000	1.000	.000	.000	.000	.000	.000	.000	.000	.000
17	1.24	.000	1.000	.000	.000	.000	.000	.000	.000	.000	.000
18	1.26	.000	1.000	.000	.000	.000	.000	.000	.000	.000	.000
19	1.18	.286	.286	.000	.000	.429	.000	.000	.000	.000	.000
20	1.07	.000	.300	.000	.000	.000	.400	.000	.000	.000	.300
21	.87	.000	.273	.000	.364	.000	.000	.000	.364	.000	.000
22	1.01	.056	.000	.222	.333	.389	.000	.000	.000	.000	.000
23	1.15	.250	.000	.000	.000	.000	.250	.000	.000	.500	.000
24	.84	.000	.300	.000	.200	.000	.000	.500	.000	.000	.000
25	1.15	.000	.333	.000	.000	.000	.000	.000	.667	.000	.000

Note: To conserve space, only 25 of the other 60 companies are shown.

that, for most companies, many of the explanatory variables are equal to zero because the firm does not compete in all segments. For example, only the first two explanatory variables for your company are nonzero, because your company competes only in the first two segments. In fact, any pure-play companies in your sample will have only one nonzero explanatory variable, and its value will be 1.0.[13]

When you run your regression, use the option in your particular software package to suppress the intercept; in other words, you don't want an intercept in your regression. The data in Exhibit 4.4 are in a spreadsheet that also includes the comparable data for the remaining firms in the sample. Using the spreadsheet regression feature, the column of betas is the Y variable; each column of weights is one of the X variables. Exhibit 4.5 reports the actual results of the regression in which the intercept is suppressed.[14]

According to these results, the estimate of the divisional beta for segment A is .83; the 95% confidence interval is from .79 to .87. The estimate of the divisional beta for segment B is 1.24, with a 95% confidence interval from 1.18 to 1.30.

Using the weight of 40% for segment A and 60% for segment B, the implied overall beta for your company is:

$$.4\ (.83)\ +\ .6\ (1.24)\ =\ 1.076$$

This compares closely to the observed overall beta of 1.10, as shown in the first row of Exhibit 4.4.

How do these results compare with the pure-play betas for segments A and B? Using companies 1 through 15, the pure-play beta for segment A is .84, with a 95% confidence interval from .77 to .90. These results are virtually identical to those of the regression approach (an estimated beta of .83 and a 95% confidence interval from .79 to .87). The story is quite different for segment B. The pure-play beta is 1.18, with a 95% confidence interval from .80 to 1.56. Compare this with the regression estimate of 1.24, and a 95% confidence interval of 1.18 to 1.30. Why are the pure-play results so different for segment B?

---

[13] Be sure to check for possible programming or data entry mistakes. Make sure that all segment weights are between zero and one, inclusive. Make sure that the segment weights sum to 1.0 for each company.

[14] Suppressing the intercept changes the interpretation of the model's R^2. The R^2 still provides a measure of how tightly clustered the observations are around the estimated equation, but it can no longer be interpreted as a coefficient of multiple correlation.

Exhibit 4.5: Regression Results for Full Sample

Multiple R	.88						
R Square	.78						
Adjusted R Square	.72						
Standard Error	.09						
Observations	61						
Analysis of Variance	df	Sum of Squares	Mean Square	F	Significance of F	
Regression	10	1.55	.15	17.70	0.00	
Residual	51	.45	.01			
Total	61	1.99				
Segment	Coefficients	Standard Error	t Statistic	P-value	Lower 95%	Upper 95%
A	.83	.02	38.02	.00	.79	.87
B	1.24	.03	41.16	.00	1.18	1.30
C	1.52	.20	7.56	.00	1.12	1.92
D	.57	.10	5.77	.00	.37	.76
E	1.21	.07	17.59	.00	1.07	1.34
F	1.06	.09	12.30	.00	.89	1.23
G	.73	.10	7.08	.00	.52	.94
H	1.05	.08	13.14	.00	.89	1.21
I	1.16	.12	9.31	.00	.91	1.41
J	1.25	.16	7.81	.00	.93	1.57

Notice that segment B has only three pure-play companies (companies 16 through 18). Any variation in the betas of those three companies will cause quite a bit of noise in the estimate of the pure-play beta. Exhibit 4.3 shows that there are 35 companies that have sales in segment B. Therefore, the regression approach can incorporate more information into the estimate of segment B's divisional beta.

If you use this regression approach to find the divisional betas for an actual company, your sample probably will have more than 61 companies and more than 10 business segments. As you add more segments, you are adding more variables to the regression. This should not be a problem if you use a mainframe computer, but it could be a problem if you use a microcomputer: as the number of variables increases, so does the likelihood that your microcomputer will be unable to perform the regression.[15] Instead of getting estimates of divisional betas, you will get a beep and an error message. Fortunately, there's a fairly simple way to handle this problem.

Suppose the computer is unable to perform the regression for the example in Exhibits 4.3 through 4.5. It's a simple matter to go into the spreadsheet of Exhibit 4.4 and reduce the number of variables by combining some columns of sales weights. For example, you could replace the two columns of segments F and G with a single column that is the sum of F and G. You might also replace columns H, I, and J with a single column containing the sum of their weights. In other words, you are creating a "super" segment that is a combination of smaller segments. This reduction in variables should allow you to perform the regression.

Your estimates of the betas for your company's division probably will be unaffected. Implementing this approach for the hypothetical sample in Exhibits 4.3 through 4.5, for example, produces a new estimate of segment A's beta equal to .83; the new estimate for segment B is 1.23. These estimates are virtually identical to the previous case including all ten segments. The "cost" of this simplification is a less accurate estimate of the betas for the "super" segments.

For example, the estimated beta for the combined segments F and G is .93; the previous estimates of segments F and G (from Exhibit 4.5) are 1.06 and .73, respectively. The consolidation costs you some information. Instead of getting separate divisional betas for segments F and G, all you get is a single estimate for the combined "super" segment of F and G. Is this a big problem for you? Probably not, because your primary objective is to measure the betas of your company's segments, which are only A and B.[16]

II. Adjusting for Leverage

Much of the discussion has been based on the assumption that each line of business has its own beta, irrespective of any differences in the firms competing in that line of business. The basis for this

---

[15] As the number of variables in your regression increases, so does the size of a matrix that the computer must invert during the computation for the regression.

[16] I am grateful to Kendall Hoyd, a manager of corporate planning at Morrison Knudsen Corporation, for making me aware of this problem.

assumption is that the production technologies are fairly standard for a particular line of business and that consumers are indifferent as to which firm produces products in this line of business. Under such conditions, the costs and revenues for a particular product line are similar for most firms. Therefore, the beta for the product line would be the same for all companies.

There is another factor that may affect the product line's beta, however, and that is capital structure. The issue of capital structure and firm value has produced a voluminous literature, some of which contributed to the Nobel prizes of Merton Miller and Franco Modigliani. A complete discussion of this literature is far beyond the scope of this book. For a general discussion of the cost of capital and firm value, see Lewellen (1976). For a discussion that is focused on how a firm should choose its capital structure, see Masulis (1988).

The rest of this book assumes that your firm's capital structure is already fixed. So the relevant question for you is: Does capital structure affect the divisional cost of equity? The academic literature is fairly consistent in answering "Yes, there is a linkage between beta and capital structure." How can you quantify that linkage? How should you adjust for capital structure when you use the pure-play or regression approach to estimate a divisional beta? The two sections following answer those questions.

II.A. The Relationship between Systematic Risk and Capital Structure

Suppose that the only element in a capital structure that affects firm value is debt, and that this is primarily because of the tax shields of debt and potential bankruptcy/agency costs. Let V_L denote the value of a firm that is partially financed with debt, V_U denote the value of an otherwise identical firm financed with no debt, and D denote the value of the debt. The value of the levered firm is:

$$V_L = V_U + GD \qquad (4.3)$$

where G is a function of debt and the tax regime.

For the case of no taxes and no bankruptcy/agency costs, G is equal to zero, and equation (4.3) reduces to the result of Modigliani and Miller (1958). When corporate taxes, τ_C, are assumed, G is equal to τ_C; this reduces equation (4.3) to the Modigliani and Miller (1963) result. For the case of corporate taxes, personal taxes on equity (τ_E) and personal taxes on debt (τ_D):

$$G = \left[1 - \frac{(1 - \tau_C)(1 - \tau_E)}{(1 - \tau_D)} \right] \qquad (4.4)$$

In this case, equation (4.3) reduces to the result of Miller (1977).[17] Reasonable values for the corporate tax rate and the personal tax rate on debt are 34% and 31%, respectively. A reasonable estimate for the effective tax rate on equity is 14% (keep in mind that increases in wealth because of stock price appreciation are not taxed until the stock is sold; therefore, the effective tax on equity is lower than the tax on debt). Under these assumptions, G, which is the gain due to debt, is equal to 17.74%. In other words, if a dollar of debt replaces a dollar of equity in the capital structure, the value of the firm increases by almost 18 cents.

Capital structure also has an impact on the systematic risk of a firm. Consider a firm with debt D and equity E, where these are market values. β_L is the beta of the firm, where the subscript L indicates that the firm has leverage in its capital structure. β_U is the beta that the firm would have if it were unlevered. Equation (4.5) defines the relationship between the levered and unlevered betas:[18]

$$\beta_L = \beta_U \left[1 + (1 - G)\frac{D}{E} \right] \qquad (4.5)$$

Notice that equation (4.5) implies that adding debt to the capital structure of a firm will increase the beta of the firm. Using three different

---

[17] Equation (4.3) is also general enough to accommodate the bankruptcy/agency costs of Yagill (1982) and Brick and Statman (1981). Riener (1985) and Taggart (1991) provide analyses that incorporate personal taxes, risky debt, and risky tax shields. See Levy and Arditti (1973, 1975), Bradford (1975), and Paul (1975) for a discussion of the impact of the tax shield due to depreciation.

[18] This assumes that the debt is not risky. See Ehrhardt and Shrieves (1992) for the more general case that the firm has preferred stock and convertible securities in its capital structure. Conine (1980) provides a model that includes risky debt, and Conine and Tamarkin (1985) extend this model to include risky preferred stock. Taggart (1991) examines models that include risky tax shields and consider personal taxes as well as corporate taxes.

The most commonly used model probably is that of Hamada (1972). This model assumes that there is only debt in the capital structure and there are only corporate taxes. The result is the same as equation (4.5), except that G is equal to the corporate tax rate, τ_c.

types of empirical tests, Hamada (1972), Mandelker and Rhee (1984), and Hill and Stone (1980) each conclude that the beta of a firm is in fact positively related to its leverage.[19]

II.B. Adjusting Estimates of Divisional Systematic Risk to Reflect Differences in Capital Structure

How should you handle the issue of capital structure when estimating divisional cost of equity? If you are estimating divisional systematic risk with one of the methods described in Section I (the pure-play approach or the multiple regression approach), there are two different approaches that you can use, and two choices within each approach.

In the first approach, you "unlever" the market betas of the firms in your sample before you estimate the line of business beta. Consider an example. You gather a sample of firms, such as those in Exhibits 4.1 or 4.3, and measure the beta for each firm. In addition, you must gather other data for the capital structure of each firm in your sample; in particular, you need estimates of each firm's equity, debt, and tax rate.[20] You then use equation (4.5) to find the unlevered beta for each firm in your sample.[21]

For example, suppose you estimate that one of the firms in your

---

[19] An alternative adjustment is the approach of Bower and Jenks (1975). They define a rate with which you should discount the after-tax cash flows of a project, not including the interest charges because of debt. Recall that Chapter 2 recommends discounting these cash flows at the weighted average cost of capital, r_c. Bower and Jenks (1975) define this rate as:

$$r_c = [r_f + \beta_U (E[r_m - r_f])] [1 - (D/V_L)].$$

Their model will give an identical cost of capital as the definition of weighted average cost of capital in Chapter 2, if you find the cost of equity using the levered beta of Hamada (1972), and if you assume that the pre-tax cost of corporate debt is equal to the risk-free rate. This may seem like a foolish assumption, but the models of both Bower and Jenks (1975) and Hamada (1972) are built on a set of assumptions that imply equality of the corporate debt rate and the risk-free rate. Therefore, in the strictest sense these two models are equivalent. Although it is somewhat ad hoc in nature, most researchers using Hamada's (1972) adjustment to find the cost of equity also use the actual cost of debt instead of the risk-free rate. In other words, they use Hamada's result without using all of his assumptions.

[20] Since the firms are publicly traded, it's easy to get an estimate of their market values of equity. If you can't get an estimate of their market value of debt, you can use the book value of debt as a proxy for the market value. You could use the statutory tax rate, but it would be better if you use the actual tax rate. You can estimate this rate by dividing the actual taxes paid by the taxable income.

[21] See note 18 for sources that describe alternative models.

sample has a beta of 1.10, a debt/equity ratio of .6, and an effective gain (G) of .18. Using equation (4.5), the unlevered beta is:

$$\beta_U = \cfrac{\beta_L}{\left[1 + (1 - G)\dfrac{D}{E} \right]} = \cfrac{1.10}{[1 + (1 - .18)(.6)]} = .737 \quad (4.6)$$

After performing this calculation for each firm in your sample, you should substitute the unlevered betas for the levered betas, and proceed with your estimation of the line-of-business betas using either the pure-play method or the regression method. Notice that the resulting line-of-business betas will be unlevered. To find the correct beta for your division, you "lever" it back up using equation (4.5), based on your firm's capital structure and tax rate.

At this point, you must make a decision about the capital structure of your division. If you believe that all divisions in your company contribute equally to the debt capacity of your company, you would use your company's debt ratio and tax rate. For example, suppose you find that the unlevered beta for the retail sales line of business is equal to .7. Suppose your firm has a division doing business in retail sales. Your firm's debt/equity ratio is .75. Because your accountants are shrewd, your firm's effective corporate tax rate is only 25%.

Using equation (4.4), the corporate tax rate of 25%, a personal debt tax rate of 31%, and a personal equity tax rate of 14%, your firm's gain due to leverage, G, is .0652. The beta for your retail sales division is:

$$\beta_L = \beta_U \left[1 + (1 - G)\frac{D}{E} \right] \quad (4.7)$$

$$= .7 \left[1 + (1 - .0652)(.75) \right] = 1.19$$

On the other hand, suppose you believe that your retail sales division is different from your other divisions with respect to the debt capacity that it brings to your firm. In other words, you believe that if this division were actually financed separately, its debt/equity ratio would be .5. Also, this division has very little in the way of other tax shields, so its effective tax rate is 34% (which gives the division a gain, G, of .1774). In this case, the beta for your division would be:

$$\beta_L = \beta_U \left[1 + (1 - G) \frac{D}{E} \right] \qquad (4.8)$$

$$= .7 \left[1 + (1 - .1774) (.5) \right] = .99$$

The second approach assumes that the division in question contributes about the same amount of debt capacity to any firm that operates this division. If this is the case, you don't need to unlever the betas in your sample before you apply either the pure-play approach or the regression approach. In either case, your resulting line of business beta is levered, where the leverage reflects the appropriate capital structure for this type of line of business. Suppose you do this, and find that the beta for the retail sales line of business is 1.02. Since you didn't unlever the betas in the sample, the estimated divisional beta of 1.02 is actually a levered beta itself.

Should you adjust this beta to reflect any differences peculiar to your firm? If you believe that the capital structure of your division is similar to the capital structure of the average division in the retail sales business, you don't need to make any adjustments. In other words, the estimated beta is appropriate for the average firm operating in this line of business, and your firm isn't significantly different from the average firm.

If you believe that your retail sales division is different from the average retail sales division with respect to the amount of debt capacity it contributes to your firm, you should make an adjustment. First, unlever the estimated retail sales beta using the average debt/equity ratio and gain to leverage, G, for the firms in your sample. Suppose these are .55 and .1774, respectively. Then the unlevered retail sales beta is:

$$\beta_U = \frac{\beta_U}{\left[1 + (1 - G) \dfrac{D}{E} \right]} \qquad (4.9)$$

$$= \frac{1.02}{\left[1 + (1 - .1774) (.55) \right]} = .702$$

You then lever this beta back up, using your division's contribution to debt capacity and gain to leverage, which in this example are .5 and .1774. This gives a divisional beta of:

$$\beta_L = \beta_U \left[1 + (1 - G) \frac{D}{E} \right] \tag{4.10}$$

$$= .702 \left[1 + (1 - .1774) (.5) \right] = .99$$

Which of these adjustments should you use? Bower and Jenks (1975) argue convincingly that different divisions do in fact support different levels of debt capacity; this is supported by the research of Bradley, Jarrell, and Kim (1984), who show that different industry groupings typically have different degrees of leverage. Taken together, this research suggests that it's not worth your effort to unlever the betas in your sample before you apply the pure-play or regression method. In other words, most divisions in the same line of business will contribute the same amount of debt capacity to their firms, which means that the estimated line-of-business beta is a pretty good estimate. Fuller and Kerr (1981) tested this premise and found that the estimated betas actually are more accurate when they do not unlever the betas in their sample.

Given these results, I recommend that you do not unlever the betas in your sample before you apply the pure-play approach or the regression approach. The result will be the appropriate beta for the typical division competing in that line of business. I recommend using this beta as an estimate of your divisional beta, unless you have some compelling reason to believe that your division is very different from the average division in that line of business with respect to debt capacity or tax liability. If you believe there is a big difference, you should use the adjustments shown in equations (4.9) and (4.10).

III. Summary and Recommendations

If your firm competes in more than one line of business, you probably shouldn't use the same cost of capital for all your projects. Using a single cost of capital can lead to the acceptance of value-reducing projects and the rejection of value-adding projects. There is no simple guideline for determining the number of different costs of capital you need. You may have multiple divisions that compete in the same line of business; it makes sense to use the same cost of capital for each of these divisions. On the other hand, you may have a single division that competes in more than one line of business; in this case, you might want multiple costs of capital for different projects within this division.

Most of the differences between product line costs of capital are the result of differences between product line systematic risks. The pure-play and the multiple regression approach can help estimate the systematic risks for your product lines. If you have 10 to 20 comparable pure-play firms, then the pure-play approach will usually provide you with a reliable estimate of the product line beta. If you have only a small number of comparable pure-play firms, you should use the multiple regression approach.

Should you adjust for leverage? Unless you believe that your division is very different from other divisions that compete in the same line of business, you are safe in ignoring adjustments for leverage. You will get the "right" estimate of the divisional beta, even without an explicit adjustment.

Appendix

Other Factors That Affect the Cost of Equity

The body of the chapter describes several factors that can affect the cost of equity. For example, the impact of capital structure on the cost of equity can be important if you are estimating divisional costs of capital. A change in capital structure also can be important if your company has recently undergone a major restructuring of its capital structure. In this case, your estimate of beta using a time series of stock returns will reflect the old capital structure, not the new one.

If your firm has recently diversified its operations, the current systematic risk of your firm may be different from the pre-diversification systematic risk. You may also experience a change in systematic risk if your firm has divested itself of any operating units. In either case, a time series of stock market returns will not accurately reflect your current level of systematic risk.

Several types of changes may affect your systematic risk: leasing, unfunded pension liabilities, accounting changes, exchange listings, and liquidity.

A-I. Leasing

In many ways, leasing is like another form of leverage; in fact, leasing is often used as a substitute for borrowing. Just as debt can affect the systematic risk of a firm's equity, you might suspect that leasing also affects the systematic risk of the equity. Yet there are significant differences in the tax treatments of debt and leasing, so the adjustments to beta that are appropriate for debt are not necessarily appropriate for leasing.

As in previous chapters, r_E denotes the cost of equity, i denotes the interest rate on debt, E denotes the market value of equity, and τ_C denotes the corporate tax rate. Long (1977) defines r_U^E as the cost of equity for an otherwise identical firm that has no leasing, L as the lease payment, and DEP as the depreciation expense that is foregone on the leased assets. He assumes that the riskiness of the firm's future capital expenditures will be similar to that of the existing assets, that the riskiness of the lease payments is similar to that of debt, and that the riskiness of the foregone depreciation is similar to that of debt. Long shows that the relationship between the lease-levered cost of equity and the unlevered cost of equity is:

$$r_E = r_E^U + (1 - \tau_C)\left(\frac{r_E^U - i}{i}\right)\frac{L}{E} + \tau_C\left(\frac{r_E^U - i}{i}\right)\frac{DEP}{E}$$

The equation shows that the lease-levered cost of equity increases as the amounts of the lease payment and foregone depreciation increase. This adjustment may be appropriate for you if you are estimating the cost of equity for a division that has substantially different leasing arrangements from the other divisions of your company.[22]

The adjustment also will be appropriate if your company recently has made a major change in its leasing arrangements. In such a case, using the past time series of returns will give you an estimate of your past systematic risk and past cost of equity. You can use the leasing adjustment in the equation to provide an estimate of the current cost of equity.

A-II. Unfunded Pension Liabilities

Another source of quasi-debt is an unfunded pension liability, which is the difference in the present value of promised future benefits and the value of funds designated for such purposes.[23] An unfunded pension liability is similar to debt in that it causes a positive current cash flow to the firm (the cash flow that otherwise would have been used to fund the future obligations) and negative future cash flows from the firm.[24] Since higher levels of debt are associated with higher

---

[22] See Schallheim (1994) for a much more detailed treatment of leasing.

[23] See Treynor (1977) and Regan (1981) for further discussion of this issue. Unfunded pension liabilities also create complications in capital budgeting studies. The pension costs should be included in the labor costs, but the impact of unfunded pension liabilities is similar to that of indirect debt. This problem is related to the appropriate definition of cash flows in Chapter 2.

[24] Two major differences between unfunded pension liabilities and debt are the implied rates and the timing of the tax deduction. Consider a firm that initially has an unfunded liability of $100. These funds must "earn" a rate of return in order to meet the future payments called for by the actuarially determined requirements of the future pension recipients. For purposes of illustration, assume that this rate is 10%, which means that the unfunded liability has an "expense" of $10 and grows to $110 during the year. This rate probably is greater than the cost of debt. Furthermore, the firm is unable to deduct the pension "expense" until the pension is actually funded. In general, these two factors mean that unfunded pension liabilities are an expensive source of debt. Notice that the deferment of a tax deduction can also occur with debt, if the firm has insufficient income

levels of systematic risk, you might expect a similar relationship between unfunded pension liabilities and systematic risk.

Malley (1983) tests this proposition. She collected data for 1973 and 1974, the two years immediately prior to enactment of the Employee Retirement Income Security Act (ERISA) of 1974; she also collected data for 1975 and 1976, the two years immediately following enactment. The samples range from 238 to 347 observations, depending on the particular year. Using McDonald's (1971) generalized growth model to estimate the cost of equity, she finds a positive and significant correlation between the cost of equity and the amount of unfunded pension liabilities for the two years after ERISA; the relationship was not significant for the two pre-ERISA years.[25]

If you have access to market returns for a period in which the unfunded pension liabilities have been stable, you don't need to worry about their impact on the cost of equity, since it will already be reflected in the market returns. If your firm has recently experienced a significant change in its unfunded pension liabilities, however, or if you are estimating the cost of equity for a nontraded firm, the presence of unfunded pension liabilities may be important.[26]

As I say in the body of the chapter, there are analytical models that allow you to incorporate the effect on the cost of equity because of debt, preferred stock, and convertible securities; Long (1977) provides a similar model for leasing. Unfortunately, there is not a similar analytical model for the impact of unfunded pension liabilities.

A-III. Accounting Changes

If your company has undergone a major change in its capital structure, the time series of stock returns may not provide an accurate estimate of the systematic risk. This also may be true if your company has undergone a major change in accounting procedures. Dhaliwal, Spicer, and Vickrey (1979) examine the impact of the 1970 SEC requirement that companies report selected data for business segments. They suggest that this requirement improves the quality of information available to investors, and so reduces the risk to the investors. Using a

---

to use the entire deduction for interest expense. I am grateful to Michael Long for making me aware of these issues.

[25] Consistent with Malley's results, Oldfield (1977) and Feldstein and Seligman (1981) find that firms with unfunded pension liabilities experienced decreases in market values.

[26] FASB No. 106 means that many firms do in fact have a significant change in their reported unfunded liabilities.

sample of 25 firms, they show that two measures of risk, beta and the total variance of returns, did decrease subsequent to implementation of the SEC requirement.

It may not be appropriate to generalize the results of a single event and a small sample to the more general case of the relationship between systematic risk and accounting changes that improve the quality of information. Even if there is such a relationship, it's not clear what you should do. Unlike the case of a change in capital structure, there is no well-accepted technique for adjusting beta to reflect accounting changes that improve the quality of information. You should be aware that such changes may affect beta, however, and you should be cautious when using data gathered prior to the change.

A-IV. Changes in Exchange Listings

Suppose your company has recently been listed on either the AMEX or the NYSE. Does this change affect your cost of equity? After all, there may be more information available for companies listed on national exchanges, and this information may reduce the perceived risk of the companies. This could be a problem in estimating your current systematic risk, since the time series of returns that you would normally use may contain data from the pre-listing period.

Does exchange listing affect systematic risk? Dhaliwal (1980) examined 16 OTC companies that became listed on either the AMEX or NYSE in 1972. Comparing these companies to a matched sample of OTC companies that did not change listing, he found that the listed companies had significantly lower measures of risk. In particular, they had lower systematic risk as measured by beta and lower standard deviation of total return.

The evidence in general is contradictory. Reints and Vandenberg (1975) examined 32 stocks that were listed initially on the NYSE in 1968; they found no change in beta. Fabozzi and Hershkoff (1979) examined approximately 100 OTC companies that were listed on the AMEX, and they found no change in beta. Phillips and Zecker (1982) performed similar tests as those of Dhaliwal (1980) on more recent data, and found no change in beta. Baker and Spitzfaden (1982) examined approximately 30 NASDAQ companies that were listed on either the AMEX or NYSE during the 1978–1980 period. They found no significant changes in beta.

Most of the empirical evidence suggests that on average there is no change in the cost of equity for companies that become listed on the AMEX or NYSE. These empirical tests are based on fairly small sample sizes and short sample periods, however. It is also possible that some companies may have positive change in systematic risk and that other companies may have negative changes, even though the average change is close to zero.

Unless you have some specific reason for believing that your company's systematic risk should change if it is listed on the AMEX or NYSE, you are probably safe in ignoring the change when you estimate your cost of equity. If you do have a specific reason, there is little in either finance theory or empirical tests to suggest how you should measure beta in the presence of such a change.

A-V. Changes in Liquidity

Amihud and Mendelson (1986, 1988, 1989a, 1989b) have conducted empirical tests demonstrating that the trading liquidity of a stock, as measured by its bid-ask spread, is associated with the expected return required by investors. In particular, stocks with greater illiquidity, as proxied by the bid–ask spread, require greater expected returns. This implies that trading liquidity has a significant impact on the cost of equity.

If your firm has recently undertaken some measure that affects the trading liquidity of its stock, your cost of equity may have been affected.[27] If this is the case, using market prices and returns from the period prior to the change in trading liquidity will not give you the correct current cost of equity. Unfortunately, there is no well-accepted analytical model for relating trading liquidity with cost of equity.

---

[27] See Amihud and Mendelson (1989b) for a discussion of actions that may affect stock liquidity.

References

Amihud, Y., and H. Mendelson. "Asset Pricing and the Bid-Ask Spread." *Journal of Financial Economics* 17 (1986): 223–249.

———. "Liquidity and Asset Prices: Financial Management Implications." *Financial Management* (Spring 1988): 5–15.

———. "The Effects of Beta, Bid-Ask Spread, Residual Risk and Size on Stock Returns." *Journal of Finance* (June 1989): 479–486.

———. "Liquidity and Cost of Capital: Implications for Corporate Management." *Journal of Applied Corporate Finance* 2(3) (1989): 65–73.

Baker, H.K., and J. Spitzfaden. "The Impact of Exchange Listing on the Cost of Equity Capital." *Financial Review* 17(3) (1982): 128–141.

Bartley, J.W. "Accounting for the Cost of Capital: An Empirical Examination." *Journal of Business Finance and Accounting* 8(2) (1982): 239–254.

Beaver, W., P. Kettler, and M. Scholes. "The Association Between Market Determined and Accounting Determined Risk Measures." *The Accounting Review* (October 1970): 654–682.

Beaver, W., and J. Manegold. "The Association Between Market Determined and Accounting Determined Risk Measures: Some Further Evidence." *Journal of Financial and Quantitative Analysis* (June 1975): 231–284.

Boquist, J., and W. Moore. "Estimating the Systematic Risk of an Industry Segment: A Mathematical Programming Approach." *Financial Management* (Winter 1983): 11–18.

Bower, R., and J. Jenks. "Divisional Screening Rates." *Financial Management* (Autumn 1975): 42–49.

Bower, R.S., and D.R. Lessard. "An Operational Approach to Risk-Screening." *Journal of Finance* (May 1973): 321–337.

Bradford, W.D. "Valuation, Leverage and the Cost of Capital in the Case of Depreciable Assets: Comment." *Journal of Finance* 30(1) (1975): 214–220.

Bradley, M., G.A. Jarrell, and E.H. Kim. "On the Existence of an Optimal Capital Structure: Theory and Evidence." *Journal of Finance* 39(3) (July 1984): 857–880.

Brick, I.E., and M. Statman. "A Note on Beta and the Probability of Default." *Journal of Financial Research* 4(3) (1981): 265–269.

Brigham, E.F. "Hurdle Rates for Screening Capital Expenditure Proposals." *Financial Management* 4(3) (1975): 17–26.

Conine, T. "Corporate Debt and Corporate Taxes: An Extension." *Journal of Finance* (September 1980): 1033–1037.

Conine, T.E., Jr., and M. Tamarkin. "Divisional Cost of Capital Estimation: Adjusting for Leverage." *Financial Management* 4(1) (1985): 54–58.

Crum, R., and K. Bi. "An Observation on Estimating the Systematic Risk of an Industry Segment." *Financial Management* (Spring 1988): 60–62.

Dhaliwal, D.S. "The Effect of Exchange-Listing on a Firm's Cost of Equity Capital." *Capital Market Working Papers,* Washington, D.C., Securities and Exchange Commission, March 1980.

Dhaliwal, D.S., B.H. Spicer, and D. Vickrey. "The Quality of Disclosure and the Cost of Capital." *Journal of Business Finance and Accounting* 6(2) (1979): 245–266.

Ehrhardt, M.C., and Y. Bhagwat. "A Full-Information Approach for Estimating Divisional Betas." *Financial Management* 20(2) (Summer 1991): 60–69.

Ehrhardt, M.C., and R.E. Shrieves. "The Impact of Warrants and Convertible Securities on the Systematic Risk of Common Equity." Working Paper, University of Tennessee, 1992.

Ezzamel, M.A. "Divisional Cost of Capital and the Measurement of Divisional Performance." *Journal of Business Finance and Accounting* 6(3) (1979): 307–319.

Fabozzi, F.J., and R.A. Hershkoff. "The Effect of the Decision to List on a Stock's Systematic Risk." *Review of Business and Economic Research* (Spring 1979): 77–82.

Feldstein, M., and S. Seligman. "Pension Funding, Share Prices, and National Saving." *Journal of Finance* (September 1981): 801–824.

Findlay, M.C., III, A.E. Gooding, and Wallace Q. Weaver, Jr. "On the Relevant Risk for Determining Capital Expenditure Hurdle Rates." *Financial Management* 5(4) (1976): 9–17.

Fuller, R., and H. Kerr. "Estimating the Divisional Cost of Capital: An Analysis of the Pure-Play Technique." *Journal of Finance* (December 1981): 997–1009.

Gitman, L.J., and V.A. Mercurio. "Cost of Capital Techniques Used by Major U.S. Firms: Survey and Analysis of Fortune's 1000." *Financial Management* 11(4) (1982): 21–29.

Gonedes, N.J. "Evidence on the Information Content of Accounting Numbers: Accounting-Based and Market-Based Estimates of Systematic Risk." *Journal of Financial and Quantitative Analysis* (June 1973): 407–443.

Gordon, M.J., and P.J. Halpern. "Cost of Capital for a Division of a Firm." *Journal of Finance* 29(4) (1974): 1153–1163.

———. "Cost of Capital for a Division of a Firm: Reply." *Journal of Finance* 32(5) (1977): 1781–1782.

Gup, B.E., and S.W. Norwood, III. "Divisional Cost of Capital: A Practical Approach." *Financial Management* 11(1) (1982): 20–24.

Hamada, R. "The Effect of the Firm's Capital Structure on the Systematic Risk of Common Stocks." *Journal of Finance* (May 1972): 435–452.

Hill, N., and B. Stone. "Accounting Betas, Systematic Operating Risk, and Financial Leverage: A Risk-Composition Approach to the Determinants of Systematic Risk." *Journal of Financial and Quantitative Analysis* (September 1980): 595–637.

Kim, S.H., T. Crick, and S.H. Kim. "Do Executives Practice What Academics Preach?" *Management Accounting* (November 1986): 49–52.

Kulkarni, M., M. Powers, and D. Shannon. "The Estimation of Product Line Betas as Surrogates of Divisional Risk Measures." *Financial Management* (Spring 1989): pp. 6–7.

Levy, H., and F.D. Arditti. "Valuation, Leverage, and the Cost of Capital in the Case of Depreciable Assets." *Journal of Finance* 28(3) (1973): 687–695.

———."Valuation, Leverage and the Cost of Capital in the Case of Depreciable Assets: A Reply." *Journal of Finance* 30(1) (1975): 221–223.

Lewellen, W.G. *The Cost of Capital*. Dubuque, Iowa: Kendall/Hunt, 1976.

Long, M.S. "Leasing and the Cost of Capital." *Journal of Financial and Quantitative Analysis* 12(4) (1977): 579–586.

Malley, S.L. "Unfunded Pension Liabilities and the Cost of Equity Capital." *The Financial Review* 18(2) (1983): 133–145.

Mandelker, G.N., and S.G. Rhee. "The Impact of the Degrees of Operating and Financial Leverage on Systematic Risk of Common Stock." *Journal of Financial and Quantitative Analysis* 19(1) (1984): 45–57.

Masulis, R.W. *The Debt/Equity Choice*. Cambridge, Mass.: Ballinger, 1988.

Maus, W.J. "How to Calculate the Cost of Capital in a Privately-Owned Company." *Management Accounting* 61(12) (1980): 20–24.

McDonald, J.G. "Required Return on Public Utility Equities: A National and Regional Analysis, 1958–1969." *Bell Journal of Economics* (Autumn 1971): 503–514.

Miller, M.H. "Debt and Taxes." *Journal of Finance* (May 1977): 261–275.

Modigliani, F., and Miller, M.H. "The Cost of Capital, Corporation Finance, and the Theory of Investment." *American Economic Review* (June 1958): 261–297.

———. "Taxes and the Cost of Capital: A Correction." *American Economic Review* (June 1963): 433–443.

Oldfield, G.S. "Financial Aspects of their Private Pension System." *Journal of Money, Credit, and Banking* (February 1977): 48–54.

Paul, R.S. "Valuation, Leverage and the Cost of Capital in the Case of Depreciable Assets: Comment." *Journal of Finance* 30(1) (1975): 211–213.

Phillips, S.M., and J.R. Zecker. "Exchange Listing and the Cost of Equity Capital." *Capital Market Working Papers*, Washington, D.C., Securities and Exchange Commission, March 1982.

Regan, P.J. "Potential Corporate Liabilities Under ERISA." *Financial Analysts Journal* (March-April 1981): 26–32.

Reints, W.W., and P.A. Vandenberg. "The Impact of Changes in Trading Location on a Security's Systematic Risk." *Journal of Financial and Quantitative Analysis* (December 1975): 881–890.

Riener, K.D. "A Pedagogic Note on the Cost of Capital with Personal Taxes and Risky Debt." *Financial Review* 20(2) (1985): 229–235.

Rosenberg, B., and W. McKibben. "The Estimation of Systematic and Specific Risk in Common Stocks." *Journal of Financial and Quantitative Analysis* (March 1973): 317–333.

Schallheim, J.S. *Leasing.* Boston: Harvard Business School Press, 1994.

Shapiro, A.C. *Modern Corporate Finance.* New York: Macmillan, 1989.

Taggart R.A., Jr. "Allocating Capital Among a Firm's Divisions: Hurdle Rates Vs. Budgets." *Journal of Financial Research* 10(3) (1987): 177–190.

———. "Consistent Valuation and Cost of Capital Expressions with Corporate and Personal Taxes." *Financial Management* 20(3) (1991): 8–20.

Treynor, J.L. "The Principles of Corporate Pension Finance." *Journal of Finance* (May 1977): 627–638.

Weaver, S.C., P.J. Clemmens, III, J. Gunn, and B. Dannenburg. "Panel Discussion on Corporate Investment: Divisional Hurdle Rates and the Cost of Capital." *Financial Management* 18(1) (Spring 1989): 18–25.

Weston, J.F., and W.Y. Lee. "Cost of Capital for a Division of a Firm: Comment." *Journal of Finance* 32(5) (1977): 1779–1780.

Wood, R.A., T.H. McInish, and K.D. Lawrence. "Estimating Divisional Betas with Diversified Firm Data." *Review of Quantitative Finance and Accounting* 2(1) (1992): 89–96.

Yagill, J. "On Valuation, Beta and the Cost of Equity Capital: A Note." *Journal of Financial and Quantitative Analysis* 17(3) (1982): 441–449.

Chapter 5

Some Advanced Issues: Flotation Costs and Long-Term Projects

You may face some complications in estimating your company's cost of capital. One major complication is the treatment of flotation costs. Should you adjust your cost of capital to reflect flotation costs, and what type of adjustment should you use? Section I addresses these issues.

A second major complication concerns the long-term nature of most projects, which typically have cash flows in many periods. Multiperiod cash flows can cause complications. For example, recall from Chapter 3 that the CAPM is a one-period model and that the CAPM cost of equity is appropriate only for discounting a one-period cash flow. How can you adjust the cost of equity so that you can discount the multiperiod cash flows of most long-term projects? How should you adjust the costs of debt and preferred stock? Section II addresses these questions.

The appendix discusses another complication, the meaning of the cost of capital in the presence of capital rationing.

I. Flotation Costs

There's an old joke about a man showing his son the harbor, and pointing out the yachts of the lawyers, the investment bankers, and the stockbrokers. The son naively asks, "Where are the clients' yachts?"

As you well know, when a company issues capital, the company's net proceeds from the issue are smaller than the gross payments from the investors. This difference may be because of explicit fees and commissions paid to lawyers and investment bankers, or it may be because of price discounts made to the underwriters. In any case, these flotation costs are not trivial. Their magnitude depends on the type of instrument being issued (debt, convertible debt, preferred stock, convertible preferred stock, common equity, and so forth), the type of issue (for example, competitive bid versus negotiated), the terms of the issue (for example, best effort versus standby agreements), and the size of the issue. The flotation costs can range from as little as .5% of the issue for a large competitively bid plain vanilla bond offering to as much as 15% of the issue for a complicated stock offering.[1] The question is, how do you handle flotation costs in the capital budgeting process?

The situation is fairly simple for debt and preferred stock, but it gets more complicated for common equity. To explain the adjustments for these three sources of financing, I start with the simplest case of debt.

I.A. The Adjusted Cost of Debt

An example will illustrate how to adjust for the cost of debt. Suppose a company issues $1 million in debt with an annual coupon rate of 12% and a maturity of five years. If the net flotation costs are 5%, the company does not actually receive the full $1 million. Instead, the company receives $950,000, which is the $1 million less the flotation costs of $50,000. What is the cost to the company of this $950,000? You know the future payments, which are nine payments of $60,000 (one every six months) and a final payment of $1,060,000 in five years.[2] Using a spreadsheet on a microcomputer, it's easy to find the internal rate of return for these cash flows. As shown in Exhibit 5.1 these cash flows produce a pre-tax annual internal rate of return of 13.40%. Notice that this is different from the 12% pre-tax cost of debt, which ignores flotation costs.

The situation is a little more complicated if you consider taxes. Flotation costs are usually amortized over the life of the loan, with the amortized expenses reducing tax liabilities. In this example, you could model the amortization charge as $50,000/10, which is $5,000 each six

---

[1] For details of the issue process and surveys of typical flotation costs, see Shapiro (1989; Chapter 13) and Brealey and Myers (1988; Chapter 15). See Pettway (1982) for a survey of flotation costs for electric utilities.

[2] You can use exactly the same approach if the bond has a sinking fund, except you replace the cash flows in Exhibit 5.1 with the cash flows of the bond with a sinking fund.

Exhibit 5.1: Flotation Costs and the Cost of Debt

		Pre-Tax Cash Flows	After-Tax Cash Flows
	Gross Proceeds =	$1,000,000	$1,000,000
	Flotation Costs =	$50,000	$50,000
Payment Date	Net Proceeds =	$950,000	$950,000
6 Months	Payment =	($60,000)	($34,000)
1 Year	Payment =	($60,000)	($34,000)
1.5 Years	Payment =	($60,000)	($34,000)
2 Years	Payment =	($60,000)	($34,000)
2.5 Years	Payment =	($60,000)	($34,000)
3 Years	Payment =	($60,000)	($34,000)
3.5 Years	Payment =	($60,000)	($34,000)
4 Years	Payment =	($60,000)	($34,000)
4.5 Years	Payment =	($60,000)	($34,000)
5 Years	Payment =	($1,060,000)	($1,034,000)
	Internal Rate of Return =	13.40%	8.03%

Notes: (1) The tax rate is 40%.
   (2) The after-tax cash flow includes the tax shield due to amortization of the flotation cost.

months.[3] The after-tax cash flows in each period would be the after-tax cost of the coupon payment adjusted by the tax shield from amortization (the signs indicate the direction of cash flow from the company's perspective):

$$-\$60,000\,(1 - .4) + \$5,000\,(.4) = -\$34,000 \qquad (5.1)$$

Exhibit 5.1 also shows the annualized internal rate of return that equates these after-tax cash flows with the net proceeds of $950,000. This after-tax cost of debt is equal to 8.03%.[4] If you ignore flotation costs, the after-tax cost of debt is equal to $(1 - .4)(.12) = 7.2\%$.

---

[3] This example uses straightline amortization to keep the example simple. If the debt is issued at an original discount of more than .25% times the years to maturity, the flotation costs must be amortized using the effective interest approach. An accountant or the Internal Revenue Service can provide details of this approach.

[4] If you multiply the pre-tax cost of debt of 13.40% (which includes the impact of flotation costs) by .6 (which is 1 − the tax rate), you get 8.04%. This is very close to the actual after-tax cost of 8.03%.

Exhibit 5.2 reports the cost of debt for several bonds, each with a 12% coupon rate but each with a different maturity. As the exhibit shows, the pre-tax cost of debt decreases and approaches 12% as the maturity increases. This is as expected, because the 5% flotation costs are amortized over a longer period of time. The after-tax cost of debt also drops and approaches the 7.2% after-tax rate that ignores flotation costs.

In general, the adjustment for flotation costs is a refinement of the basic unadjusted cost. In other words, usually the adjusted and unadjusted costs will not be very different. However, this doesn't imply that you shouldn't make the adjustment. The information needed to make the adjustment is readily available, and the adjustment itself doesn't require much effort or computer processing time. To paraphrase the film maker, Spike Lee, you should do the right thing (*especially if the right thing is relatively easy to do*).[5]

I.B. The Adjusted Cost of Preferred Stock

Consider preferred stock that is not perpetual but that instead has a sinking fund with a final redemption date. In this case, you can use the same procedure as in the case of debt. You amortize the flotation costs and specify the cash flows of the company in each period. The cost of the preferred is the internal rate of return that equates this finite stream of future cash flows with the net proceeds of the issue.

If the preferred stock doesn't have a sinking fund but instead is perpetual preferred, you must use a different procedure. An example illustrates this procedure.

Suppose a company issues $1 million of preferred stock with an annual dividend rate of 10%; flotation costs are 6% of the issue. The

Exhibit 5.2:   Flotation Costs and Maturity of Debt: The Impact on the Cost of Debt

Maturity (in years)	Pre-Tax Cost of Debt	After-Tax Cost of Debt
5	13.40%	8.03%
10	12.90%	7.73%
20	12.69%	7.59%
30	12.65%	7.56%

---

[5] The italics are mine.

net proceeds to the company are $940,000, which is the $1 million less the flotation costs of $60,000. If the company pays quarterly dividends, the quarterly dividend payment is $25,000. The cost to the company is the internal rate of return that equates the present value of all future dividends with the net proceeds. Since all future payments are constant, you can use the perpetuity valuation model:

$$P_N = \frac{D}{r_P} \qquad (5.2)$$

where P_N denotes the net proceeds after flotation costs, D denotes the quarterly dividend, and r_P denotes the quarterly cost of preferred stock. Since you know the net proceeds (P_N) and the dividend (D), you can solve equation (6) for the cost of preferred (r_P):

$$r_P = \frac{D}{P_N} = \frac{D}{P_0 (1 - F)} \qquad (5.3)$$

where P_0 and F denote the gross proceeds and the flotation costs as a percentage of the issue.

Using the values in this example, the adjusted cost of the preferred is:

$$r_P = \frac{\$25,000}{\$940,000} = 2.66\% \qquad (5.4)$$

Multiplying the quarterly rate of 2.66% by four gives an annual rate of 10.64%.[6] Notice that this is higher than 10%, the annualized cost of preferred stock if flotation costs are ignored.[7]

I.C. The Adjusted Cost of Common Equity

Section I.C.1 describes the adjustment to the cost of equity based on the adjusted discount rate approach. Section I.C.2 compares the costs of new equity and retained earnings. Section I.C.3 compares the adjusted discount rate approach with an alternative, the adjusted net present value approach.

---

[6] As an alternative, you could find the compounded annual cost, which is $(1 + .0266)^4 - 1$, or 11.07%.

[7] You could also find the adjusted cost of preferred by dividing the unadjusted cost of preferred by $1 - F$. In this case, the calculation would be $10\%/(1 - .06) = 10.64\%$.

I.C.1. Applying the Adjusted Discount Rate Method

The most common method of adjustment relies on the dividend growth model, which is described in detail in Chapter 3. Recall that the dividend growth model expresses the cost of equity (r_E) as a function of next period's dividend (D_1), today's price (P_0), and the expected growth rate in dividends:

$$r_E = \frac{D_1}{P_0} + g \tag{5.5}$$

A simple example illustrates the adjustment for flotation costs.[8] Suppose a company can issue stock for $26 per share (and you ignore flotation costs). For ease of exposition, assume that the company will pay an annual dividend. The first dividend will be $2.08, and the dividend is expected to grow at an annual rate of 4%. The dividend growth model provides an estimate of the unadjusted cost of equity:

$$r_E = \frac{\$2.08}{\$26} + .04 = 12.00\% \tag{5.6}$$

Now consider an identical situation except that flotation costs are 7% of the issue proceeds.[9] The future cash flows of the company remain the same, but the proceeds are no longer $26 per share. The net proceeds, P_N, are reduced by the flotation costs, F. Incorporating this into equation (5.5) yields:[10]

$$r_E = \frac{D_1}{P_N} + g = \frac{D_1}{P_0 (1 - F)} + g \tag{5.7}$$

Using the flotation cost of 7%, the adjusted cost of equity is:

$$r_E = \frac{\$2.08}{\$26 (1 - .07)} + .04 = 12.60\% \tag{5.8}$$

Notice that the cost of equity with flotation costs, 12.60%, is slightly higher than the cost without flotation costs, 12%.[11]

---

[8] For more discussion of this approach, see Brigham and Gapenski (1991b) or textbooks by Clark, Hindelang, and Pritchard (1989, pp. 181–186); Brigham and Gapenski (1991a, pp. 294–301); Gitman, Joehnk, and Pinches (1985, pp. 705–706); or Martin, Petty, Keown, and Scott (1991, p. 267).

[9] Flotation costs are not deductible for tax purposes.

[10] Notice that if the growth rate is zero, the adjusted cost of common equity is the same as the adjusted cost of the preferred stock in equation (5.3).

[11] If you have had multiple equity offering with different flotation costs, you should find a separate adjusted cost of equity for each issue, and then compute a weighted

Suppose your company doesn't pay dividends. In this case, you certainly can't use the dividend growth model. How should you adjust the cost of equity to reflect flotation costs if you aren't using the dividend growth model to estimate your unadjusted cost of equity? An example shows how you do this if you use the CAPM to estimate your unadjusted cost of equity.

To understand the CAPM adjustment, it helps to begin with a closer look at the dividend growth model. Consider a stock with no expected growth in dividends. Let r_{NG} denote the no-growth cost of equity, which is defined as:

$$r_{NG} = \frac{D_1}{P_0} \tag{5.9}$$

After substituting the no-growth cost of equity from equation (5.9) into equation (5.7), the adjusted cost of equity for a stock with growth is:

$$r_E = \frac{r_{NG}}{(1 - F)} + g \tag{5.10}$$

As equation (5.10) demonstrates, the adjusted cost of equity, r_E, is just the sum of the adjusted no-growth cost of equity and the growth rate in dividends. Notice that the growth rate in dividends is equal to the growth rate in earnings, given a constant dividend payout rate.

When you view it from this perspective, the underlying logic of the adjustment procedure in equation (5.10) is apparent. First, you decompose the unadjusted cost of equity into two components. The first component reflects the cost of equity due to the assets and earnings already in place (r_{NG}); the second component reflects the cost of equity due to expected growth. The adjustment procedure is straightforward: (1) adjust the no-growth cost of equity to reflect the flotation costs; and (2) add this adjusted no-growth cost of equity to the growth rate, which results in the adjusted cost of equity.

The adjustment for the dividend growth model cost of equity suggests a similar adjustment for the CAPM cost of equity. For example, suppose the CAPM cost of equity is 11.5% and the estimated growth rate in earnings is 4.5%. This implies that the no-growth cost of equity

---

average of these adjusted equity costs. See Brigham, Aberwald, and Gapenski (1985) for details.

is 11.5% − 4.5% = 7.0%.[12] If flotation costs are equal to 6%, the adjusted cost of equity is:

$$r_E = \frac{.07}{(1 - .06)} + .045 = 11.95\% \qquad (5.11)$$

I.C.2. Retained Earnings versus New Equity

You incur flotation costs only when you make a new issue. What effect does this have on the cost of reinvested earnings? To keep this discussion as simple as possible, let's assume that your firm is financed only with equity and debt. The flotation cost is incurred at the time that new equity is issued. Presumably, the new capital is used to undertake new projects. When you choose the appropriate rate to discount the cash flows of the new projects, it's obvious you should use the adjusted cost of equity in computing your weighted average cost of capital. It might not be quite as obvious, but you also should use this adjusted cost of capital for any subsequent projects financed with the reinvested earnings of the original projects. In other words, you don't consider "retained earnings" as a separate source of financing; see Chapter 3 for further discussion of this point.

For this simple firm, the only two sources of financing are equity and debt. You should use the market values of the equity and debt when you estimate the weights for the cost of capital, and you should apply the adjusted cost of equity to the equity weight.[13] You don't have to worry about decomposing future investments into the portion due to issued equity and the portion due to reinvested equity. The adjusted cost of equity already accommodates this.

It's important that you understand this point, because some authors suggest an alternative adjustment, which can lead to some confusion. In this alternative approach, you adjust the cost of new equity, r_{NE}, by:[14]

$$r_{NE} = \frac{r_E}{(1 - F)} \qquad (5.12)$$

The alternative approach of equation (5.12) will always produce a higher adjusted cost of new equity than the conventional approach

---

[12] Keep in mind that this is not the dividend yield. It is simply the difference in the estimated cost of equity and the growth rate in earnings.

[13] Actually, you should use the proportions of debt and equity in your target market capital structure instead of the current market values. See Chapter 3 for discussion of this issue.

[14] See Shapiro (1989, p. 289) or Lewellen (1976, pp. 88–106) for an example of this approach.

described by equation (5.10). There is an explanation for this apparent contradiction. The alternative approach requires that you explicitly consider retained earnings as a separate source of financing; unlike the cost of new equity, the cost of retained earnings does not include flotation costs. If you include this lower cost of the retained earnings when you calculate the weighted average cost of capital, the alternative approach leads to the same capital budgeting conclusions as the conventional approach. In other words, both methods are correct.

If both are correct, which one should you use? When there is a choice, you should always use the easiest approach. The conventional approach is easier, because it doesn't require any effort to specify weights and costs for retained earnings. Therefore, you should use the conventional approach, unless there is some compelling reason for you to do otherwise.[15]

I.C.3. The Adjusted Net Present Value Method

An alternative to the adjusted discount method is the adjusted net present value approach. In the adjusted net present value approach, the cost of capital is not adjusted to reflect flotation costs. Instead, you use the unadjusted cost of capital to discount the cash flows of a prospective project, but you adjust those cash flows to reflect the flotation costs.[16]

Which of these methods should you use? If you are raising capital for a specific project and will return that capital to investors at the completion of the project, then you should use the adjusted net present value method. If you are raising capital that will be continually reinvested in the firm, you should use the adjusted cost of capital method.

In reality, neither assumption (return of all capital at the completion of the project versus perpetual reinvestment of all capital) is correct. Yet very few companies return capital after the completion of each project, but most companies do reinvest capital for long periods of time. This means that the adjusted discount rate approach is generally a better choice than the adjusted net present value approach. Therefore, I recommend you use the adjusted discount rate approach, as described earlier in the chapter.[17]

---

[15] For further discussion of this issue within the context of utility rate setting, see Patterson (1981, 1983), Arzac and Marcus (1981, 1983), Bierman and Hass (1984), and Howe and Beranek (1992).

[16] See Keane (1976, 1978) for discussions of this concept.

[17] See Ehrhardt (1993) for a detailed and tedious review of the adjusted net present value approach; this review also compares and contrasts the adjusted discount rate approach

II. The Cost of Capital for Long-Term Projects

One of the most commonly used methods for estimating the cost of equity is the CAPM approach. As Chapter 3 explains, the CAPM is a one-period model. In other words, CAPM provides the correct cost of equity for discounting a cash flow that occurs in one period. Most projects, of course, typically have cash flows in many different future periods. How can you adjust the one-period CAPM cost of equity to accommodate the multiperiod nature of future cash flows? Are other methods of estimating the cost of equity still appropriate for discounting multiperiod cash flows? What about the costs of the other components of the capital structure?

These are the questions addressed in this section. Section II.A explains the problem in more detail, Section II.B explains how to adjust the cost of equity, and Section II.C discusses the costs of debt and preferred stock.

II.A. The Problems Caused by the Term Structure of Interest Rates

To understand the problems caused by the multiperiod cash flows of real projects, it helps to begin with the valuation of a bond. The insights from bond valuation are applicable to the valuation of real projects.

Bond valuation begins with spot rates, but what are spot rates? Suppose you know the current price of a default-free bond that makes no payments between now and its maturity date. At maturity, you are guaranteed to receive the bond's face value, since there is no default risk. Let P_t denote the price of this default-free zero-coupon bond that matures at time t; F_t denotes its face value at maturity. The spot rate for this t-period bond is the discount rate that makes the current price of the bond equal to the present value of its face value:

$$P_t = \frac{F_t}{(1 + R_t)^t} \qquad (5.13)$$

where R_t is the t-period spot rate. In other words, the spot rate is the internal rate of return for this default-free zero-coupon bond.

---

and the adjusted net present value approach. Alternatively, you could go to the original sources, which are Ezzell and Porter (1976); Copeland and Weston (1988); Hubbard (1984); PonArul (1990); Brigham and Gapenski (1991); Shrieves (1984); Wirth and Wright (1987); Howe (1982); and Howe and Patterson (1985).

The following example illustrates this. Suppose that a default-free zero-coupon bond pays $1,000 at its maturity in one year. If the current price on the bond is $962.34, the one-year spot rate is given by the equation:

$$\$962.34 = \frac{\$1000}{(1 + R_1)^1} \tag{5.14}$$

Solving equation (5.14) gives a one-year spot rate of $R_1 = 3.91\%$.

Data for spot rates are readily available. For example, *The Wall Street Journal* reports the prices of U.S. Treasury STRIP bonds, which are default-free zero-coupon instruments. In fact, the price of the bond in the example is actually the reported price for a one-year STRIP.[18] If you use this data source, you don't even have to convert prices to spot rates, because *The Wall Street Journal* also reports the "yields" of the STRIPs. Keep in mind that the yield is the internal rate of return, and the internal rate of return for a default-free zero-coupon instrument is the spot rate.

The relationship between the spot rate and maturity is defined as the term structure of interest rates. At the time of writing, the 10-year spot rate was 7.58%, and the 20-year spot rate was 8.33%. This term structure is not flat, in the sense that the spot rates are different for different maturities. To see how the term structure might affect the evaluation of a project, consider first how it affects the valuation of a coupon-paying bond. The price of a coupon-paying bond is just the present value of its coupon and principal payments, but each payment should be discounted by the appropriate spot rate:

$$P = \sum_{t=1}^{T} \frac{C_t}{(1 + R_t)^t} \tag{5.15}$$

where P is the current price of the bond, T is the total number of payments, and C_t is the total payment of the bond at time t. For all except the last payment date, C_t is the coupon payment; for the last payment, C_T is the sum of the coupon and the principal.

---

[18] Prices are actually reported as though the bond has a face value of $100. The bid and ask prices are reported in increments of 1/32. For example, on November 11, 1992, the reported bid price was 96:07 and the reported ask price was 96:08 for a STRIP maturing on November 15, 1993. The average of the bid and ask prices, converted to decimal and not 32nds, and converted to $1,000 face value and not $100 face value, is 962.34.

Given a set of hypothetical spot rates, an example illustrates bond valuation. Exhibit 5.3 shows these spot rates.[19]

Consider a simple default-free bond that has an annual coupon payment of $100 and matures in five years with a principal payment of $1,000; this is Bond 1 in Exhibit 5.3. Let C_t denote the cash flow of the bond; C_5 includes the principal payment. The price of a bond, P, is the present value of the payments. As shown in Exhibit 5.3, the price of this five-year bond is $1,037.33.

The yield of a bond, Y, is the internal rate of return based on the observed price and the cash flows. It is simply the value of Y that makes the following equation true:

$$P = \sum_{t=1}^{T} \frac{C_t}{(1 + Y)^t} \tag{5.16}$$

Exhibit 5.3 shows that the yield of this bond is 9.04%. Notice that the yield is between the smallest spot rate of 6.00% and the largest spot rate of 9.25%; in fact, the yield is a complicated nonlinear average of all the spot rates.[20]

Exhibit 5.3: An Example of Bond Valuation*

		Bond 1		Bond 2	
Year	Spot Rates	Payments	PV of Payments	Payments	PV of Payments
1	6.00%	$100	$94.34	$1,000	$943.40
2	7.50%	$100	$86.53	$1,000	$865.33
3	8.25%	$100	$78.83	$1,000	$788.34
4	9.00%	$100	$70.84	$1,000	$708.43
5	9.25%	$1,100	$706.78	$1,000	$642.53
		Price =	$1,037.33	Price =	$3,948.03
		Yield =	9.04%	Yield =	8.43%

*PV means present value.

---

[19] Keep in mind that these are spot rates and not implied forward rates; i.e., the two-year spot rate of 7.5% is the rate of return that would be earned by a zero-coupon bond maturing in two years.

[20] Actual bond data also support this conclusion. At the time of writing, the term structure of spot rates began at about 3.91% and increased to about 7.58% for the ten-year spot rate. The reported yield for the 11 5/8% coupon-paying bond that matured in ten years (November of 2002) had a yield of 6.96%, which is between the spot rates of 3.91% and 7.58%.

If you didn't know the spot rates but you knew the yield, you could find the price by discounting all the future cash flows with a "cost of capital" equal to the yield. But would it be appropriate to use this same cost of capital to find the price of another bond?

The answer is "no." Consider a second default-free bond with a maturity of five years. Suppose this bond makes equal payments of $1,000 in each year. Using the first bond's "cost of capital" of 9.04%, the estimated price of the second bond is:

$$P = \frac{\$1000}{(1 + .0904)} + \frac{\$1000}{(1 + .0904)^2} + \frac{\$1000}{(1 + .0904)^3}$$

$$+ \frac{\$1000}{(1 + .0904)^4} + \frac{\$1000}{(1 + .0904)^5} \qquad (5.17)$$

$$= \$3,885.69$$

The true price, however, should be based on the term structure of interest rates, as shown in equation (5.15). Exhibit 5.3 shows the correct price of Bond 2, which is $3,948.03. Using the cost of capital for the first bond results in an incorrect estimate of price for the second bond. This is because the yield of the second bond, which is the second bond's "cost of capital," is actually 8.43%, which is lower than the 9.04% "cost of capital" for the first bond. Even though both bonds are default-free, the timing of the cash flows will lead to different costs of capital if the term structure is not flat.

This point is also applicable to real projects. Suppose the two sets of cash flows in Exhibit 5.3 represent the cash flows of two projects. Since both projects are default-free, you might be tempted to use the same cost of capital to find the present values of the two projects. This can lead to an incorrect decision. For example, suppose the initial cost of the second project is $3,900. If you use the cost of capital from the first project, 9.04%, you would incorrectly conclude that the second project's value is $3,885.69, which is less than the acquisition cost. Therefore, you would reject the project. In fact, the true value of the project is $3,948.03, which is greater than the acquisition cost. In this case, using the wrong cost of capital would cause rejection of a value-adding project. The following sections show how to avoid making this type of mistake.

II.B. Estimating the Cost of Equity

The next three sections describe: (1) the adjustments that are necessary if you use the CAPM to estimate the cost of equity; (2) the adjustments that are necessary if you use the dividend growth model to estimate the cost of equity; and (3) the impact of inflation.

II.B.1. Adjusting the CAPM Cost of Equity

If you use the CAPM to estimate the cost of equity, you must make three decisions: (1) how to estimate beta; (2) what to use as a proxy for the risk-free rate; and (3) what to use as a proxy for the market risk premium.

The derivation of the CAPM assumes that investors are maximizing utility over the next investment period; therefore, CAPM is a one-period model. If the term structure is flat, and the term structure will not shift or change over time, the future investment environment truly is equivalent to a series of independent single periods.[21] Therefore, the CAPM is appropriate, and you can estimate the systematic risk, beta, just as Chapter 3 demonstrates. Your choice for a proxy of the risk-free rate is also simple, since the term structure is flat. The flat term structure means that all U.S. Treasury instruments have the same yield, so you simply pick a yield and use it as the risk-free rate.

If the term structure is not flat or constant over time, which it doesn't appear to be, you must make some decisions. If you're currently using the CAPM, you must decide whether to switch to another model. After all, a nonfixed term structure implies that all future periods will not be identical investment environments, because interest rates are changing. This violates an assumption underlying the derivation of CAPM and casts doubt on the validity of the resulting model. You might consider some alternative models of CAPM that do incorporate this nonstochastic term structure, such as the intertemporal CAPM of Merton (1973) or the term-risk structure model of Dothan and Williams (1980). These models are typically very difficult to implement, which might explain why most practitioners and researchers continue to use the original CAPM, even when they know that the term structure is shifting over time and is often sloped either upward or downward.

Suppose that you, too, decide to stay with the original CAPM. How do you estimate the cost of equity and find the net present value of a project? An example demonstrates the answer to this question.

Consider a project with a stream of cash flows for a finite number of future periods. Assume the project has five annual expected cash

---

[21] This also assumes that there are no changes in beta. In reality, beta could change if there are changes in investor risk preferences or production technologies.

flows of $1,000 each. Your first step is to estimate the beta of this project. You can use the techniques of Chapter 3 (or Chapter 4 if the project is in a different line of business from the rest of your company) to estimate beta.[22] For this example, suppose that the appropriate beta is 1.0.

Keep in mind that by staying with the original CAPM, you have implicitly assumed that the systematic risk is the same for each cash flow in each future period.[23] Given the nonflat term structure, however, you know that the risk-free rate is not constant for each time period. The question is "What adjustment should you make to the risk premium and the risk-free rate in the CAPM model?"

The most theoretically appealing adjustment is to use a different cost of equity for each period in which there is a cash flow.[24] This requires an estimate of the risk-free rate and the market risk premium for each period. It's very easy to determine the appropriate risk-free rate for each period: these are the spot rates from Exhibit 5.3. Exhibit 5.4 shows the cash flows of the project and the spot rates for each year.

How should you estimate the market risk premium? Ideally, you would like the expected risk premium for each year. Let R_{mt} denote the market return for a t-period return interval, R_{ft} the risk-free rate for a t-period return, and $E[R_{mt} - R_{ft}]$ the expected market premium for a t-period return. You know from Chapter 3 that you typically estimate the risk premium by using a long time series of historical returns. You take the arithmetic average market return and subtract the arithmetic average risk-free rate.

The average market return is readily available from sources such as Ibbotson and Sinquefield (1989), but it is not as easy to find historical averages for the spot rates. For example, Ibbotson and Sinquefield report only the yields on T-bills, long-term (2-year) T-bonds, and medium-term (10 years) T-bonds. For the years 1926–1987, the average market premium relative to T-bills was 8.3%, the premium relative to

---

[22] The suggested estimation techniques in Chapter 3 use either daily or monthly returns to estimate beta. Because you are trying to estimate the cost of equity for longer-term cash flows, it might seem reasonable to use yearly returns (or even longer returns) when you estimate beta. If returns are truly independently distributed, you should get the same beta whether you use short-term or long-term returns. If returns are not independently distributed, using long-term returns exposes you to estimation bias due to the "intervaling effect." See Smith (1978) and Levhari and Levy (1977) for more discussion of the intervaling effect.

[23] This also implies that the firm maintains the same leverage ratios. See Chapters 2 and 4 for further discussion of the relationship between systematic risk and leverage.

[24] See Fama (1977); Beranek (1978); Grinyer (1976, 1980); Haley and Schall (1978); and Keane (1975) for additional discussion of this issue.

Exhibit 5.4: Cost of Equity for a Long-Term Project
(finding the present value of a project)

Year	Spot Rate	Market Premium	Cost of Equity	Cash Flow of Project	Present Value of Payment
1	6.00%	8.2%	14.20%	$1,000.00	$875.66
2	7.50%	8.1%	15.60%	$1,000.00	$748.31
3	8.25%	8.0%	16.25%	$1,000.00	$636.53
4	9.00%	7.9%	16.90%	$1,000.00	$535.48
5	9.25%	7.8%	17.05%	$1,000.00	$455.14

Total Present Value of Project =	$3,251.12

"Average" Cost of Equity of Project =	16.31%

Note: The project beta is equal to 1.0%.

10-year T-bonds was 7.3%, and the premium relative to 20-year T-bonds was 6.8%.

Although it is only an approximation, you can use the T-bill premium and the ten-year premium to interpolate and find estimates of the one-year, two-year, three-year, four-year, and five-year premiums. These estimates are shown in Exhibit 5.4.

Let r_{Et} denote the cost of equity for each period. Using the values for the risk-free rate and the market premium in each period, you can use equation 5.18 to estimate the cost of equity for each period:

$$r_{Et} = R_t + \beta \, (E[R_{mt} - R_{ft}]) \qquad (5.18)$$

Exhibit 5.4 shows the cost of equity for each of the five years, based on the beta of 1.0, the risk premiums, and the spot rates. Exhibit 5.4 also shows the present value of the project's future cash flows, assuming the project is financed only with equity. For this project, the present value is $3,251.12.

If you wanted to find a single cost of equity for this project, it would have to be 16.31%. This is analogous to the yield of the bond example in Exhibit 5.3. As in the case of the bonds, any other average cost of equity would give an incorrect present value. It's also true that the 16.31% average cost of equity from this project would be incorrect for another project with the same beta but with a different pattern of cash flows. As Keane (1977) notes, the cost of equity for any particular project will depend on the timing and size of that project's cash flows.[25]

As the example indicates, there are risks of using a single cost of equity, but the practice is common among practitioners and researchers, perhaps because of its simplicity. A frequently used approach is to proxy the risk-free rate with the current yield on either a 10–year or 20–year T-bond.[26] It is also common to proxy the market premium with the historical market premium relative to either a 10–year or 20–year T-bond.[27]

For this example, suppose that the current yield on a 10–year T-bond is 9.5%. Using this as the risk-free rate and the market premium relative to a 10–year T-bond, the estimate of the cost of equity is:

$$r_E = 9.5\% + 1.0 \, (7.3\%) = 16.8\% \tag{5.19}$$

If you use this cost of equity in the example of Exhibit 5.4, you would estimate the present value of the cash flows to be $3,214.11. This would underestimate the present value of the project by about 1.1% ($3,214.11 present value for the approximation versus $3,251.12 for the true present value). As you see, the difference between the true value (using a cost of equity at each different time) and the approximated value (using a single cost of equity) is usually very small, and you might be willing to live with an error of this magnitude. Nevertheless, you should try to be as accurate as possible, and the adjustments in Exhibit 5.4 are not very complicated.

II.B.2. Adjusting the Dividend Growth Model Cost of Equity

What if you use another model, such as the dividend growth model? What adjustments should you make when you estimate the cost of equity for a long-term project? Recall that the dividend growth

---

[25] Keane (1978) also points out that a mismatch in the maturities of the project and the instruments that finance the project may cause problems when estimating the cost of capital.

[26] Recall that the yield on a bond is actually a complicated average of all the spot rates.

[27] For example, Copeland, Koller, and Murrin (1990) suggest using the yield on a 10–year bond as the risk-free rate and the geometric average of the stock market premium relative to a long-term T-bond. Ibbotson and Sinquefield (1989) suggest using the yield on a 20–year T-bond as the risk-free rate and using the arithmetic average of the stock market premium relative to a 20–year T-bond.

model estimates the cost of equity on the basis of a series of future dividend payments. Usually these payments grow at a geometric rate for an infinite number of periods. Therefore, if your project is generating an infinite number of cash flows that grow at a geometric rate, the dividend growth model cost of equity is just right. But if your project doesn't have cash flows with this pattern, and it probably won't, the dividend growth model cost of equity probably is not quite correct. Unfortunately, if you use a model other than the CAPM, there is little in the literature that will help you accommodate a nonflat or nonfixed term structure.

II.B.3. Inflation and the Cost of Equity

Shakespeare said that a rose by any other name would smell as sweet. Unfortunately, that isn't true for prices: a price is *not* a price, if there is inflation. For example, suppose that the price of a house last year was $70,000 and the price of a house this year is $72,100. Has the price changed? The answer is yes and no. The answer is yes, because the *nominal* price has changed. The nominal price, which is the price you actually observe, has changed from $70,000 to $72,100. Suppose inflation, which is the rate of change in prices, was 3% last year. The *real* price can be found by:

$$\text{Real Price } = \frac{\text{Nominal Price}}{(1 + \text{Inflation Rate})} = \frac{\$72,000}{(1 + .03)} = \$70,000 \quad (5.20)$$

In this example, the real price of the house hasn't changed: it was $70,000 last year, and it is $70,000 this year.

The conventional wisdom is that you can accommodate inflation in a capital budgeting study with one of two methods. In the "real" approach, you express all the future cash flows on a real basis, and then discount these real cash flows by the appropriate real cost of capital. In the "nominal" approach, you express the future cash flows on a nominal basis, and then discount these nominal cash flows by the appropriate nominal cost of capital.

Should you use the real approach, or should you use the nominal approach? Each approach is theoretically sound, if you are careful to implement it correctly.[28] Therefore, the choice of method boils down to which one is easier to implement.

---

[28] See Rappaport and Taggart (1982) for a demonstration that each method is theoretically sound, if it is applied correctly.

To estimate the future cash flows of a project, the nominal approach is somewhat easier. This is because many components of the cash flows usually are expressed on a nominal basis. For example, rent, insurance, and depreciation usually are expressed in nominal values. You also might have existing contracts for the purchase of raw materials or the sale of your product, and these contracts usually are in nominal terms. If you use the nominal approach, you don't have to make any adjustments in these values; using the real approach causes an extra set of calculations because you must convert these nominal costs to real costs.[29]

Which is easier to estimate, the nominal discount rate or the real discount rate? Unfortunately, there are difficulties in estimating both rates. All things considered, however, it's a little easier to estimate the nominal rate. This is because most approaches for estimating the real discount rate begin with the nominal rate.[30] If you use the nominal approach, you can avoid these extra adjustments needed to convert the nominal rate to the real rate. Therefore, I recommend using the nominal approach, unless there is a compelling reason to do otherwise.

Unfortunately, the techniques that are described in the previous chapters for estimating the cost of equity may not be exactly appropriate if there is inflation. This is because inflation may affect systematic risk, the market premium, or the appropriate risk-free rate.

If you believe that inflation expectations are fully captured in the nominal default-free spot rates, and that inflation doesn't affect the systematic risk of equity or the market risk premium, you can estimate the cost of equity the same way you would in the case of a nonflat, nonfixed term structure; see Section II.B.1.

If you are not willing to accept these assumptions, the situation becomes more complicated. There are several models that incorporate inflationary expectations into estimates of systematic risk. Two such models are those of Friend, Landskroner, and Losq (1976) and Mehta, Curley, and Fung (1984).[31] These models require additional inputs such

---

[29] There are other inputs that usually are forecast on a nominal basis. For example, the price of a high-technology product usually decreases over time, and you typically model this expected price decrease in your forecast. In most cases, you model this in nominal prices, not real prices.

[30] See Cooley, Roenfeldt, and Chew (1975) and Findlay, Frankle, Cooley, Roenfeldt, and Chew (1976) for a discussion of procedures necessary to adjust a nominal rate to a real rate.

[31] There are several asset pricing models that explicitly incorporate inflation. For example, Long (1974) extends the work of Merton (1973) to include inflation as well as term structure volatility. Cox, Ingersoll, and Ross (1985a, 1985b) provide very general models

as the covariances of the market index, the risk-free rate, and the company's returns with inflation. Using reasonable values for the inputs to the models, the adjusted systematic risk is frequently very close to the CAPM estimate of systematic risk. Therefore, unless you expect very high levels of inflation, you are probably safe in using the CAPM estimate of systematic risk.[32]

II.C. Estimating the Cost of Debt and Preferred Stock

Since you adjust the cost of equity for long-term projects, should you not also adjust the cost of debt? If the project is typical of the other projects that your firm undertakes, you don't have to make any special adjustment for the cost of debt, even if the term structure isn't flat. Keep in mind that your cost of debt should be based on the *current* rate at which you can issue debt, not the historical rate on your existing debt. The current rate at which you can issue debt already reflects the current shape of the term structure, so there is no need to make additional adjustments to the cost of debt.[33] There is also no need to adjust the cost of preferred stock, for the same reasons that you don't need to adjust the cost of debt.

What if the project is very different from the other projects that your firm undertakes? Should you use a different cost of debt for this project? To understand the answer to this question, it may be helpful to consider the case of a company with two different divisions in different lines of business. First, suppose that each of these divisions is actually a separate stand-alone company, financed with its own debt and equity. Of course, different lines of business support different levels

---

of asset pricing that can incorporate inflation. These models are extremely difficult to implement, however.

[32] See Lewellen and Ang (1982) and Howe (1992) for further discussion of inflation and capital budgeting.

[33] Term structures are normally upward-sloping, which means that the cost of long-term debt is usually more than the cost of short-term debt. This is not a problem if you have short- and long-term debt in your capital structure. You will simply treat the short- and long-term debt as two different sources of financing, each with its own cost. The issue does raise an interesting question with respect to your firm's choice of capital structure. Since short-term debt usually has a lower coupon rate, why don't firms simply finance with short-term debt and not long-term debt?

A complete answer is beyond the scope of this book, but one reason is flotation costs. Financing exclusively with short-term debt increases the total amount of flotation costs that the firm will incur, because the firm must refinance more often. A second reason is refinancing risk and its impact upon the debt capacity of the firm; see Brick and Ravid (1991) for details. Also, see Barnea, Haugen, and Senbet (1980) and Flannery (1986) for other explanations related to agency theory and asymmetric information.

of debt capacity. Therefore, each stand-alone company has its own target debt/equity ratio.

The equity in each stand-alone company has its own beta, which gives each company a different cost of equity. Suppose also that each company has a different bond rating, and the bonds issued by each company have different maturities. In this case, the cost of debt for the first stand-alone company is different from the cost of debt for the second company. But what happens to the costs of equity and costs of debt for the original company that consists of the two divisions?

The cost of equity is simply the average of the two costs of equity of the two divisions. This is because the company's beta is the average of the two divisional betas, as shown in Chapter 4.[34]

But what about the company's cost of debt? Suppose the company has a single issue of debt that is secured by the entire company's ability to generate revenues, which is typical of most conventional debt. First, it is highly unlikely that the company's bond rating will be the average of the bond ratings of the two divisions. If the cash flows of the two divisions are not perfectly positively correlated, the combined cash flows of the company are not nearly as risky from a lender's perspective. In other words, the total cash flows of the company during any particular year might well be positive even if the cash flows from one division are negative. Therefore, the company might well have a higher bond rating and, consequently, a lower cost of debt than either division.

Theoretically speaking, it would be desirable to assign each division a cost of debt based on the division's contribution to the firm's overall bond rating. Unfortunately, there is no well-accepted method for making such an allocation. Therefore, it is common to use the company's bond rating for estimating the cost of debt of each project. If you are not comfortable with this because you have projects with very different degrees of risk, you will have to use your own judgment in choosing bond ratings for each project.

Finally, should you assume that different projects are financed by debt of different maturities? In theory, firms should match the maturity of the debt to the duration of the project's cash flows.[35] In reality, most firms finance many different projects with a single debt issue. In fact, it's often hard to associate a project with any particular debt issue.

---

[34] This assumes that the target leverage ratio of the firm is the average of the leverage ratios of the two divisions; see Chapter 4 for further discussion of this issue. If this is not true, it would be more accurate to state that the unlevered beta of the company is the average of the unlevered betas of the two divisions.

[35] See Brick and Ravid (1991) for a discussion of this issue.

Therefore, in practice it's common to use the maturity of the firm's debt when finding the cost of debt for all projects, rather than assuming a different maturity for each project.[36] In most cases the cost of debt is not directly related to the project's cash flows. In general, the debt is secured by the cash-generating ability of the firm itself, not by the cash flows of a single project, so it is reasonable to use the firm's cost of debt for each project. In other words, you don't have to make any special adjustments for the cost of debt.

II.D. Summary and Recommendations

What adjustments should you make to the cost of capital when the term structure is not flat? The good news is that usually you don't need to make any adjustments to the cost of debt or preferred stock. The bad news is that there is no perfect adjustment for the cost of equity. The best you can hope for is an approximation that will minimize the resulting errors in your capital budgeting studies.

If the term structure slopes upward or downward by more than a percentage point or two, you should use a modified CAPM cost of equity as described in Section II.B. Using the methods of Chapter 3 to estimate the systematic risk is likely to produce some small bias in the resulting estimate of beta, since the CAPM is based on assumptions of nonstochastic interest rates, but the alternative models that explicitly incorporate nonstochastic interest rates are extremely difficult to implement. Therefore, I suggest you use the methods of Chapter 3 to estimate systematic risk, and hope that the bias because of nonstochastic interest rates is small.

---

[36] Of course, if you have a project that actually is supported by identifiable debt of a specific maturity, you should use this maturity when you estimate the project's cost of debt.

Appendix

Capital Rationing and the Cost of Capital

Suppose there is a firm that is not going to grow any more and you need to calculate the cost of capital based on the assets that are already in place. In other words, you need to find the capitalization rate that will equate the market value of the firm with the discounted value of the future cash flows generated by the assets in place. For a firm like this, the concept of capital rationing is irrelevant, because the firm is never going to raise any additional capital or reinvest in new assets.

Let's hope for the sake of your job security that your firm is not like this one, but that your firm is instead a thriving, growing, going concern. This means your firm will raise capital and reinvest in productive assets on a regular basis.[37] After all, the primary reason you need to measure the cost of capital is probably to use it in determining the optimal investment policy; i.e., in which assets should you invest, and which projects should you undertake?

Suppose you can reliably estimate the future cash flows of all potential projects in your investment opportunity set. Using the cost of capital as a discount rate, you can easily estimate the net present value of each project. It is entirely likely that your firm will not be able to accept all the positive NPV projects, because most firms face constraints. How do you choose the "best" group of projects from the investment opportunity set? In other words, how do you allocate, or ration, your capital among the potential projects? Unlike the case in the no-growth company, the issue of capital rationing is very important in this instance.

You may be wondering why your company can't immediately accept all positive NPV projects. It could be because the company doesn't have enough experienced management to undertake all the projects simulta-

---

[37] Even if your firm doesn't explicitly raise capital on a regular basis, it still raises capital implicitly. Financing investments with retained earnings instead of external capital is implicitly equivalent to the process of paying out cash in the form of dividends to stockholders and simultaneously raising capital from the same stockholders, if transactions costs and agency costs are neglected.

neously, or not enough engineering support or trained personnel. You might have physical constraints, such as the size of the facilities, that make it impossible for you to accept all projects.[38] Notice that you can eliminate each of these constraints in the long term, but this is not a long-term problem: you must decide which projects to accept now.

One potential approach is to formulate the decision as a linear programming problem.[39] Your basic objective would be to maximize your net present value, subject to the constraints that you face in each year. Following is a simple example to illustrate this capital budgeting problem.

Let's assume your only constraints are budgetary in nature, and that you have only a limited amount of funds available each year. Let b_t denote the amount of funds available in year t; your planning horizon starts at $t = 0$, which is the current date, and goes out to $t = T$. Let c_{it} denote the cash flow during period t that is caused by an investment of \$1 in project i. During the early years of a project's life, the cash flows (c_{it}) are likely to be negative, while they typically will be positive during the latter years. The net present value of \$1 invested in project i is:

$$NPV_i = \sum_{t=0}^{T} \frac{c_{it}}{(1 + r_c)^t} \qquad (A1)$$

where NPV_i is the net present value of \$1 invested in project i, and r_c is the cost of capital.

Suppose you have N possible projects; let x_i denote the number of dollars invested in project i.[40] The objective function is to maximize total net present value, which is just the sum of the net present values of the total investment in all the projects:

$$\text{Max} \sum_{i=1}^{N} NPV_i \, x_i \qquad (A2)$$

The sum of the amount budgeted in each year and the net cash flows due to the total investment in projects must be greater than or

---

[38] There are also some companies whose managers simply do not want to go the capital markets, particularly if it requires adding debt.

[39] See Weingartner (1963, 1966) for an early application of linear programming techniques to capital budgeting. Myers and Pogue (1974) and Myers (1974) also provide interesting financial planning models. Several textbooks, such as Clark, Hindelang, and Pritchard (1989), give excellent treatments of this topic.

[40] This implies that projects are divisible with respect to scale. You can modify this program to reflect projects that must be either rejected or accepted in their entirety. You can also modify it to reflect projects that are mutually exclusive or mutually dependent.

equal to zero, because you can't spend more than you have. The amount invested in each project must be nonnegative. This gives a system of constraints:

$$b_i + \sum_{i=1}^{N} c_{it} x_i \geq 0 \qquad \text{for } t = 1,T \qquad \text{(A3)}$$

$$x_i \geq 0 \qquad \text{for } i = 1,N$$

The solution to this linear program is a set of values for the x_i. If x_i is zero, you don't invest any money in project i. If x_i is positive, that is the amount that you invest in project i.[41]

For example, suppose you are considering a total of ten possible projects. The solution to the linear program of (A2) and (A3) is $x_1 = 100,000$, $x_2 = 500,000$, and all the other x's equal zero.[42] This means you should invest $100,000 in the first project, $500,000 in the second project, and nothing in any of the other projects.

You might wonder what all this has to do with the cost of capital. To see the connection, you need to see the dual program to the linear program in equations (A2) and (A3). Loosely speaking, a dual program is simply another linear program that must be true if the original program has a solution. To make the notation a little less complicated, let the discount rate for period t, based on the cost of capital, be d_t:

$$d_t = \frac{1}{(1 + r_c)^t} \qquad \text{(A4)}$$

Keep in mind that this discount rate measures the relative value between $1 paid in the future and $1 now, based on the company's cost of capital.

This changes the problem from a simple linear program to a mixed integer program. See Clark, Hindelang, and Pritchard (1989) for details.

[41] There are more realistic versions of this type of financial planning. See Weingartner (the find horizon model), Myers and Pogue (1974), and Myers (1974) for examples. Hughes and Lewellen (1974) criticize the linear programming approach to financial planning.

[42] Incidentally, most good spreadsheet programs for the microcomputer will now solve reasonably large linear programs.

The dual program is:

$$\text{Min} \quad \sum_{t=1}^{T} b_t \, L_t$$

$$\text{s.t} \quad \sum_{t=1}^{T} - c_{it} \, L_t \geq \sum_{t=1}^{T} d_t \, L_t \quad \text{for } i = 1, N \qquad \text{(A5)}$$

$$L_t \geq 0$$

The dual variables are denoted by L_t. These dual variables correspond to the constraints in (A3), and can be interpreted loosely as the amount of change in the objective function, given a change in the constraints.[43] To put it a little differently, any particular dual variable L_t is the amount that the net present value of the objective function increases if there is an extra \$1 of available funds in period t. Therefore, the dual variable L_t can be interpreted as the present value factor for period t. But this is exactly the same interpretation as the discount rate d_t.

Since the dual variable L_t and the discount rate d_t have the same economic interpretation, you might expect that the dual program in equation (A5) would give values of L_t that are equal to d_t. Burton and Damon (1974), however, show mathematically that L_t and d_t cannot be equal.[44]

This is the dilemma: if you have capital rationing, it's not clear that the cost of capital is a meaningful concept. It certainly can't be interpreted as a rate that equates a dollar in the future with a dollar today, which casts doubt on its use in finding the net present value of a project.

This really calls into question the whole issue of capital rationing and the meaning of the cost of capital. If the cost of capital is truly the rate that investors demand, then in well-functioning capital markets you should always be able to raise funds for positive NPV projects. Investors may demand a high return, but they are willing to invest in projects that have a positive NPV based on the investors' required rate

---

[43] For a more detailed discussion of linear programming and interpretation of dual variables, see any good operations research text such as Hillier and Lieberman (1974) or Bazaraa and Jarvis (1977).

[44] This is always true, except for the trivial case in which $L_t = d_t = 0$. See Baumol and Quandt (1965); Carleton (1969); Elton (1970); Myers (1972); Merville and Tavis (1973); and Weingartner (1977) for further discussion of this issue.

of return; in fact, that's a tautological definition of the required rate of return. Therefore, firms should never face capital rationing if the cost of capital is defined correctly.

The reality is that most managers in firms do face capital rationing. Unfortunately, there's no easy way to accommodate theory and reality.[45] All I can suggest is that if your firm consistently rejects many projects with positive NPVs, you need to re-examine your cost of capital, and your firm needs to reconsider its financial resourcing policies.

---

[45] Taggart (1987) provides an interesting discussion of the role that the cost of capital plays in capital rationing.

References

Arzac, E.R., and M. Marcus. "Flotation Cost Allowance in Rate of Return Regulation: A Note." *Journal of Finance* 36(5) (December 1981): 1199–1202.

―――. "Flotation Cost Allowance in Rate of Return Regulation: A Reply." *Journal of Finance* 38(4) (September 1983): 1339–1341.

Barnea, A., R.A. Haugen, and L.W. Senbet. "A Rationale for Debt Maturity Structure and Call Provisions in the Agency Theoretic Framework." *Journal of Finance* 35(5) (1980): 1223–1234.

Baumol, W.J., and R.E. Quandt. "Investment and Discount Rates Under Capital Rationing—A Programming Approach." *The Economic Journal* 75(298) (June 1965): 317–329.

Bazaraa, M.S., and J.J. Jarvis. *Linear Programming and Network Flows.* New York: Wiley, 1977.

Beranek, W. "Some New Capital Budgeting Theorems." *Journal of Financial and Quantitative Analysis* (December 1978): 809–823.

Bierman, H., Jr., and J.E. Hass. "Equity Flotation Cost Adjustment in Utilities' Cost of Service." *Public Utilities Fortnightly* (March 1, 1984): 46–49.

Brealey, R.A., and S.C. Myers. *Principles of Corporate Finance* 3d ed. New York: McGraw-Hill, 1988.

Brick, I.E., and S.A. Ravid. "Interest Rate Uncertainty and the Optimal Debt Maturity Structure." *Journal of Financial and Quantitative Analysis* 26(1) (1991): 63–82.

Brigham, E.F., D. Aberwald, and L.C. Gapenski. "Common Equity Flotation Costs and Rate Making." *Public Utilities Fortnightly* (May 2, 1985): 28–36.

Brigham, E.F., and L.C. Gapenski. *Financial Management: Theory and Practice,* 6th ed. Hinsdale, Ill.: Dryden Press, 1991.

―――. "Flotation Cost Adjustments." *Financial Practice and Education* (Fall/Winter 1991): 29–34.

Burton, R.M., and W.W. Damon. "On The Existence of a Cost of Capital Under Pure Capital Rationing." *Journal of Finance* 29(4) (1974): 1165–1173.

Carleton, W.T. "Linear Programming and Capital Budgeting Models: A New Interpretation." *Journal of Finance* 24(5) (December, 1969): 825–833.

Clark, J.J., T.J. Hindelang, and R.E. Pritchard. *Capital Budgeting: Planning and Control of Capital Expenditures.* Englewood Cliffs, N.J.: Prentice Hall, 1989.

Cooley, P.L., R.L. Roenfeldt, and I. Chew. "Capital Budgeting Procedures Under Inflation." *Financial Management* (Winter 1975): 18–27.

Copeland, T., T. Koller, and J. Murrin. *Valuation: Measuring and Managing the Value of Companies.* New York: Wiley, 1990.

Copeland, T.E., and J.F. Weston. *Financial Theory and Corporate Policy* 3d ed. Reading, Mass.: Addison-Wesley, 1988.

Cox, J.C., J.E. Ingersoll, and S.A. Ross. "An Intertemporal General Equilibrium Model of Asset Prices." *Econometrica* 53(2) (1985a): 363–384.

———. "A Theory of the Term Structure of Interest Rates." *Econometrica* 53(2) (1985b): 385–407.

Dothan, U., and J. Williams. "Term-Risk Structures and the Valuation of Projects." *Journal of Financial and Quantitative Analysis* 15 (November 1980): 875–906.

Ehrhardt, M.C. "Flotation Costs and the Cost of Capital: A Comparison of the Adjusted Discount Rate Approach and the Adjusted Net Present Value Approach." Working Paper, University of Tennessee, 1993.

Elton, E.J., "Capital Rationing and External Discount Rates." *Journal of Finance* 25(3) (June 1970): 573–584.

Ezzell, J.R., and R.B. Porter. "Flotation Costs and the Weighted Average Cost of Capital." *Journal of Financial and Quantitative Analysis* 11(3) (1976): 403–413.

Fama, E.F. "Risk-Adjusted Discount Rates and Capital Budgeting Under Uncertainty." *Journal of Financial Economics* 5 (1977): 3–24.

Findlay, M.C., III, A.W. Frankle, Philip L. Cooley, Rodney L. Roenfeldt, and It-Keong Chew. "Capital Budgeting Procedures Under Inflation: Cooley, Roenfeldt, and Chew vs. Findlay and Frankle." *Financial Management* (Autumn 1976): 83–90.

Flannery, M.J. "Asymmetric Information and Risky Debt Maturity Choice." *Journal of Finance* 41(1) (1986): 19–38.

Friend, I., Y. Landskroner, and E. Losq. "The Demand for Risky Assets Under Uncertain Inflation." *Journal of Finance* (December 1976): 1285–1297.

Gitman, L.J., M.D. Joehnk, and G.E. Pinches. *Managerial Finance.* New York: Harper & Row, 1985.

Grinyer, J.R. "The Cost of Equity, the CAPM, and Management Objectives Under Uncertainty." *Journal of Business Finance and Accounting* 3(2) (1976): 101–121.

———. "The Term Structure and the Irrelevance of the Firm's Cost of Capital: A Comment." *Journal of Business Finance and Accounting* 7(2) (1980): 305–310.

Haley, C.W., and L.D. Schall. "Problems With the Concept of the Cost of Capital." *Journal of Financial and Quantitative Analysis* 13(5) (1978): 847–870.

Hillier, F.S., and G.J. Lieberman. *Operations Research* 2d ed. San Francisco: Holden-Day, 1974.

Howe, K.M. "A Note on Flotation Costs and Capital Budgeting." *Financial Management* (Winter 1982): 30–33.

Howe, K.M., and W. Beranek. "Issue Costs and Regulated Returns: A General Approach." *Journal of Regulatory Economics* 4 (1992): 365–378.

Howe, K.M., and J.H. Patterson. "Capital Investment Decisions Under Economies of Scale in Flotation Costs." *Financial Management* (Autumn 1985): 61–69.

Hubbard, C.M. "Flotation Costs in Capital Budgeting: A Note on the Tax Effect." *Financial Management* (Summer 1984): 38–40.

Hughes, J.S., and W.G. Lewellen. "Programming Solutions to Capital Rationing Problems." *Journal of Business Finance and Accounting* 1(1) (1974): 55–74.

Ibbotson, R.G., and R.A. Sinquefield. *Stocks, Bonds, Bills and Inflation: Historical Returns (1926-1987).* Charlottesville, Va: The Financial Analysts Research Foundation, 1989.

Keane, S.M. "Some Aspects of the Cost of Debt." *Accounting and Business Research* (Autumn 1975): 298–304.

———. "The Investment Discount Rate—In Defence of the Market Rate of Interest." *Accounting and Business Research* (Summer 1976): 228–236.

———. "The Irrelevance of the Firm's Cost of Capital as an Investment Decision Tool." *Journal of Business Finance and Accounting* 4(2) (1977): 201–216.

———. "The Cost of Capital as a Financial Decision Tool." *Journal of Business Finance and Accounting,* 5(3) (1978): 339–354.

Levhari, D., and H. Levy. "The Capital Asset Pricing Model and the Investment Horizon." *The Review of Economics and Statistics* 59 (1977): 92–104.

Lewellen, W.G. *The Cost of Capital.* Dubuque, Iowa: Kendall/Hunt, 1976.

Lewellen, W.G., and J.S. Ang. "Inflation, Security Values, and Risk Premia." *Journal of Financial Research* 5(2) (Summer 1982): 105–123.

Long, J.B., Jr., "Stock Price, Inflation, and the Term Structure of Interest Rates." *Journal of Financial Economics* 1(2) (1974): 131–170.

Martin, J.D., J.W. Petty, A.J. Keown, and D.F. Scott, Jr. *Basic Financial Management,* 5th ed. Englewood Cliffs, N.J.: Prentice-Hall, 1991.

Mehta, D.R., M.D. Curley, and H. Fung. "Inflation, Cost of Capital, and Capital Budgeting Procedures." *Financial Management* 13(4) (1984): 48–54.

Merton, R.C. "An Intertemporal Capital Asset Pricing Model." *Econometrica* (September 1973): 867–888.

Merville, L.J., and L.A. Tavis. "A Generalized Model for Capital Investment." *Journal of Finance* 27(1) (March 1973): 109–118.

Myers, S.C. "A Note on Linear Programming and Capital Budgeting." *Journal of Finance* 27(1) (March 1972): 89–92.

———. "Interactions of Corporate Financing and Investment Decisions—Implications for Capital Budgeting." *Journal of Finance* (May 1974): 1–25.

Myers, S.C., and G.A. Pogue. "A Programming Approach to Corporate Financial Management." *Journal of Finance* (March 1974): 579–599.

Patterson, C.S. "Issue Costs in the Estimation of the Cost of Equity Capital." *Public Utilities Fortnightly* 108 (July 16, 1981): 28–32.

———. "Flotation Cost Allowance in Rate of Return Regulation: A Comment." *Journal of Finance* 38(4) (September 1983): 1335–1338.

Pettway, R.S. "A Note on the Flotation Costs of New Equity Capital Issues of Electric Companies." *Public Utilities Fortnightly* 109 (March 18, 1982): 68–69.

PonArul, R. "Treatment of Flotation Cost of Equity in Capital Budgeting." *Journal of Financial Education* 19 (1990): 44–45.

Rappaport, A., and R.A. Taggart, Jr. "Evaluation of Capital Expenditure Proposals Under Inflation." *Financial Management* (Spring 1982): 5–13.

Shapiro, A.C. *Modern Corporate Finance.* New York: Macmillan, 1989.

Shrieves, R.E. "The Optimal Investment Decision with Capital Market Transaction Costs." Working paper, University of Tennessee, 1984.

Smith, K.V. "The Effect of Intervalling on Estimating Parameters of the Capital Asset Pricing Model." *Journal of Financial and Quantitative Analysis* 13 (1978): 313–332.

Taggart, R.A., Jr. "Allocating Capital Among a Firm's Divisions: Hurdle Rates vs. Budgets." *Journal of Financial Research* 10(3) (1987): 177–190.

Weingartner, H.M. *Mathematical Programming and the Analysis of Capital Budgeting Problems.* Englewood Cliffs, N.J.: Prentice-Hall, 1963.

———. "Criteria for Programming Investment Project Selection." *Journal of Industrial Economics* 15(1) (November 1966): 65–76.

———. "Capital Rationing: Authors in Search of a Plot." *Journal of Finance* 32(5) (1977): 1403–1431.

Wirth, A., and F.K. Wright. "New Issue Costs and Project Evaluation: Ezzell and Porter Revisited." *Journal of Business Finance and Accounting* 14(3) (Autumn 1987): 393–407.

Chapter *6*

The Cost of Capital for Regulated Companies: Utilities and Deposit-Taking Financial Institutions

*I*have assumed so far that your company competes in an industry where prices are for the most part determined by the competitive forces of the free market. I have also assumed that your company is free to choose which products and services it will provide. Chapter 6 examines a different issue: the cost of capital for companies in regulated industries.

The techniques illustrated in the previous chapters may not be directly applicable to companies operating in a regulated industry. If your company is one, you may need to modify these techniques when you estimate the cost of capital. There are two reasons for this. First, product characteristics and production technologies in regulated industries often differ from those of nonregulated industries. For example, the products and services of a bank are quite different from those of a manufacturer. These differences may affect the method used in estimating the cost of equity; e.g., a multifactor model that includes interest rates is especially appropriate for a deposit-taking financial institution.

Second, the process of regulation itself may affect the appropriate technique for estimating the cost of capital. In the case of an electric utility, regulators typically determine the prices the company charges. Because the revenue stream is not completely determined by market forces, perhaps the stock returns are not completely determined by market forces. Therefore, you may need to modify the methods described in the previous chapters.

163

Section I discusses issues associated with the cost of capital for utilities, which face regulation with respect to the prices that they can charge. Section II focuses on deposit-taking financial institutions, which face regulation with respect to the services and products that they can provide. The techniques used for estimating the cost of capital for companies in these regulated industries are similar, but not always identical, to the techniques of the previous chapters.

I. The Cost of Capital for Utilities

Most utilities, whether they provide their customers electricity or local telephone service, share a common feature: their products and services can be provided "best" by a single company. For example, it doesn't make economic sense for two different companies to place telephone poles and telephone lines along the same street. It is instead more cost-effective for a single company to provide local telephone service within a specific geographic area. Therefore, government agencies allow only one company to provide local service telephone within that area. If regulation stopped at this point, the single provider of local telephone service would probably charge much higher prices than it would if it were competing against other companies in a free market. To prevent this loss of consumer welfare, regulators also set limits on the prices that the single provider can charge.

How do regulators determine the allowable prices? In many ways, regulation is a balancing act.[1] If prices are too high, consumers experience a transfer in welfare to the owners of the utility. If prices are too low, however, investors suffer a loss in wealth, and the utility will be unable to attract sufficient financing for replacement, expansion, or improvement of its physical assets. Plant deterioration ultimately leads to reductions in the level and quality of services demanded by consumers. Therefore, regulators attempt to establish prices that balance the conflicting goals of consumers and investors. In other words, the prices cannot be so high that consumers pay unfair charges, nor so low that investors fail to receive an adequate rate of return.[2]

---

[1] The United States Supreme Court established this principle in two widely cited cases. The first is *Bluefield Water Works* v. *P.S.C.*, 262 U.S. 679 (1923), and the second is *F.P.C.* v. *Hope Natural Gas Co.*, 320 U.S. 591 (1944). See Kolbe, Read, and Hall (1984) for detailed discussion of these two landmark cases.

[2] Under "perfect" regulation, prices are set at the same level that would prevail in perfect competition: price = marginal revenue = marginal cost.

What is the relationship between the allowable rate of return set by regulators and the weighted average cost of capital described in the previous chapters? Are there characteristics unique to utilities that affect the choice of method when estimating the costs of the components in a utility's capital structure? These are the questions that sections I.B, I.C, and I.D address. First, however, we define the allowable rate of return within the context of the regulatory process.

I.A. The Regulatory Process and the Allowable Rate of Return

The rate-making process is extremely complicated, requiring forecast of demand from consumers, estimation of production costs, and determination of capital costs. A thorough treatment is far beyond the scope of this chapter. In fact, an entire literature is devoted to the determination of capital costs.[3] Here I describe only the distinctive features of the process, with an emphasis on their linkage to the cost of capital.

Public utilities cannot change the prices they charge without approval from the applicable regulatory commission.[4] Typically a utility must file a formal request with the regulatory commission. A hearing follows this request, at which time the regulatory commission makes a decision with respect to the requested price. The primary objective of regulatory review is to set a price that is sufficient to cover the costs of production, the costs of taxes, the costs of interest payments, and the costs to investors of equity.

In a typical rate case hearing, a necessary step is the establishment of a rate base.[5] This rate base is usually the sum of the book values of debt (D_B) and equity (E_B).[6]

---

[3] See Gordon (1974) or Kolbe, Read, and Hall (1984) for a thorough treatment of this topic.

[4] There are a few exceptions. For example, some utilities also compete in nonregulated businesses, and they can change prices for these nonregulated products and services. Also, some jurisdictions permit prices to go into effect prior to the rate case hearing, subject to refund pending the ultimate decision of the regulatory commission. See Kolbe, Read, and Hall (1984) for more details.

[5] There is no uniform process used by all commissions. I describe a typical process, but it is by no means common to all rate case hearings. See Kolbe, Read, and Hall (1984) for descriptions of other processes.

[6] Other sources of financing, such as preferred stock, are also included. For clarity of exposition, however, the discussion assumes all financing is by common equity and debt.

The next step is to estimate the components of the allowable cost of capital. The cost of debt is the weighted average of the coupon rates on all of the company's existing debt. This historical pre-tax cost of debt, i_H, is frequently called the "embedded cost of debt." The commission also establishes an allowable cost of equity, r_{AE}; section I.C discusses this process in detail.

The allowable weighted average cost of capital is:

$$r_{AC} = \left(\frac{E_B}{E_B + D_B}\right) r_{AE} + \left(\frac{D_B}{E_B + D_B}\right) (1 - \tau) i_H \qquad (6.1)$$

where r_{AC} denotes the allowable cost of capital, and τ is the corporate tax rate.[7]

The commission multiplies the allowable cost of capital by the rate base to determine the allowable after-tax revenues. The commission adds tax expenses (ignoring the tax shield due to the interest payments), estimated production costs, and other expenses to these after-tax revenues.[8] The resulting figure is analogous to the net sales of a manufacturer. The commission divides this figure by the forecasted demanded quantity, and the result is the allowable price.

This might be an appropriate process for regulators, because the objective of the regulatory commission is to determine the allowable price. Yet this allowable cost of capital is different from the weighted average cost of capital as defined in Chapters 2 and 3.

I.B. Differences between the Weighted Average Cost of Capital and the Allowable Cost of Capital

Chapter 2 defines the weighted average cost of capital as:[9]

$$r_C = \left(\frac{E}{E + D}\right) r_E + \left(\frac{D}{E + D}\right) (1 - \tau) i \qquad (6.2)$$

where E is the market value of equity, D is the market value of debt, r_E is the cost of equity, and i is the current rate at which you could issue debt.

---

[7] Most commissions actually use a pre-tax embedded interest rate. As I describe, the after-tax rate used in equation (6.1) results in exactly the same allowable prices as the pre-tax embedded interest rate. I use the after-tax rate here because it lends itself more directly to comparison with the weighted average cost of capital as defined in Chapter 2.

[8] If the commission uses the pre-tax cost of debt, it then adds all tax expenses, not just those net of the tax shield because of interest payments.

[9] Remember, these cash flows do not include any cash flows because of debt.

What are the differences between the allowable cost of capital in equation (6.1) and the weighted average cost of capital in equation (6.2)? One obvious difference is the use of book weights for the allowable cost of capital and market weights for the weighted average cost of capital. As discussed in Chapter 3, the book value of debt and the market value of debt are usually similar, unless market interest rates have changed considerably.

The market value of equity and the book value of equity are often similar for utilities. In fact, some researchers argue that regulators should set prices so that the market and book values of equity are equal, that this is equivalent to setting the allowable rate of return equal to the market-determined weighted average cost of capital.[10] Whether regulators actually pursue this goal is debatable, but it is true that book and market values of equity for utilities are often very similar.[11] If there are significant differences between book and market values, the allowable cost of capital generally will be different from the weighted average cost of capital.

A second difference between the allowable cost of capital in equation (6.1) and the weighted average cost of capital in equation (6.2) is the interest rate. The interest rate for the allowable cost of capital is the embedded historical rate, not the current rate. If more debt must be raised in order to accept a proposed project, it is clearly wrong to use the historical interest rate in deciding whether to accept or reject the project. Unless the historical and current rates happen to be equal, using the allowable cost of capital can lead to erroneous capital budgeting decisions.

For example, suppose the current rates are higher than the embedded historical rates, which means that the allowable cost of capital is lower than the weighted average cost of capital. What happens if you use the allowable cost of capital?

Let's assume you are considering a project that has a positive net

---

[10] Kolbe, Read, and Hall (1984) outline this argument; they also claim that if flotation costs are incorporated, the market value of equity should be slightly higher than the book value. There are others, such as Gordon (1974), who argue that regulators should not use market values, because the regulatory process itself contributes to the market value. For example, suppose the current market value of equity is below the current book value of equity because product prices are too low. If stockholders believe the regulatory commission is going to adjust prices in order to equate the market and book value, the market value will immediately increase to equal the book value. But if they are equal, the regulatory commission might believe that no price adjustment is necessary. If this is the case, the stock price will revert to its original level. As you can see, there is no end to this circle of cause and effect.

[11] See Brigham and Crum (1978), Carleton (1978), and Myers (1972) for further discussion of this point.

present value if you use the allowable cost of capital but that has a negative NPV if you use the weighted average cost of capital. If you accept the project and finance it partially with new debt at the current rate, shareholders will experience an immediate decline in wealth because of the adoption of a negative NPV project. It is true that at the next rate case hearing the resulting allowable cost of capital will reflect the updated embedded cost of debt, but this does not fully restore the loss in wealth to the shareholders because price adjustments are not retroactive.[12]

Despite the best intentions of regulatory agencies, lags between the filing of a request for a rate change and the implementation of the rate change can affect the returns realized by investors. To mitigate the impact of this regulatory lag, many regulatory agencies permit utilities to pass on unexpected increases in fuel costs to customers without a rate hearing.[13] As Clarke (1978) shows, if regulators allow firms to use an automatic adjustment clause but also hold total expected profits constant, there is a decrease in the systematic risk of the firm's assets. This decrease in systematic risk causes a decrease in the cost of equity. Therefore, if regulators have recently allowed your firm to implement an automatic adjustment clause, historical returns from the period prior to the change will not accurately reflect the new cost of equity. It would be difficult for you to implement Clarke's analytical model to determine the change in systematic risk, but you should be aware that adoption of the adjustment clause may reduce your systematic risk.

I.C. The Cost of Equity For Utilities

Chapters 3, 4, and 5 describe techniques for estimating the cost of equity for nonregulated firms. Are there any special adjustments or modifications that should be applied when estimating the cost of equity for a regulated utility?

One fundamental issue is whether the CAPM can be used to estimate the cost of equity for a utility.[14] There is no doubt that the regula-

---

[12] See Myers (1972) for further discussion on problems because of the embedded cost of debt.

[13] See Sarikas (1975) and Schiffel (1975) for details concerning the automatic fuel adjustment clause. West and Eubank (1976) argue that other automatic adjustments should be allowed, including an automatic adjustment in the cost of capital.

[14] For a discussion of flotation costs and the estimated cost of capital for utilities, see Arzac and Marcus (1981, 1983); Bierman and Hass (1984); Brigham, Aberwald, and Gapenski (1985); Patterson (1981, 1983); Howe and Beranek (1992); and Pettway (1982). See Linke and Zumwalt (1984) for several adjustments necessary to convert the quarterly dividend growth model cost of equity into an appropriate allowable cost of equity.

tory process itself affects the expected cash flows of a utility, which almost certainly affects the distribution of expected stock returns. Carleton (1978) argues that the impact of the regulatory process alters the expected return distribution to the extent that application of the CAPM is no longer valid. In fact, he suggests that no asset pricing model is valid unless that model explicitly takes into account the regulatory process.[15] Other authors, for various reasons, also argue that the CAPM should not be used to estimate the cost of equity for a utility. On the other hand, many other authors argue that the CAPM can be used. Unfortunately, there is no definitive answer.[16]

If you don't use the CAPM, then what are the alternatives? One choice is the dividend growth model. This model usually is well-suited to utilities, as most utilities have relatively large and relatively stable dividends. You can apply this model directly, as it is explained in Chapter 3, to utilities.[17] Three other choices are the three-moment model, which incorporates skewness, the arbitrage pricing theory (APT) model, and an interest rate index model. Sections I.C.1 and I.C.2 explain the three-moment and APT models. Section II.A explains the interest rate index model within the context of financial institutions, but you can use the same approach to apply the model to utilities.

I.C.1. The Three-Moment Model

The CAPM approach assumes that expected stock returns have a normal distribution. Brigham and Crum (1978), however, argue that regulators limit the upside potential for investors in regulated firms, which would cause skewness in the expected stock returns for utilities. For this reason, Conine and Tamarkin (1985) suggest that the Kraus

---

[15] Carleton (1977) provides a version of the dividend growth model that does explicitly incorporate the regulatory process.

[16] Myers (1972) argues that the CAPM can be used, while Breen and Lerner (1972) argue against its use. See Brigham and Crum (1977, 1978); Sharpe (1978); McEnally (1978); Myers (1978); Gilster and Linke (1978); and Carleton (1978) for an interesting exchange on the topic of the CAPM's validity for estimating a utility's cost of equity, and whether that cost can be used in rate case hearings. Litzenberger, Ramaswamy, and Sosin (1980) also discuss the use of the standard CAPM and several modifications in estimating the cost of equity.

[17] One potential modification is to replace the market value of the stock's price with the book value of the stock's price. The rationale for this modification is that regulators are going to apply the rate of return to book equity, so the rate itself should be derived from the book equity. Keep in mind that book prices and market prices usually are close to one another for utilities, so this modification might not produce a large change in the estimated cost of equity.

and Litzenberger (1976) three-moment asset pricing model, which accommodates skewness in expected returns, is appropriate for utilities.
    This is the three-moment model:

$$r_E = r_f + b_1\beta + b_2\gamma \tag{6.3}$$

where beta (β) and gamma (γ) are the measures of risk, and b_1 and b_2
are the risk premiums for those two sources of risk. Beta has the same
interpretation as the traditional CAPM beta. That is, beta is:

$$\beta = \frac{\text{COVARIANCE } [R_i, R_m]}{\text{VARIANCE } [R_m]} \tag{6.4}$$

    Let R_{it} and R_{mt} denote the security return and the market return
in period t, respectively. If you have a sample of T observations, the
estimate of beta is:

$$\beta = \frac{\sum_{t=1}^{T} (R_{it} - \overline{R}_i)(R_{mt} - \overline{R}_m)}{\sum_{t=1}^{T} (R_{mt} - \overline{R}_m)^2} \tag{6.5}$$

    Gamma (γ) is a measure of risk attributable to skewness. Gamma
is:

$$\gamma = \frac{\text{COSKEWNESS}[R_i, R_m]}{\text{SKEWNESS}[R_m]} \tag{6.6}$$

$$= \frac{\sum_{t=1}^{T} (R_{it} - \overline{R}_i)(R_{mt} - \overline{R}_m)^2}{\sum_{t=1}^{T} (R_{mt} - \overline{R}_m)^3}$$

    Conine and Tamarkin use 60 months of data from the period
1976–1980 to estimate the two measures of risk (beta and gamma) for
each company in a sample containing 60 utilities. They assume that
investors have a specific type of utility function, which allows them
to estimate value of b_1 and b_2; see the appendix of their paper for
details.
    Conine and Tamarkin use their estimates of the parameters in
equation (6.3) to calculate the three-moment cost of equity for each of
the 60 utilities. They also estimate the CAPM cost of equity for these

same companies. They find a mean CAPM cost of equity for their sample of 15.81% and a mean three-moment cost of equity of 17.16%. Their evidence suggests that the CAPM approach for estimating the cost of equity may be inadequate for utilities, given the skewness in utilities' stock returns.

I.C.2. The Arbitrage Pricing Theory Model

The CAPM suggests that a stock's expected return is a function only of the company's systematic risk with respect to the market portfolio. The arbitrage pricing theory (APT) (discussed in the appendix to Chapter 3) suggests instead that a stock's expected return might be a function of more than one source of systematic risk. Bower, Bower, and Logue (1984) apply APT to a sample of utilities and find that it leads to significantly different estimates of the cost of equity.

Bower, Bower, and Logue use factor analysis on a sample containing all nonutility stocks on the New York and American Stock exchanges (factor analysis is also discussed in the appendix to Chapter 3). They extract four time series containing T observations each of "factor scores." Let F_{1t}, F_{2t}, F_{3t}, and F_{4t} denote the value of the factor scores on each date t. Bower, Bower, and Logue perform this regression on stock returns for a sample of utilities:

$$r_{it} = b_{i0} + b_{i1}F_{1t} + b_{i2}F_{2t} + b_{i3}F_{3t} + b_{i4}F_{4t} + e_{it} \qquad (6.7)$$

where e_{it} is an error term, and b_{i0}, b_{i1}, b_{i2}, b_{i3}, and b_{i4} are the regression coefficients.

APT states that the expected return on a security is:

$$r_E = r_f + b_{i1}RP_1 + b_{i2}RP_2 + b_{i3}RP_3 + b_{i4}RP_{4t} \qquad (6.8)$$

where RP_1, RP_2, RP_3, and RP_4 are the risk premiums for the four different sources of risk.

Bower, Bower, and Logue estimate the risk premiums by applying the Fama and MacBeth (1973) techniques of cross-sectional regressions on the sample of nonutility stocks; see the appendix of Chapter 3 for further details on this methodology. Using equation (6.8), Bower, Bower, and Logue estimate an APT cost of equity of 10.9% for electric utilities and 13.7% for gas distribution utilities during the period 1971–1979. These are substantially different from the CAPM costs of equity for electric utilities and gas distribution utilities, which Bower, Bower, and Logue calculate as 13.2% and 11.8%, respectively.[18]

Their further tests of the explanatory power of APT versus CAPM indicate that APT provides a much higher degree of explanatory power, which leads them to conclude that the APT costs of equity are superior to the CAPM costs of equity.

I.C.3. Holding Companies versus Subsidiaries

Finally, there is a special problem related to the organizational form of the company. If the utility is a holding company, you must first decide whether you can estimate a single cost of equity for the entire company, or whether you should estimate a separate cost of equity for each of the subsidiaries. Pettway and Jordan (1983) show that you should estimate a separate cost of equity if the subsidiaries have different risks or if the parent company has issued its own debt. If this is the case, you can use the techniques of Chapter 4, subject to the modifications described in this section, to estimate the divisional cost of capital. Otherwise, you can estimate a single cost of capital for the holding company.

I.D. Capital Structure and the Cost of Equity for Utilities

As discussed in Chapter 4, the relationship between capital structure and the cost of equity for nonregulated firms is complex, and many theories have been offered to explain the relationship. Unfortunately, empirical tests have not yet unambiguously confirmed any single theory.[19]

Despite the lack of incontrovertible evidence and support, the Modigliani and Miller (1963) model frequently is used:

$$r_E = r_U + (1 - \tau)(r_U - i)\left(\frac{D}{E}\right) \qquad (6.9)$$

where r_U is the cost of equity for an unlevered firm.

If you accept the premise that this model is correct for nonregulated firms, does that mean the model is also correct for regulated firms? In

---

[18] These estimates of the CAPM cost of equity are lower than those of Conine and Tamarkin (1985).

[19] For a thorough treatment of the debt/equity choice, see Masulis (1988). Interestingly, many of the early tests of the relationship between debt and the cost of capital were conducted using data for utilities. For example, see Modigliani and Miller (1966) and

other words, can you use this model to find the new cost of equity if a utility has had a recent change in leverage? Or can you use this model to estimate the cost of equity for a utility via the pure-play type of adjustments described in Chapter 4?

Gordon (1967) claims the answer is no. If a utility has changed its leverage, Gordon argues that the regulatory commission will change the prices charged to consumers in such a way that the model in equation (6.9) is no longer correct. In particular, he argues that regulators maintain a constant expected ratio of after-tax earnings (the earnings are before subtracting interest payments, but the tax includes the tax shield of the interest payments) to book assets. This means that the return on assets is not invariant with respect to leverage. Gordon shows that incorporating this assumption leads to:

$$r_E = r_U + (r_U - i)\left(\frac{D}{E}\right) \qquad (6.10)$$

Notice that the tax rate does not appear in the Gordon model.

Which model is right? That depends on the ratio of pre-tax earnings to expected pre-tax earnings, and whether it is independent of leverage. Elton and Gruber (1971) assume that most of the uncertainty in pre-tax earnings is the result of the random nature of future sales. They show that the ratio of pre-tax earnings to expected pre-tax earnings is independent of the degree of leverage, which implies that the Modigliani and Miller model of equation (6.9) is correct. However, Gordon and McCallum (1972) assume that most of the uncertainty is caused by the regulation process itself. Adopting this assumption, Gordon and McCallum show that the ratio of pre-tax earnings to expected pre-tax earnings is not independent of leverage, which means that equation (6.10) is the correct model.[20]

Because there is no incontrovertible empirical evidence to confirm or reject either model, you will have to use your own judgment. If you need to adjust the cost of equity of a utility to reflect the impact of leverage, I suggest you use both methods, and then conduct sensitivity analysis when you use the two values for the adjusted cost of equity.

Robichek, Higgins, and Kinsman (1973); both studies find a positive relationship between debt and the cost of equity.

[20] See Brennan (1972) and Elton and Gruber (1972) for further discussion of this issue.

II. The Cost of Capital for Deposit-Taking Financial Institutions

Deposit-taking financial institutions, such as banks and S&Ls, have much more discretion in pricing decisions than do public utilities. Regulation, however, does have an impact on their cost of capital, particularly with respect to deposit insurance and FDIC forbearance. Differences in products and production technologies between financial institutions and manufacturers also affect the appropriate models for estimating the cost of equity. Section II.A explains techniques for estimating the cost of equity for deposit-taking financial institutions. Section II.B discusses the impact of deposit insurance.[21]

II.A. Estimating the Cost of Equity for a Financial Institution

The stock returns of financial institutions are extremely sensitive to changes in market interest rates. This sensitivity suggests that a single-factor model such as the CAPM may not be adequate for estimating the cost of equity for financial institutions. As the appendix of Chapter 3 explains, there are many different ways to incorporate interest rate risk into a multifactor model. Rather than discuss all possible approaches, this section instead explains one particular approach in detail.[22]

Flannery and James (1984a) suggest a model for the stock returns of a financial institution:[23]

$$R_{it} = a_i + \beta_i R_{mt} + b_i R_{jlt} + \varepsilon_{it} \qquad (6.11)$$

where R_{it} is the return on company i in period t, R_{mt} is the return on the stock market in period t, R_{jlt} is a measure of the jth interest rate index in period t, ε_{it} is an error term, and a_i, β_i, and b_i are the regression

---

[21] The discussion in this section is limited to deposit-taking financial intermediaries, such as banks and S&Ls. For a discussion of the cost of capital in the context of insurance companies, see Cummins and Nye (1972); Forbes (1972); Haugen and Kroncke (1971); Launie (1971, 1972); Lee and Forbes (1980); and Quirin and Waters (1975).

[22] For examples of multifactor interest rate model, see Fogler, John, and Tipton (1981); Oldfield and Rogalski (1981); Ehrhardt (1991); Stone (1974); Lloyd and Shick (1977); and Sweeney and Warga (1983, 1986). Merton (1973) develops an intertemporal CAPM. Under certain simplifying assumptions, his model implies that stock returns are a function of bond portfolios as well as the market stock portfolio.

[23] See Flannery and James (1984b) for another description of this process.

coefficients. Notice that β_i is the measure of systematic market risk, and b_i is the measure of the company's interest rate risk.

How do you measure the interest rate index, R_{jIt}? Flannery and James use three different measures. Their first measure, R_{1It}, begins with the return on a Government National Mortgage Association (GNMA) 8% certificate; let $R_{GNMA,t}$ denote this return. Since returns on interest rate instruments are often autocorrelated, Flannery and James "remove" the autocorrelation by estimating a third-order autoregressive model:

$$R_{GNMA,t} = c_0 + c_1 R_{GNMA,t-1} + c_2 R_{GNMA,t-2} + c_3 R_{GNMA,t-3} + \omega_t \qquad (6.12)$$

where ω_t is an error term, and where c_0, c_1, c_2, and c_3 are regression coefficients.

The error from this equation, ω_t, is not correlated with the lagged returns on the GNMA certificate. Therefore, Flannery and James define the first measure of the interest rate index, R_{1It}, as:

$$R_{1It} = \omega_t \qquad (6.13)$$

This results in an interest rate index that captures only the unanticipated interest rate changes. Using this measure of interest rate risk, Flannery and James estimate equation (6.11) for each financial institution in their sample to get estimates of the institution's market risk (β_i) and interest rate risk (b_i).

Flannery and James repeat this procedure for two other interest rate indexes. One is the return on the one-year Treasury bill. They use the Treasury bill returns in equation (6.12) and then define the interest rate index, R_{2It}, by equation (6.13).

Their last index begins with the yield relative on an index of seven-year Treasury bonds. This variable, $R_{TBOND,t}$, is defined as:

$$R_{TBOND,t} = -\left[\frac{Y_t - Y_{t-1}}{Y_{t-1}}\right] \qquad (6.14)$$

where Y_t is the yield on the index of seven-year Treasury Bonds. Flannery and James remove the autocorrelation by using equation (6.12), and they define the index, R_{3It}, with equation (6.13).

Flannery and James find that the interest rate index, for all three definitions, is significant in equation (6.11). In other words, interest rate sensitivity is an important element in explaining the volatility of a financial institution's stock returns.[24] Using a similar approach for a sample of utilities, Sweeney and Warga (1986) find that utility stock returns also are sensitive to changes in interest rates.

Can you use the Flannery and James results to estimate the expected return on the financial institution's stock, which would give you its cost of equity? The answer is yes, if you make a few additional assumptions. Suppose that the expected return is a function of the two sources of risk for the stock; i.e., systemic market risk and interest rate risk. From equation (6.11), you know that β_i measures systematic market risk, and b_i measures interest rate risk. If you knew the risk premium for systematic market risk, RP_m, and the risk premium for interest rate risk, RP_I, then you could estimate the cost of equity as:

$$r_E = r_f + \beta_i RP_m + b_i RP_I \qquad (6.15)$$

How can you get estimates of the two risk premiums, RP_m and RP_I? Just as in the case of the APT model for utilities in Section I.C.2, you could use the Fama-MacBeth (1973) cross-sectional regression approach. The appendix of Chapter 3 provides further details on this technique.

Flannery and James provide an example of a multifactor model that incorporates interest rate risk. As they show, the results are fairly robust to the choice of the interest rate index. They also show that this type of model explains the returns of financial institutions much better than the CAPM. Whether you use the Flannery–James model or another model with a different definition of the interest rate index, you should explicitly incorporate interest rate risk when you estimate the cost of equity for a financial institution.

II.B. The Impact of Deposit Insurance on the Cost of Capital

A major difference between financial institutions and nonfinancial firms is the existence of deposit insurance. Osterberg and Thomson (1990) examine the relationship between the cost of capital and the presence of deposit insurance guarantees and regulatory forbearance. They develop analytical models similar to those of Chen (1978).

When there is no deposit insurance, Osterberg and Thomson show that the cost of debt is a function of the risk-free interest rate, the

---

[24] Flannery and James (1984) find that the interest rate sensitivity, b_i, is significantly related to the difference in the average maturity of the bank's assets and liabilities.

systematic risk of the firm's cash flows, and the probability of bankruptcy (which relates to leverage in the capital structure). The cost of equity is a function of the risk-free interest rate, the systematic risk of the firm's cash flows, the payments due to debt, and the probability of bankruptcy.

Their results for firms with deposit insurance and firms without deposit insurance are identical if deposit insurance is fairly priced; i.e., there is no change in the cost of debt or the cost of equity. This is not so when the deposit insurance is mispriced. When deposit insurance is underpriced, this is equivalent to a subsidy from the government. This subsidy increases the value of the debt and lowers its cost. Osterberg and Thomson show that the value of equity will not decrease; in all likelihood, the value of equity will increase, and the cost of equity will decrease.[25] The result is definitely a lower weighted average cost of capital.

When they examine the effect of regulator forbearance and bailout policy in addition to underpriced deposit insurance, Osterberg and Thomson find that the cost of debt falls even more, but that there is no further change in the cost of equity. The net effect is a further decrease in the cost of capital.

These results imply that a change in the degree of mispricing or in regulator forbearance will change a bank's cost of capital. Notice that changes in mispricing can occur if the bank changes the riskiness of its asset mix, even though there may be no change in the explicit price of the insurance. If your firm is a bank, and you have reason to believe that the degree of mispricing or regulator forbearance has changed, analysis using historical data prior to the change will not result in your bank's current cost of capital. Although the Osterberg and Thomson model is useful for identifying the direction of the change in the cost of capital, it is probably not feasible to use the model to identify the size of the change. You should, however, be aware of the model's implications: changes in the mispricing of deposit insurance will change your bank's cost of capital.

III. Summary and Recommendations

There are special issues associated with the cost of capital for regulated industries, whether the regulation is in the form of price controls or in constraints on allowable products and services. For companies

---

[25] Magen (1971) finds no positive relationship between the cost of equity and the degree of financial leverage. This could be because of the presence of deposit insurance.

facing price regulation, such as utilities, the CAPM probably is not the best choice for estimating the cost of equity. For theoretical reasons, the three-moment skewness model, the multifactor APT model, or an interest rate index model are better choices. Empirical studies support this conclusion.

Deposit-taking financial institutions face a different type of regulation. Regulators limit these institutions in the types of products and services that they can provide. The nature of the allowable products and services means that the stock of these institutions is very sensitive to changes in interest rates. Therefore, multifactor models that explicitly incorporate interest rate risk are more appropriate than the CAPM for estimating the cost of equity for financial institutions.

References

Arzac, E.R., and M. Marcus. "Flotation Cost Allowance in Rate of Return Regulation: A Note." *Journal of Finance* 36(5) (December 1981): 1199–1202.

———. "Flotation Cost Allowance in Rate of Return Regulation: A Reply." *Journal of Finance* 38(4) (September 1983): 1339–1341.

Bierman, H., Jr., and J.E. Hass. "Equity Flotation Cost Adjustment in Utilities' Cost of Service." *Public Utilities Fortnightly* (March 1, 1984): 46–49.

Bower, D., R. Bower, and D. Logue. "Arbitrage Pricing Theory and Utility Stock Returns." *Journal of Finance* (September 1984): 1041–1054.

Breen, W.J., and E. M. Lerner. "On the Use of β in Regulatory Proceedings." *Bell Journal of Economics and Management Science* (Autumn 1972): 612–621.

Brennan, M.J. "Valuation and the Cost of Capital for Regulated Industries: A Comment." *Journal of Finance* 27(5) (1972): 1147–1149.

Brigham, E.F., D. Aberwald, and L.C. Gapenski. "Common Equity Flotation Costs and Rate Making." *Public Utilities Fortnightly* (May 2, 1985): 28–36.

Brigham, E.F., and R.L. Crum. "Use of the CAPM in Public Utility Rate Cases." *Financial Management* (Summer 1977): 7–15.

———. "Reply to Comments on the Use of the CAPM in Public Utility Rate Cases." *Financial Management* (Autumn 1978): 72–76.

Carleton, W.T. "Testimony on Carolina Power & Light Company's Fair Rate of Return." *North Carolina Utilities Commission* Docket Number E-2, Sub. 297, April 1977.

———. "A Highly Personal Comment on the Use of the CAPM in Public Utility Rate Cases." *Financial Management* 7(3) (Autumn 1978): 57–59.

Chen, A. "Recent Developments in the Cost of Debt Capital." *Journal of Finance* 33(3) (1978): 863–877.

Clarke, R.G. "The Impact of a Fuel Adjustment Clause on the Regulated Firm's Value and Cost of Capital." *Journal of Financial and Quantitative Analysis* 13(4) (1978): 745–757.

Conine, T.E., Jr., and M. Tamarkin. "Implications of Skewness in Returns For Utilities' Cost of Equity Capital." *Financial Management* 14(4) (1985): 66–71.

Cummins, J.D., and D.J. Nye. "The Cost of Capital of Insurance Companies: Comment." *Journal of Risk and Insurance* 39(3) (1972): 487–491.

Ehrhardt, M. "Diversification and Interest Rate Risk." *Journal of Business Finance and Accounting* 18(1) (January 1991): 43–59.

Elton, E.J., and M.J. Gruber. "Valuation and the Cost of Capital for Regulated Industries." *Journal of Finance* 26(3) (1971): 661–670.

———. "Valuation and the Cost of Capital for Regulated Industries: Reply." *Journal of Finance* 27(5) (1972): 1150–1155.

Fama, E.F., and J. MacBeth. "Risk, Return, and Equilibrium: Empirical Tests." *Journal of Political Economy* 81 (May–June 1973): 607–636.

Flannery, J.M., and C.M. James. "The Effect of Interest Rate Changes on the Common Stock Returns of Financial Institutions." *Journal of Finance* 39(4) (September 1984): 1141–1153.

———. "Market Evidence on the Effective Maturity of Bank Assets and Liabilities." *Journal of Money, Credit, and Banking* 16(4) (November 1984): 435–445.

Fogler, H.R., K. John, and J. Tipton. "Three Factors, Interest Rate Differentials and Stock Groups." *Journal of Finance* 36(2) (May 1981): 323–335.

Forbes, S.W. "The Cost of Capital of Insurance Companies: A Comment." *Journal of Risk and Insurance* 39(3) (1972): 491–492.

Gilster, J.E., Jr., and C.M. Linke. "More on the Estimation of β for Public Utilities: Biases Resulting from Structural Shifts in True Beta." *Financial Management* 7(3) (Autumn 1978): 60–65.

Gordon, M.J. "Some Estimates of the Cost of Capital to the Electric Utility Industry, 1954–57: Comment." *American Economic Review* (December 1967): 1267–1278.

———. *The Cost of Capital to a Public Utility*. East Lansing, Mich.: MSU Public Utilities Studies, 1974.

Gordon, M.J., and J.S. McCallum. "Valuation and the Cost of Capital for Regulated Utilities: Comment." *Journal of Finance* 27(5) (1972): 1141–1146.

Haugen, R.A., and C.O. Kroncke. "Rate Regulation and the Cost of Capital in the Insurance Industry." *Journal of Financial and Quantitative Analysis* 6(5) (1971): 1283–1305.

Howe, K.M., and W. Beranek. "Issue Costs and Regulated Returns: A General Approach." *Journal of Regulatory Economics* 4 (1992): 365–378.

Kolbe, A.L., J.A. Read, and G.R. Hall. *The Cost of Capital: Estimating the Rate of Return for Public Utilities*. Cambridge, Mass.: MIT Press, 1984.

Kraus, A., and R. Litzenberger. "Skewness Preference and the Valuation of Risky Assets." *Journal of Finance* (May 1976): 1085–1100.

Launie, J.J. "The Cost of Capital of Insurance Companies." *Journal of Risk and Insurance* 38(2) (1971): 263–268.

———. "The Cost of Capital of Insurance Companies: Reply." *Journal of Risk and Insurance* 39(3) (1972): 492–495.

Lee, C.F., and S.W. Forbes. "Dividend Policy, Equity Value, and Cost of Capital Estimates for the Property and Liability Insurance Industry." *Journal of Risk and Insurance* 47(2) (1980): 205–222.

Linke, C.M., and J.K. Zumwalt. "Estimation Biases in Discounted Cash Flow Analyses of Equity Capital Cost in Rate Regulation." *Financial Management* 13(3) (1984): 15–21.

Litzenberger, R., K. Ramaswamy, and H. Sosin. "On the CAPM Approach to the Estimation of a Public Utility's Cost of Equity Capital." *Journal of Finance* 35(2) (1980): 369–383.

Lloyd, W.P., and R.A. Shick. "A Test of Stone's Two-Index Model of Return." *Journal of Financial and Quantitative Analysis* 12(3) (1977): 363–376.

Magen, S.D. "Cost of Capital and Dividend Policies in Commercial Banks." *Journal of Financial and Quantitative Analysis* 6(2) (1971): 733–746.

Masulis, R.W. *The Debt/Equity Choice.* Cambridge, Mass.: Ballinger, 1988.

McEnally, R.W. "On the Use of the CAPM in Public Utility Rate Cases: Comment." *Financial Management* 7(3) (Autumn 1978) 69–70.

Merton, R. "An Intertemporal Capital Asset Pricing Model." *Econometrica* (September 1973): 867–888.

Modigliani, F., and M. Miller. "Taxes and the Cost of Capital: A Correction." *American Economic Review* (June 1963): 433–443.

———. "Some Estimates of the Cost of Capital to the Electric Utility Industry, 1954–57." *American Economic Review* (June 1966): 333–391.

Myers, S.C. "The Application of Finance Theory to Public Utility Rate Cases." *Bell Journal of Economics and Management Science* 3 (Autumn 1972): 58–97.

———. "On the Use of Modern Portfolio Theory in Public Utility Rate Cases: Comment" *Financial Management* 7(3) (Autumn 1978): 66–68.

Oldfield, G., Jr., and R. Rogalski. "Treasury Bill Factors and Common Stock Returns." *Journal of Finance* (May 1981): 337–350.

Osterberg, W.P., and J.B. Thomson. "Deposit Insurance and the Cost of Capital." *Research in Finance* 8 (1990): 255–270.

Patterson, C.S. "Issue Costs in the Estimation of the Cost of Equity Capital." *Public Utilities Fortnightly* 108 (July 16, 1981): 28–32.

———. "Flotation Cost Allowance in Rate of Return Regulation: A Comment." *Journal of Finance* 38(4) (September 1983): 1335–1338.

Pettway, R.H. "A Note on the Flotation Costs of New Equity Capital Issues of Electric Companies." *Public Utilities Fortnightly* 109 (March 18, 1982): 68–69.

Pettway, R.H., and B.D. Jordan. "Diversification, Double Leverage, and the Cost of Capital." *Journal of Financial Research* 6(4) (1983): 289–300.

Quirin, G.D., and W.R. Waters. "Market Efficiency and the Cost of Capital: The Strange Case of Fire and Casualty Insurance Companies." *Journal of Finance* 30(2) (1975): 427–445.

Robichek, A., R.C. Higgins, and M. Kinsman. "The Effect of Leverage on the Cost of Equity Capital of Electric Utility Firms." *Journal of Finance* 28(2) (1973): 353–367.

Sarikas, R.H. "What Is New in Adjustment Clauses." *Public Utilities Fortnightly* 95 (June 19, 1975): 32–36.

Schiffel, D. "Electric Utility Regulation: An Overview of Fuel Adjustment Clauses." *Public Utilities Fortnightly* 95 (June 19, 1975): 23–31.

Sharpe, W.F. "On the Use of the CAPM in Public Utility Rate Cases: Comment." *Financial Management* 7(3) (Autumn 1978): 71.

Stone, B.K. "Systematic Interest-Rate Risk in a Two-Index Model of Returns." *Journal of Financial and Quantitative Analysis* 9(5) (1974): 709–721.

Sweeney, R.J., and A.D. Warga. "Interest-Sensitive Stocks: An APT Application." *Financial Review* 18(4) (1983): 257–270.

———. "The Pricing of Interest Rate Risk: Evidence from the Stock Market." *Journal of Finance* 41(2) (1986): 393–410.

West, D.A., and A.A. Eubank, Jr. "An Automatic Cost of Capital Adjustment Model for Regulating Public Utilities." *Financial Management* 5(1) (1976): 23–31.

Chapter 7

The Cost of Capital in a Global Economy

Very few companies are unaffected by the globalization of the business environment. Some companies have manufacturing facilities in foreign countries, some companies market their products to foreign consumers, some companies buy raw materials or components from foreign companies, and some companies secure financing from foreign financial markets. These companies obviously are integrated into the global economy.

For other companies, the integration may be less obvious, although no less important. For example, a company may produce products that face competition from international firms. This company clearly is affected by the global economy. Also, every company that issues publicly traded equity or debt is affected by the global economy, because the capital markets themselves are affected by international events.

What impact does globalization have on measuring the cost of capital for an international project? That is the question this chapter addresses. Section I provides a brief overview of general issues associated with globalization. Section II focuses upon measuring the cost of capital for an international project. Section III is a brief summary.

I. Globalization and the Cost of Capital

Most companies compete in product, factor, and financial markets that are increasingly global in scope. Competition in global product and factor markets alters the riskiness of a company's revenue stream, which in turn affects the value and riskiness of claims on the revenue stream, such as equity. Also, global financial markets allow new possibilities with respect to sources of financing. Sections I.A and I.B address these two issues.[1]

I.A. The Effect of Globalization on the Cost of Equity

Globalization can affect the cost of equity two different ways: first, through the international financial markets; second, through the expansion of production and sales into the international economy. Sections I.A.1 and I.A.2 discuss each of these effects on the cost of equity.

I.A.1. Globalization of Financial Markets

Before addressing the effect of globalization on the cost of equity, it's useful to consider first the effect of international portfolio diversification from the perspective of an investor. One of the basic premises of modern portfolio theory is that investors are not compensated for risk that can be diversified away.[2] The degree of diversification possible between any set of securities depends on the correlation between the returns on those securities, with more diversification resulting when there is lower correlation. There is considerable evidence that the returns across international stock markets are not highly correlated.[3] For example, Tucker, Becker, Isimbabi, and Ogden (1992) report a correlation between the U.S. stock market and the Japanese stock market of only .277 during the 1986–1990 period. This evidence suggests that investing in an international portfolio offers the possibility of added

---

[1] A third issue is the extent to which theoretical models and empirical tests based on the U.S. economy and financial markets are applicable to companies in other countries. For example, Rao and Litzenberger (1971) find that the relationship between leverage and the cost of capital is different between utilities in India and utilities in the United States; they attribute these differences to the less-developed capital market in India (see Sarma and Rao (1971) for an alternative interpretation of the Litzenberger and Rao results). Other differences are due to the corporate and personal tax systems in other countries, which are often different from the tax systems in the United States. For example, Lawrenz (1976) and Ashton (1989) show the effect that these different tax systems have on the cost of equity; Kent and Theobald (1980–1981) discuss the imputation tax system and show that it produces a different version of the dividend growth model. As these studies indicate, not all U.S. results are applicable to all countries. However, a thorough treatment of this issue is beyond the scope of this book.

[2] This concept is well accepted today because of the work of Nobel prize winners Markowitz (1952) and Sharpe (1964).

[3] See textbooks by Tucker, Becker, Isimbabi, and Ogden (1992, Chapter 8); Tucker, Madura, and Chiang (1991, Chapter 9); Eiteman, Stonehill, and Moffett (1992, Chapter 13, written by C.S. Eun); and Shapiro (1986, Chapter 4; and 1992, Chapter 16) for a thorough discussion of this issue. Isimbabi (1992) also provides a comprehensive survey of this issue. Also, see Eun and Resnick (1984); Roll (1988); Solnik (1974); and Lessard (1976) for further details.

diversification. In fact, a fully diversified international portfolio can be half as risky as a fully diversified domestic portfolio, because a major portion of domestic systematic risk can be diversified away with an international portfolio. The result is an internationally diversified portfolio with significantly lower risk than a domestic portfolio with the same level of expected return.

What does this have to do with the cost of equity? The theoretical implication is that the domestic stock market is not the appropriate set of securities within the context of the Markowitz efficient frontier. This theoretical implication is confirmed by numerous empirical studies showing that the internationally diversified market portfolio is significantly different from the traditional domestic market portfolio.[4]

The appropriate definition of the market portfolio directly affects use of the capital asset pricing model to estimate the cost of equity.[5] If you use the CAPM to estimate the cost of equity for your company, which index should you use for your systematic risk? Recall from Chapter 3 that you estimate the CAPM systematic risk, β_i, using the time series regression:

$$(R_{it} - R_{ft}) = a_0 + \beta_i(R_{mt} - R_{ft}) + e_{it} \qquad (7.1)$$

where R_{it} is the return on company i in period t, R_{ft} is the risk-free rate in period t, R_{mt} is the return on the market portfolio in period t, a_0 is the estimated intercept from the regression, β_i is the estimated slope of the regression, and e_{it} is the estimated error in the regression.

How should you define the return on the market portfolio, R_{mt}? Should you use an index on a domestic market portfolio such as those described in Chapter 3? Or should you use an index on an international market portfolio, such as the Morgan Stanley World Index or the Capital International World Index, which are value-weighted indexes of international stocks? How should you define the risk-free rate and the market risk premium?

As Shapiro (1983) notes, the answers to these questions depend on the degree of integration in the international financial markets.[6] If your

---

[4] For example, see Eun and Resnick (1985) and Solnik and Noetzlin (1982).

[5] See Chapter 3 for further discussion of the CAPM, or see Markowitz (1952) or Sharpe (1964) for the original development of the concept of efficient frontiers and the CAPM. For further details, see textbooks such as Shapiro (1989) or Brealey and Myers (1988). Cohn and Pringle (1973) provide a specific discussion about incorporation of international diversification into the CAPM.

[6] My discussion assumes that the CAPM is the correct asset pricing model; the only question is whether a domestic CAPM or an international CAPM is appropriate.

domestic financial market is not at all integrated into international financial markets, the prices in your financial market will be determined independently of prices in other financial markets. This means that the investors who are setting the prices in your market behave as if they had no knowledge of other international markets. Therefore, the equilibrium asset prices conform to a "domestic" CAPM, which means that you should use your domestic market portfolio and a domestic risk-free rate when you estimate your company's systematic risk. On the other hand, if all financial markets are fully integrated, prices in all financial markets are determined by a single set of investors who view the world as a single market. Therefore, you should use an index on the world market when you estimate your company's systematic risk.

How integrated are international equity markets? Tucker, Becker, Isimbabi, and Ogden (1992, Chapter 8) show that the gross purchases and sales of U.S. stocks by nonresidents grew from $75.2 billion in 1980 to $1,036.3 billion in 1991; a similar growth rate also occurred for other major non-U.S. stock exchanges. Does this phenomenal growth in international investing activity imply that equity markets are now fully integrated? Isimbabi (1992, p. 130) notes in a comprehensive review of empirical literature that the evidence is mixed: the "findings of some of the tests do indicate what casual observation suggests, i.e., partial segmentation." In other words, international equity markets are neither fully segmented nor fully integrated.

The implication of these empirical facts is that a single-index model with a domestic index isn't appropriate, and neither is a single-index model with an international index. A reasonable alternative is to use both indexes in a two-factor model.[7] An example would be:

$$R_{it} = a_0 + \beta_{iD} R_{Dt} + \beta_{iW}R_{Wt} + e_{it} \tag{7.2}$$

where R_{Dt} and R_{Wt} are returns on the domestic and world index, respectively. β_{iD} and β_{iW} are the two measures of risk.

If λ_D and λ_W denote the risk premiums for the two sources of risk, then the cost of equity is:

$$r_E = a_0 + \beta_{iD}\lambda_D + \beta_{iW}\lambda_W \tag{7.3}$$

---

[7] International data are often more difficult to obtain than purely domestic data. See Copeland, Koller, and Murrin (1990, Appendix B) for a description of data sources.

where r_E is the cost of equity. You can estimate the values of the risk premiums, λ_D and λ_W, using the techniques for multifactor models, as shown in the appendix of Chapter 3.[8]

It's entirely possible that the measure of world risk, β_{iw}, might be negligible for your company. In other words, your company's returns are affected by international financial markets only to the extent that the domestic financial market is affected by international financial markets. If this is the case, you can use the original CAPM model of equation (7.1), with the domestic market index as the market return, R_{mt}.

How can you tell if world risk, β_{iw}, is negligible? The easiest way is to use the regression's test for the significance of the estimate of the measure of world risk, β_{iw}; i.e., use the t-test that determines the probability that $\beta_{iw} = 0$. Unfortunately, this easiest way is also the wrong way. If the domestic index and the world index are correlated, the regression of equation (7.2) will have an econometric problem called multicollinearity. The result is that the test of significance for the estimated coefficient is not valid. Given the likely presence of multicollinearity, how can you determine whether the measure of world risk, β_{iw}, is significant?

A quick-and-dirty method is to run the original CAPM of equation (7.1) with the domestic index, and then to run the two-index model of equation (7.2).[9] If the adjusted R^2 from the regression of the two-factor model of equation (7.2) isn't substantially higher than the adjusted R^2 of the regression of the single-index CAPM of equation (7.1), the world index does not add much explanatory power. This technique is not econometrically precise, but it is easy and will at least give you an estimate of the extra explanatory power provided by the world index.

A better approach is to "orthogonalize" the world index with respect to the domestic index. To do this, you first would run the regression:

$$R_{Wt} = b_0 + b_1 R_{Dt} + u_{it} \qquad (7.4)$$

where b_0 and b_1 are the estimated regression coefficients, and u_{it} is the estimated regression error. You then substitute the error from equation

---

[8] See Tucker, Madura, and Chiang (1991, Chapter 10) for more discussion of this type of two-index model; Agmon and Lessard (1977) and Yang, Wansley, and Lane (1985) also demonstrate applications of this type of model.

[9] This is actually a "stepwise" regression, which is an option in many regression software packages.

(7.4), u_{it}, for the world index in equation (7.2). This procedure results in modification of the regression in equation (7.2) as follows:

$$R_{it} = a_0 + \beta_{iD}R_{Dt} + B_{iW} u_{it} + e_{it} \qquad (7.5)$$

where B_{iW} is the orthogonalized coefficient.

If the usual t-tests from the regression of equation (7.5) show that B_{iW} is not significantly different from zero, the impact of any international sources of risk, other than those already captured by the domestic index, is negligible, and you can safely use the single-index model of the original CAPM of equation (7.1).[10]

I.A.2. Globalization of Operations and Sales

Globalization with respect to the factor and product markets might also affect the cost of equity. This type of globalization can occur if your firm purchases raw materials or components from nondomestic suppliers, manufactures products at nondomestic locations, or sells to nondomestic customers. This globalization will almost certainly have some effect on the riskiness of your company's revenue stream. The question is, how will it affect the riskiness of your company's equity? More specifically, how will it affect your cost of equity?

This result may be somewhat surprising, but globalization with respect to the factor and product markets usually decreases the systematic risk of equity.[11] You might wonder how this can be, given that international operations present sources of economic, political, and financial risk not encountered by domestic firms. For example, many transactions are conducted in foreign currencies, which expose multinational corporations to risk caused by exchange rate volatility. This exchange rate volatility also causes accounting exposure, because most firms must consolidate financial statements of international affiliates. Multinational firms often face additional political risks, ranging from restrictions on the repatriation of dividends, royalties, and fees to exces-

---

[10] Another alternative for estimating the cost of equity is to use an international version of the arbitrage pricing theory model; see the appendix of Chapter 3 for further discussion of domestic APT models. As Isimbabi (1992) states, the empirical evidence is mixed. For example, Christofi and Philippatos (1987) find evidence of one common international factor, while Cho, Eun, and Senbet (1986) conclude that the joint hypothesis of integrated markets and an international APT is not valid, except perhaps in the case of regionally segmented capital markets. In summary, the evidence suggests that a single-factor model probably isn't adequate, but there is no well-accepted method for incorporating international factors into a multifactor asset pricing model.

[11] See Fatemi (1984) and Jacquillat and Solnik (1978) for details.

sive regulatory intervention through tax changes and price controls to outright expropriation or nationalization.

Why are the effects of these extra sources of international risk on the systematic risk of the company's equity typically so small? First, there are many effective techniques for mitigating these additional sources of risk, and most multinational firms are skilled in using these techniques.[12] For example, many firms have sophisticated programs to hedge against exchange rate risk. Firms also can protect themselves from expropriation risk by purchasing insurance from the Overseas Private Investment Corporation, a United States government agency. Even if a multinational corporation cannot eliminate all of the extra international risks, it is unlikely that these types of international risks are correlated with the risk of the market index. Therefore, these risks probably do not increase the *systematic* risk of the stock.[13]

Second, the revenue stream of any company is a function of raw material prices, production costs, and product sales. Since factor costs and sales demand are not perfectly correlated among international markets, the revenue stream for a multinational firm tends to be less volatile than the revenue stream of a similar but purely domestic firm. Also, this revenue stream usually is less correlated with the market index, at least if the index is the domestic index. The net result typically is a reduction in systematic risk, which leads to a lower cost of equity according to the CAPM.[14]

In contrast to conventional wisdom, investors do not require, and do not get, a higher rate of return for investing in an international product. In fact, the cost of equity for a multinational firm usually is lower than that of a similar domestic firm.[15]

---

[12] See Eiteman, Stonehill, and Moffett (1992) or Shapiro (1992) for thorough descriptions of these additional sources of risk and the ways to manage them.

[13] Of course, the CAPM may not be the appropriate model for a multinational firm facing significant expropriation risk. As Tucker points out (in personal correspondence), expropriation risk is not diversifiable in the same sense as other typical nonsystematic risks. For example, suppose you hold a portfolio containing stocks of multinational firms. If one foreign country expropriates the foreign operations of one stock in your portfolio, it is unlikely that another foreign country will appropriate additional operations to a different firm in your portfolio. In other words, cash flows from expropriation risk are always negative, which means that the CAPM might not be appropriate. See Mahajan (1990), who uses option pricing theory to model expropriation risk. Also, Chapter 8 discusses strategic projects and some valuation techniques for embedded real options.

[14] For example, see Fatemi (1984), who shows that a sample of multinational firms has a slightly lower mean beta than a comparable sample of purely domestic firms. The mean beta is lower whether the market index is a domestic or an international index.

[15] If your company has recently changed its level of international involvement, using a time series of historical returns may not result in an accurate estimate of your company's current beta. There is no technique to transform a pre-change beta into the post-change beta, other than to wait for returns from a period after the change (although the direction

I.B. Global Sources of Financing: The Cost of Capital in an International Financing Package

Can you reduce your firm's cost of capital through a strategy of international financing? The usual sources of financing for a domestic firm once were limited to domestic banks, the domestic bond market, and the domestic equity markets. This limitation no longer holds. Many firms now raise capital in numerous different markets using a variety of different financial instruments. A comprehensive description of these new sources of financing is beyond the scope of this book, but you should be aware of the alternatives that are now available.[16]

International banks have always played a critical role in financing international trade through the creation of letters of credit and bankers' acceptances. Many international banks now provide financing for general corporate needs as well. The Foreign Bank Market entails the creation of loans from a domestic bank, denominated in the local domestic currency, to a nondomestic company for use abroad. An example would be a loan from a German bank, denominated in deutschemarks, to a French company for use in financing inventory at a French warehouse. Notice that this is different from a loan from a domestic bank to the local affiliate of a foreign parent, such as a loan from a German bank to the Germany subsidiary of a French parent, with the proceeds of the loan used to renovate the office facilities of the German subsidiary. The latter is a local loan, as the borrower is located in the same country in which the loan proceeds are used.

Another example of international banking is the Eurocurrency market, in which domestic banks accept deposits and make loans, called Euroloans, that are not denominated in the local domestic currency. For example, a firm in the United States might borrow money from a bank, or syndicate of banks, in Great Britain, with the loan denominated in dollars. A related activity is the creation of Note Issuance Facilities (NIF) by financial institutions. In the simplest case, a foreign company issues an instrument much like commercial paper. This Euro-commercial paper is denominated in the currency of the issuer, but distributed by the local financial institution providing the NIF. In other cases, the NIF provides a service much like a line of credit. Another important instrument in the international debt market is the Euro-medium-term

---

of the expected change is downward). Fatemi's (1984) results suggest as a rule of thumb a decrease in beta on the order of .10.

[16] See Tucker, Madura, and Chiang (1991), particularly Chapters 7–11. Eiteman, Stonehill, and Moffett (1992) and Shapiro (1992) also provide thorough discussions of this topic.

note. Similar to a U.S. Treasury note, this security spans the maturity gap between short-term and long-term Eurocurrency debt.

In the foreign bond market, a nondomestic company issues debt that is denominated in the local currency. For example, a U.S. company could issue debt in Great Britain that is denominated in pounds. This type of issue is different from those of the Eurobond market, in which the debt is denominated in a nondomestic currency. An example of the Eurobond market is a U.S. company that issues debt in Great Britain, with the debt denominated in dollars.

Each of the international markets has its own set of standard conventions with respect to features such as the typical maturities, currency denominations, or fixed versus floating interest rates. There is now a thriving market in "swaps" that allows issuers to "mix-and-match" the terms from different markets. See Beidleman (1991, 1992) and Tucker, Madura, and Chiang (1991, Chapter 16) for a more thorough treatment of swaps.

Changes also have occurred in the international equity markets. During the last decade, these equity markets have experienced phenomenal growth with favorable expansion/investment opportunities in major world regions, increased public offerings by foreign companies, and collective governmental efforts to deregulate foreign markets. The total value of all stock markets in 1980, expressed in U.S. dollars, was $2.32 billion; by 1989 this figure had reached $9.67 billion.

Patterns of trading have changed as well. For example, some firms issue equity in foreign markets, particularly if their own domestic markets are too small to absorb the new issue. Other firms list their equity on several international stock exchanges.[17,18] Another change is the increase of trading hours; for example, many exchanges are adding trading after normal daytime working hours in an attempt to capture the trading volume occurring at other exchanges in different time zones.

How do these changes and innovations in the world's financial markets affect your company's cost of capital? If all financial markets were perfectly integrated, and if there were no frictions or barriers to

---

[17] An indirect mechanism through which a non-U.S. firm might trade in the United States is the American Depository Receipt (ADR). A foreign custodial bank holds the shares and issues certificates of ownership to the investor. See Tucker, Madura, and Chiang (1991) for more details on ADRs. Also, see Tucker (1987) for a comparison of ADRs and direct ownership of foreign shares.

[18] Despite recent improvements, stock exchanges still are not completely internationalized. For example, many exchanges still place restrictions on foreign investors. Other barriers appear to be cultural rather than institutional. An example of this is the recent delisting of GM from the Tokyo Stock Exchange because of a lack of volume.

trading, these changes would have no effect on your cost of capital. But markets are not perfectly integrated, which means that differences in the relative supply of funds in domestic and foreign capital markets can cause differences in those markets' costs of capital. In other words, it matters where you raise capital.

Different government regulations and different tax regimes, which are often complex when it comes to international finance, can cause the costs of capital in one market to differ from the costs of capital in other markets. Also, many capital markets have different degrees of liquidity and different numbers of participating investors. This fact is significant, because theoretical work by Merton (1987) suggests that a firm can lower its cost of capital by increasing its investor base. Alexander, Eun, and Janakiramanan (1986) and Howe and Madura (1990) test this hypothesis by examining firms that increase their investor base by listing their shares in the other markets. They find that these firms do in fact reduce their cost of equity, although the change is not statistically significant in the Howe and Madura (1990) study.

Here is the bottom line: if your company does not now engage in any international financing, there is a reasonable chance that you can reduce your cost of capital through an appropriate international financing package. If you are considering going overseas for part of your company's financing, you should see Shapiro (1992) for an excellent description of the issues involved in establishing an optimal global capital structure. You should also see Stonehill and Dullum (1983), who present a fascinating case study of Novo Industri A/s. The evidence suggests that Novo was able to decrease its cost of capital through its international financing strategy. Perhaps your company can do the same.

II. Measuring the Cost of Capital for an International Project

There are two different classes of international business activities. The first class includes activities such as importing raw materials, component parts, or finished goods from nondomestic vendors; it also includes exporting products to nondomestic customers. These activities require skills in international marketing and exchange rate management, but the basic principles of capital budgeting are the same as for a purely domestic project: estimate project cash flows, and then discount them at the appropriate cost of capital.

Just as the principles of capital budgeting are unchanged, the approaches for estimating the appropriate cost of capital are unchanged.

For example, you could use the CAPM to measure the risk of the project. Since the covariances between the market index and import/export prices probably are fairly low, the beta of an import/export project may actually be lower than that of a purely domestic project.[19] Therefore, this type of international project might actually have a lower cost of capital than a similar domestic project. It's important to recognize that the cost of capital might be different from that of a purely domestic project, but that for this type of project, the capital budgeting techniques and the approaches for estimating the cost of capital are essentially the same as those applicable to a purely domestic project.

The second class of international projects includes activities such as establishment of a nondomestic subsidiary or direct investment in real assets located in a nondomestic country. How do you evaluate this type of international project? Section II.A explains how you should estimate the cost of capital under a set of simple assumptions. Section II.B extends the analysis to a more complicated case with more realistic assumptions.

II.A. The Cost of Capital Under Simplifying Assumptions

A domestic company is considering a project at a wholly owned foreign subsidiary. The foreign subsidiary will finance the project with a combination of capital from its parent, retained earnings from its local operations, and debt from its local lenders. Here are the simplifying assumptions:

(1) international financial markets are perfectly integrated, which means that risk premiums are identical in all markets;[20]

(2) there are no barriers to repatriation of earnings;

(3) there are no additional taxes on repatriated earnings;

(4) there are no foreign government subsidies on the local debt;

(5) the subsidiary may not deduct interest payments to the parent;

---

[19] If the international vendors or customers embody considerable default risk in an international project, the relevant measure of risk probably is not defined by the CAPM systematic risk. Of course, this is true for domestic as well as international projects. In either case, it might be more appropriate to use the option pricing techniques described in Chapter 8.

[20] Perfectly integrated markets would ensure identical risk premiums, since any differences would lead to arbitrage opportunities. Identical risk premiums could also be the result of redundant investment opportunities in international capital markets; in other words, the types of investments available in the international markets are similar to those available (or replicable) in domestic markets.

(6) the values of the currencies in the two countries are perfectly correlated; and

(7) the corporate tax rate is the same in both countries.

The appropriate criterion for deciding whether to accept or reject the project is the impact the project will have on the value of the parent's equity. But how can you determine whether the project adds value to the parent's equity? You can use an appropriate weighted average cost of capital to find the net present value of the after-tax cash flows of the project. If the NPV is positive, the project adds value to the parent's equity; if the NPV is negative, the project reduces the value of the parent's equity. But how do you measure this appropriate weighted average cost of capital?

Under the simplifying assumptions, the appropriate weighted average cost of capital for this foreign project is simply the same weighted average cost of capital that you would use to find the NPV for a similar domestic project. To see this, consider the individual elements that make up the weighted average cost of capital.

In an integrated financial market, the risk premium that investors demand does not depend on the location of the project. Therefore, the cost of equity for this foreign project is the same cost of equity for a similar domestic project.

The pre-tax cost of debt for the local loan is the same as the pre-tax cost of domestic debt. This result occurs because of the integration of the financial markets, the absence of foreign government subsidies on the subsidiary's debt, the perfect correlation between the two currencies, and the implicit assumption that the parent will guarantee the subsidiary's local debt. With identical corporate tax rates, the after-tax cost of debt is the same for the subsidiary's debt as for the parent's debt. Because the two currencies are perfectly correlated, there is no need to adjust the subsidiary's debt to reflect expected changes in the exchange rates.

The appropriate weights should be based on the parent company's target leverage ratio using market values; the use of local debt is irrelevant, because any additional local debt in the subsidiary displaces an equal amount of the parent's debt.[21] The same reasoning applies to the use of the subsidiary's retained earnings. In the absence of any barriers to repatriation or differential tax treatment, the subsidiary's retained earnings are just another part of the parent's equity. Analogous to the

---

[21] See Chapters 2 and 3 for a similar discussion with respect to the debt of a purely domestic company.

case of local debt, the use of the subsidiary's retained earnings displaces equity somewhere else in the parent. Taken together, these assumptions imply that the parent's target leverage ratio is appropriate for this foreign project.

Under the simple assumptions with regard to the tax codes, the composition of the capital that the parent supplies to the subsidiary is irrelevant. It doesn't matter whether the parent structures the provided capital as debt, equity, or some mixture.

The net result of the simplifying assumptions is that the weighted average cost of capital for the foreign project is identical to the parent's weighted average cost of capital.

II.B. The Cost of Capital Under More Realistic Assumptions

Unfortunately, the real world is not nearly as simple. One major difference is a wedge between the cash flows realized by the subsidiary and the cash flows realized by the parent. For example, additional taxes on repatriated earnings cause a deviation between the subsidiary's cash flows and the parent's cash flows.[22] Also, there often are legal constraints on remittances to the parent, which further contribute to this wedge. Even in the absence of legal constraints, many firms choose to limit repatriation of earnings for political reasons. As shown in Bradley (1977), reinvestment of subsidiary earnings reduces the likelihood of foreign government intervention or expropriation.[23]

If such a wedge exists, should you evaluate the project from the perspective of the subsidiary or the parent? Finance theory states that your objective is to maximize the wealth of the stockholders, which means that you should evaluate the cash flows to the parent.

A second major issue is the composition of the funds that the parent provides to the subsidiary. For example, the parent can lend to the subsidiary, can invest equity in the subsidiary, or can provide a mixture of debt and equity.[24] Unlike the previous simplified case, the composi-

---

[22] See Booth (1990) for a detailed discussion of this issue.

[23] Mahajan (1990) uses option pricing theory to value the threat of expropriation; as he shows, companies can reduce the risk of expropriation by increasing the cost of exercising the expropriation option.

[24] There is also the issue of using leasing as a substitute for debt. Section 861 of the IRS Code (as of 1992) stipulates that interest expense be allocated to domestic and international operations on the basis of the value of domestic and international assets. In general, this ruling means that domestic leasing is preferable to domestic borrowing when multinational firms finance assets used in the United States. I am grateful to Michael Long for making me aware of this issue.

tion of the capital does affect the cash flows received by the parent. Tax effects make a difference, and foreign governments often place fewer limitations on the "interest" paid to the parent than on "dividends" remitted to the parent.[25] This difference also brings into question the capital structure of the subsidiary. Some advocate a capital structure for the subsidiary that is identical to the capital structure of the parent. Others suggest that the subsidiary should have a capital structure similar to that of its local competitors. A third, and more convincing, solution is to find the optimal financing mix, which may be different from both the parent and local competitors.[26]

A third major issue is the treatment of "international risk." One source is exchange rate risk. Should you adjust the cash flows to reflect this risk, or should you adjust the discount rate? Should you adjust the discount rate for the expropriation/intervention risk inherent in countries with less stable governments?

Unfortunately, there is no single unified theory of international valuation that is accepted by all practitioners and researchers. Following are descriptions of several different approaches for estimating the cost of capital under certain specific conditions.

II.B.1. Exchange Rate Uncertainty and the Cost of Capital

Consider a project that is an investment in real assets located in a foreign country. Unlike the situation in Section II.A, the domestic and foreign currencies are not perfectly correlated, which causes a problem called "exchange rate risk." The project will generate cash flows denominated in the local currency, but it should be valued from the perspective of the parent. Therefore, the present value of the project should be denominated in the parent's currency. One approach is to convert all expected future cash flows from the local currency into the parent's currency. There are two problems with this approach. First, many of the project's cash flows will occur in the future: What exchange rate should you use to convert these cash flows? You could use the current exchange rate, which may be a decent estimate of the expected future exchange rates, but you can be certain that the actual future exchange rates will vary quite a bit. This brings up the second issue, which is how you accommodate this exchange rate risk. Specifically, should you adjust the cost of capital?

---

[25] Many firms can minimize their exposure to international taxes through optimal "licensing" and transfer pricing decisions. See Shapiro (1986) for details.

[26] See Shapiro (1978) for further discussion.

Ang and Lai (1989) present an approach that completely finesses the problem of exchange rate uncertainty. Instead of explicitly adjusting either the future cash flows or the discount rate for exchange rate risk, they recommend that you find the present value of the project's future cash flows in the local currency using a local cost of capital. Using the current spot exchange rate, you can easily translate this present value from the local currency to the home currency. If the translated value is greater than the cost of the project, you should accept the project.[27]

With respect to the cost of capital that you use to discount the project's cash flows, Ang and Lai suggest that you use the "applicable local discount rate for the project."[28] This is the rate that a local competitor with an optimal local capital structure would use to discount the project. Recall from Section II.A that, in perfectly integrated markets, the local discount rate of the foreign subsidiary and the domestic discount rate of the parent will be identical. Therefore, you don't have to modify the techniques described in Chapters 3–5 when you estimate the cost of capital for the project. You simply use this rate to find the present value of the project's expected future cash flows, denominated in the subsidiary's local currency. You then convert the present value to the currency of the parent using the current exchange rate.

If markets are segmented, the domestic discount rate for a similar domestic project might differ from the foreign discount rate.[29] The difference in discount rates might be the result of different optimal capital structures, different risk premiums, or different term structures. In this situation, Ang and Lai suggest using a discount rate appropriate for a similar domestic project rather than the local discount rate.[30] Once again, you can use the techniques of Chapters 3–5. You still find the present value of the project denominated in the local currency, and you still convert it using the current exchange rate.

Ang and Lai also consider one further complication. Suppose there is a wedge between the subsidiary's cash flows and the parent's cash flows, perhaps because of restrictions on repatriated dividends. In this case, Ang and Lai suggest discounting the parent's cash flows instead of the subsidiary's cash flows. The cash flows are still denominated in the local currency, and you still convert the present value into the parent's currency using the current exchange rate.

---

[27] Copeland, Koller, and Murrin (1990, Chapter 10) recommend a similar approach.

[28] See Ang and Lai (1989), p. 72.

[29] See Adler (1974, 1977) and Goldberg and Lee (1977) for further discussion of segmented markets.

[30] Eiteman, Stonehill, and Moffett (1992), p. 497, also make this suggestion.

II.B.2. Repatriated Earnings, Local Borrowing, and the Cost of Capital

Shapiro (1978a) suggests a somewhat different approach to estimate the cost of capital, one that explicitly considers differential taxation on repatriated earnings and local borrowing by the subsidiary.[31]

The first source of funds used to finance the subsidiary is the parent.[32] These funds have a cost equal to the parent's weighted average cost of capital. Let r_C denote this cost; you can compute this cost using the techniques in Chapters 2–5.

The second source is the retained earnings of the subsidiary. Let τ_I denote any incremental taxes due on foreign dividends remitted to the parent. Let r_E denote the cost of equity for a domestic project that is similar to the foreign project. Shapiro shows that the cost of retained earnings, r_{RE}, is:[33]

$$r_{RE} = (1 - \tau_I)r_E \qquad (7.6)$$

The third source of funds is direct foreign borrowing by the subsidiary from local sources. Let i_{FD} denote the rate on the locally secured debt, τ_F the foreign corporate tax rate, and d the expected currency devaluation relative to the domestic currency.[34] The after-tax cost of foreign debt, r_{FD}, is:[35]

$$r_{FD} = i_{FD}(1 - d)(1 - \tau_F) - d \qquad (7.7)$$

Let r_{CF} denote the weighted average cost of capital that you should use to discount the cash flows received by the parent from the foreign

---

[31] See Shapiro (1975) for a detailed discussion of the after-tax costs of different forms of debt, including intracorporate loans, Eurodollar loans, local currency loans, discounting bills, and swap loans.

[32] The prevailing tax codes might cause the cash flows to the parent to depend on whether the funds are debt or equity, but the riskiness of the cash flows is independent of the composition of the capital. Therefore, the debt/equity choice does not affect the cost of these funds.

[33] This technique assumes that the foreign project doesn't affect the riskiness of the parent's other assets. See Shapiro (1978a) for the appropriate adjustment if there is a change in the riskiness of the assets already in place.

[34] For example, suppose the debt matures at time 1. Let e_0 denote the current spot exchange rate (one unit of local currency equals e_0 dollars) and let e_1 denote the expected future exchange rate. The rate of expected devaluation, d, is $d = (e_0 - e_1)/e_0$. The best method for estimating e_1 is to use an observed value of a forward contract on the exchange rate. Notice that this method requires a forward contract with a maturity date equal to the date of the debt maturity, which precludes application of the approach to long-term debt. See Shapiro (1992, Chapter 12) for further details.

[35] Strictly speaking, this adjustment is valid only for short-term debt. See Shapiro (1992, Chapter 19, Appendix) for the case of long-term debt.

project. If the target debt ratio of the parent is to remain constant, the addition of foreign debt displaces debt somewhere else in the parent. This means that you must make an adjustment when you calculate the foreign weighted average cost of capital, r_{CF}. Suppose the parent has a target debt ratio of L; i.e., $D/(D + E) = L$, where D and E are the market values of the parent's debt and equity, respectively. The parent's cost of equity is r_E, and the parent's after-tax cost of debt is r_D. Let w_{RE} denote the portion of the project that is financed by the subsidiary's retained earnings, and let w_{FD} denote the portion of the project financed with local debt. Shapiro (1978a) provides a formula for the foreign weighted average cost of capital such that the parent's debt ratio remains constant:

$$r_{CF} = r_C - (r_E - r_{RE})w_{RE} - (r_D - r_{FD}) \tag{7.8}$$

An example will illustrate this procedure. Suppose a parent company is considering a project at one of its foreign subsidiaries. The parent has a pre-tax cost of debt equal to 10% and a tax rate of 40%. Therefore, the parent's after-tax cost of debt, r_D, is 6%. The parent's cost of equity, r_E, is 12%. With a target debt ratio of 50%, the parent's weighted average cost of capital is 9%.

The additional foreign tax on repatriated dividends is 15%. Using equation (7.6), the cost of the subsidiary's retained earnings is:

$$r_{RE} = (1 - .15)(.12) = 10.2\% \tag{7.9}$$

The foreign tax rate on debt, τ_F, is 50%. The interest rate on the foreign debt, i_{FD}, is 24%, and the expected rate of devaluation, d, is 6%. Using equation (7.7), the after-tax cost of foreign debt, r_{FD}, is:

$$r_{FD} = .24(1 - .06)(1 - .5) - .06 = 5.28\% \tag{7.10}$$

Suppose the subsidiary's retained earnings will provide 40% of the funds for the project, and the subsidiary's local borrowing will provide 10% of the funds. Using equation (7.8), the appropriate cost of capital for this foreign project, r_{CF}, is:

$$r_{CF} = .09 - (.12 - .102)(.4) - (.06 - .528)(.1) = 8.21\% \tag{7.11}$$

In this example, the appropriate cost of capital for the foreign project is actually lower than the cost of capital for a domestic project.

This is because of the slightly lower after-tax cost of foreign debt versus domestic debt (5.28% versus 6%) and the fact that it is "cheaper" to reinvest the subsidiary's earnings than to remit them to the parent. Keep in mind that this is only an example, and the cost of capital for a foreign project may not always be lower than the cost of capital for a domestic project.

III. Summary and Recommendations

With the explosion of new services and financial instruments in the global financial markets, it is possible you can reduce your firm's cost of capital by undertaking a global financing package.

Second, even if your firm does not engage in any explicit international activities, it is possible that your firm's cost of equity is affected by international events. This may be the case if some of your competitors are foreign firms. If this is so, you might need to estimate your cost of equity by using the two-index model of equation (7.2) that includes the traditional domestic market index and a world index. Also, if your firm does engage in explicit international activities, you should consider using this type of model when estimating your cost of equity.

Third, you probably should not add a risk premium when evaluating certain types of international projects, such as those that involve only import/export activities. In fact, these projects are likely to be less risky than similar purely domestic projects, because the cash flows from import/export activities probably are not highly correlated with the domestic market. These projects have low systematic risk, and should consequently have a lower cost of equity despite their exposure to international risks.

Fourth, your decision on whether to accept or reject a project should be based on the cash flows of the project from the parent's perspective, not from the perspective of the subsidiary. Evaluating the project from the perspective of the subsidiary is equivalent to valuing the project as though it were an independent company headquartered in the foreign country. This information is useful, but not enough of a basis for accepting or rejecting a project. If cash flows back to the parent are not sufficient to recover the parent's cost of capital, you should reject the project even if it looks good from the subsidiary's perspective.[36]

---

[36] A survey by Stanley and Block (1983) found that 48% of the responding companies evaluated the project from the subsidiary's perspective, 36% from the parent's perspec-

Fifth, you should adjust the project's cost of capital to reflect any barriers to the remittance of dividends and any effects due to local borrowing. Section II.B.2 describes these techniques.[37]

Finally, in two instances the weighted average cost of capital may not be appropriate. For some projects, there is more information available with respect to cash flows than there is with respect to the appropriate costs of capital. For this reason, many researchers advocate a capital budgeting technique that does not require a weighted average cost of capital. The appendix to this chapter describes this technique, which is called the adjusted net present value approach.[38]

There is no well-accepted method for incorporating certain types of international risk, such as the risk of expropriation, into the weighted average cost of capital. If a project faces significant expropriation risk, the embedded option techniques of Chapter 8 might be more appropriate than discounted cash flow techniques.

---

tive, and 16% from both. Surveys also indicate that a high percentage of firms use discounted cash flow techniques. Stanley and Block (1984) report that over 80% of their respondents use either a net present value approach or an internal rate of return approach; similar high percentages are also reported by Oblak and Helm (1980), Bavishi (1981), and Shao and Shao (1992).

[37] Bavishi reports that of those firms using discounted cash flow techniques, 43% use their worldwide cost of capital and 27% use the local cost of capital; the remaining 30% use subjective judgment in choosing the cost of capital for the foreign project. Oblak and Helm (1980) and Stanley and Block (1984) report similar figures.

[38] Shao and Shao (1992) surveyed 188 foreign subsidiaries of U.S.-based multinational firms. The respondents stated that the most difficult stage of project evaluation involves estimation of project cash flows; they considered estimation of the discount rate to be the easiest part of the procedure. As Shao and Shao note, this may be because the parent companies tend to exert a significant amount of influence in setting minimum cost of capital requirements for their foreign subsidiaries.

Appendix

The Adjusted Net Present Value Approach

Many projects have side effects that are not directly related to the actual operations of the project. One example is the tax shield associated with debt. The weighted average cost of capital accommodates the value of this tax shield by incorporating the relatively low after-tax cost of debt in the weighted average cost of capital. Big tax shields decrease the cost of capital, which leads to higher present values for the project.

An alternative to the weighted average cost of capital approach is the adjusted net present value (ANPV) approach.[39] The first step in the ANPV approach is to estimate the cost of unlevered equity, which is the cost of equity that the firm would have if the firm had no leverage; notice that this is not the cost of capital.[40] The second step is to estimate the cash flows that are generated directly by the operations of the project. The "base net present value" is the net present value of the installation costs and the operating cash flows discounted at the unlevered cost of equity. Other rates are used to discount the cash flows that are generated by any side effects, such as the tax shield of debt. The adjusted present value of the project is the sum of the base NPV and the NPV of side effects.

International projects often have many side effects. For example, foreign governments often provide subsidies on local debt. Holland (1990) suggests that the adjusted present value of an international project is:

Present value of the project = the present value of the capital outlays
+ the present value of the remittable after-tax operating cash flows
+ the present value of the tax savings from depreciation

---

[39] See Myers (1974), Brealey and Myers (1988), and Shapiro (1989) for a more detailed description of this approach.

[40] Chapter 4 describes the technique for estimating this unlevered cost of equity.

+ the present value of financial subsidies
+ the present value of the project's
contribution to the corporate debt
capacity
+ the present value of other tax savings
+ the present value of extra remittances
+ the present value of residual plant
and equipment.

An advantage to this approach is that it allows separate specification of the different contributors to cash flows. It also allows you to
specify different discount rates for the different components of the
cash flows. After applying the different discount rates to the separate
components of the cash flows, you can directly observe the contribution
to value made by the various components. See Shapiro (1978b, 1983)
for further discussion of the use of the adjusted net present value
technique in valuing international projects. Shapiro (1992, Chapter 18)
provides a comprehensive example that illustrates the technique.

References

Adler, M. "The Cost of Capital and Valuation of a Two-Country Firm." *Journal of Finance* 29(1) (1974): 119–132.

———. "The Cost of Capital and Valuation of a Two-Country Firm: Reply." *Journal of Finance* 32(4) (1977): 1354–1357.

Agmon, T., and D. Lessard. "Investor Recognition of Corporate International Diversification." *Journal of Finance* (September 1977): 1049–1055.

Alexander, G.J., C.S. Eun, and S. Janakiramanan. "International Listings and Stock Returns: Some Empirical Evidence." Working Paper, University of Minnesota, May 1986.

Ang, J.S., and T. Lai. "A Simple Rule for Multinational Capital Budgeting." *The Global Finance Journal* 1(1) (1989): 71–75.

Ashton, D.J. "The Cost of Capital and the Imputation Tax System." *Journal of Business Finance and Accounting* 16(1) (1989): 75–88.

Bavishi, V.B. "Capital Budgeting Practices at Multinationals." *Management Accounting* (August 1981): 32–35.

Beidleman, C.R. *Interest Rate Swaps.* Homewood, Ill.: Business One–Irwin, 1991.

———. *Cross Currency Swaps.* Homewood, Ill.: Business One–Irwin, 1992.

Booth, L.D. "Taxes, Funds Positioning, and the Cost of Capital for Multinationals." *Advances in Financial Planning and Forecasting* 5(2) (1990): 245–270.

Bradley, D. "Managing Against Expropriation." *Harvard Business Review* (July–August 1977): 75–83.

Brealey, R.A., and S.C. Myers. *Principles of Corporate Finance,* 3rd ed. New York: McGraw-Hill, 1988.

Cho, D.C., C.S. Eun, and L.W. Senbet. "International Arbitrage Pricing Theory: An Empirical Investigation." *Journal of Finance* 41(2) (June 1986): 313–329.

Christofi, A.C., and G.C. Philippatos. "An Empirical Investigation of the International Arbitrage Pricing Theory." *Management International Review* 27(1) (1987): 13–22.

Cohn, R.A., and J.J. Pringle. "Imperfections in International Financial Markets: Implications for Risk Premia and the Cost of Capital to Firms." *Journal of Finance* 28(1) (1973): 59–66.

Copeland, T., T. Koller, and J. Murrin. *Valuation: Measuring and Managing the Value of Companies.* New York: Wiley, 1990.

Eiteman, D.K., A.I. Stonehill, and M.H. Moffett. *Multinational Business Finance,* 6th ed. Reading, Mass.: Addison-Wesley, 1992.

Eun, C.S., and B.G. Resnick. "Estimating the Correlation Structure of International Share Prices." *Journal of Finance* (December 1984): 1311–1324.

———. "Currency Factors in International Portfolio Diversification." *Columbia Journal of World Business* (Summer 1985): 45–53.

Fatemi, A.M. "Shareholder Benefits from Corporate International Diversification." *Journal of Finance* (December 1984): 1325–1344.

Goldberg, M.A., and W.Y. Lee. "The Cost of Capital and Valuation of a Two-Country Firm: Comment." *Journal of Finance* 32(4) (1977): 1348–1353.

Holland, J. "Capital Budgeting for International Business: A Framework for Analysis." *Managerial Finance* (November 1990): 1–6.

Howe, J., and J. Madura. "The Impact of International Listings on Risk: Implications for Capital Market Integration." *Journal of Banking and Finance* 14(6) (1990): 1133–1142.

Isimbabi, M.J. "Comovements of World Securities Markets, International Portfolio Diversification, and Asset Returns: A Survey of Empirical Evidence." Ch. 4 in *Recent Development in International Banking & Finance*, Vol. VI, Sarkis J. Khoury, ed. Cambridge, Mass.: Blackwell, 1992.

Jacquillat, B., and B.H. Solnik. "Multinationals are Poor Tools for Diversification." *Journal of Portfolio Management* (Winter 1978): 8–12.

Kent, D., and M. Theobald. "The Imputation System, Cost of Capital and Dividend Policy." *Accounting and Business Research* 11(41) (1980–81): 61–65.

Lawrenz, D.W. "The Effects of Corporate Taxation on the Cost of Equity Capital." *Financial Management* 5(1) (1976): 53–57.

Lessard, D.R. "World, Country, and Industry Relationships in Equity Returns: Implications for Risk Reduction Through International Diversification." *Financial Analysts Journal* (January/February 1976): 32–38.

Mahajan, A. "Pricing Expropriation Risk." *Financial Management* (Winter 1990): 77–86.

Markowitz, H. "Portfolio Selection." *Journal of Finance* (March 1952): 77–91.

Merton, R.C. "A Simple Model of Capital Market Equilibrium with Incomplete Information." *Journal of Finance* (July 1987): 483–510.

Myers, S.C. "Interactions of Corporate Financing and Investments Decisions: Implications for Capital Budgeting." *Journal of Finance* 29(1) (March 1974): 1–25.

Oblak, D.J., and R.J. Helm, Jr. "Survey and Analysis of Capital Budgeting Methods Used by Multinationals." *Financial Management* (Winter 1980): 37–41.

Rao, C.U., and R.H. Litzenberger. "Leverage and the Cost of Capital in a Less Developed Capital Market: Comment." *Journal of Finance* 26(3) (1971): 777–782.

Roll, R. "The International Crash of 1987." *Financial Analysts Journal* (September–October 1988): 19–35.

Sarma, L.V., and K.S. Hanumanta Rao. "Leverage and the Cost of Capital in a Less Developed Capital Market: Reply." *Journal of Finance* 26(3) (1971): 783–785.

Shao, L.P., and A.P. Shao. "Capital Budgeting and Risk Analysis: An Exploratory Study of the Techniques Adopted by Foreign Subsidiaries of U.S. Multinational Enterprises." Working Paper, Fordham University, 1992.

Shapiro, A.C. "Evaluating Financing Costs for Multinational Subsidiaries." *Journal of International Business Studies* (Fall 1975): 25–32.

———. "Capital Budgeting for the Multinational Corporation." *Financial Management* (Spring 1978a): 7–16.

———. "Financial Structure and Cost of Capital in the Multinational Corporation." *Journal of Financial and Quantitative Analysis* 13(2) (1978b): 211–226.

———. "International Capital Budgeting." *Midland Journal of Corporate Finance* 1(1) (Spring 1983): 26–45.

———. *International Corporate Finance: A Survey and Synthesis.* Tampa, Fla.: Financial Management Association, 1986.

———. *Modern Corporate Finance.* New York: Macmillan, 1989.

———. *Multinational Financial Management,* 4th ed. Boston: Allyn and Bacon, 1992.

Sharpe, W.F. "Capital Asset Prices: A Theory of Market Equilibrium Under Conditions of Risk." *Journal of Finance* (September 1964): 425–442.

Solnik, B.H. "Why Not Diversify Internationally Rather Than Domestically?" *Financial Analysts Journal* (July–August 1974): 48–54.

Solnik, B.H., and B. Noetzlin. "Optimal International Asset Allocation." *Journal of Portfolio Management* (Fall 1982): 11–21.

Stanley, M., and S. Block. "An Empirical Study of Management and Financial Variables Influencing Capital Budgeting Decisions for Multinational Corporations in the 1980's." *Management International Review* 23(3) (1983): 61–72.

———. "A Survey of Multinational Capital Budgeting." *Financial Review* 19(1) (1984): 36–54.

Stonehill, A.I., and K.B. Dullum. *Internationalizing the Cost of Capital: The Novo Experience and National Policy Implications.* New York: Wiley, 1983.

Tucker, A. "International Investing: Are ADR's an Alternative?" *AAII Journal* (November 1987): 10–12.

Tucker, A., K. Becker, M. Isimbabi, and J. Ogden, *Contemporary Portfolio Theory and Risk Management.* St. Paul, Minn.: West Publishing, 1992.

Tucker, A.L., J. Madura, and T.C. Chiang. *International Financial Markets*. St. Paul, Minn.: West Publishing, 1991.

Yang, H., J. Wansley, and W. Lane. "Stock Market Recognition of Multinationality of a Firm and International Events." *Journal of Business Finance and Accounting* (Summer 1985): 233–274.

Chapter **8**

Valuing Strategic Options: When the Discounted Cash Flow Approach Doesn't Work

The discounted cash flow approach is a powerful and frequently used tool for finding the value of projects. As Chapter 2 shows, the discounted cash flow approach can help identify the value-adding projects that you should implement and the value-decreasing projects that you should avoid. The discounted cash flow approach also is popular because it is intuitive and easy to understand: you estimate the expected future cash flows, and use the right discount rate to find the present value.

Although the concept is simple, in practice the approach may be hard to apply. After all, it is often very difficult to estimate the expected future cash flows of a project. Even if you can estimate those cash flows, it's not always easy to find the right discount rate. Despite these difficulties, the logic underlying the discounted cash flow approach is valid, which explains why it's usually worthwhile for you to undergo the arduous process of estimating cash flows and discount rates.

Sometimes, however, it's *impossible* to estimate the appropriate discount rate. And if you can't estimate the discount rate, you certainly can't use the discounted cash flow approach. This chapter should help identify the types of projects for which the discounted cash flow approach is inappropriate. For such projects, usually there isn't any well-accepted alternative method for quantifying the project's value, but there are guidelines that allow you to make qualitative judgments about the values of these projects.

Section I identifies the types of projects for which the discounted cash flow approach is inappropriate; in general, these are strategic projects that have embedded real options. Section II explains why discounted cash flow techniques are not appropriate for projects with embedded options. Section III describes how you can value certain types of strategic projects and how you can make qualitative judgments about the value of embedded real options.

I. What Are Embedded Real Options?

Suppose you're considering a project that uses a new and innovative technology. The project has a short life cycle of two years, and you conduct a traditional discounted cash flow analysis based on this two-year life. The net present value is negative. Should you reject the project? That depends on the volatility of the expected technological developments. To see this, consider the following example.

Suppose that you expect only minor improvements in the new technology, but there exists a small chance of a major technological breakthrough during the next two years. If the breakthrough occurs, another project that begins in two years would have a positive NPV. What is today's expected present value of the project that begins in two years? It's pretty much the same as the NPV of the project that begins now, as the probability of a breakthrough is small. Therefore, you might think that neither project is worth accepting.

However, let's assume that you accept the current project. If a breakthrough doesn't occur, you could abandon the project at the end of its two-year life. But if a breakthrough does occur, at the end of the original project's life you could incorporate these technological improvements in an improved project for the next two years. But here's the catch: you can't implement the improved project unless you have first implemented the original project. This is because you will be too far back on the learning curve to implement the improved technology on a timely basis.

Therefore, this original project actually has two components. The first is a straight project, which has a negative NPV. The second is an embedded real option to incorporate new technology, and the embedded option has a positive value. The total value of the original project is the sum of the negative NPV and the positive embedded option. This total value might well be positive, in which case you should accept the original project. A conventional discounted cash flow analysis ignores the value of the embedded real option and could lead you to reject a value-adding project.[1]

The same type of reasoning applies to a new product line. At the time of a product's introduction, you might not know whether the market demand for the product will be large enough for you to make a profit. Suppose you don't enter the new market, but that your competitors do. If at some later date the market does grow, you might not be able to enter the market successfully because your competitors have already established name recognition and customer loyalty. Therefore, the decision to enter the market early gives you an option to take advantage of a high-growth market, should that occur.

Notice that you can't base your decision on the expected market growth. Even if the expected growth in the market isn't large enough to justify the new product line, the option to take advantage of possible high growth might justify a decision to enter the market. To see this, suppose there is an equal chance of low growth and high growth. If the growth turns out to be low, you terminate the product line. But if the growth is high, you can expand your capacity.

In other words, the expected growth is not nearly as important as the *unexpected* growth. You could lose your initial investment if the market demand unexpectedly turns out to be low, but you might make a killing if the market demand unexpectedly turns out to be high. Your loss is limited, but your possible gain could be enormous. If you base your decision just on the expected market growth, you ignore the possibility of hitting a home run.

There are also situations in which the option to defer investment has value. For example, suppose you have the opportunity to purchase a license that gives you exclusive rights to manufacture and sell a laser disc with a game that can be played on the new interactive television systems. If you decide to market this game, you will incur a startup cost at your current manufacturing facility. Suppose that the current anticipated volume of disc sales, based on the number of consumers who own interactive television systems, is too low to justify your total initial costs, which are the sum of the license costs and the manufacturing startup costs. Does this mean you shouldn't purchase the license?

Keep in mind that you don't have to begin producing the disc immediately. You could purchase the license now, but wait a year before retooling your facility. If the number of consumers owning interactive

---

[1] See Kester (1984) and Trigeorgis and Mason (1987) for further discussion of the concept of embedded options.

television systems increases enough, it may be profitable to retool your facility and begin selling the game. In other words, you're not just purchasing a license; you also are buying an option to defer startup costs until you resolve some of the uncertainty in the market. This option might be so valuable that you should purchase the license.

Many other projects, such as advertising, flexible manufacturing systems, and R&D, also incorporate real options. In fact, if a project allows managerial intervention, then the project almost certainly has an embedded real option.[2]

Why can't you use discounted cash flow techniques to value real options? Simply put, it's because having a real option embedded in a project alters the project's appropriate cost of capital. Then why can't you just use the altered cost of capital? This is impossible, because no one knows how to estimate this altered cost of capital. The next section explains this in more detail.

II. Why You Can't Estimate the Cost of Capital for Embedded Real Options

One of the fundamental principles of modern finance is that there is a relationship between risk and expected return. Unfortunately, modern finance has been unable to establish this risk–return relationship for the type of risk inherent in a real option. To show you why this is so, it's helpful to start with some types of risk for which the risk–return relationship is known. It's also helpful to draw analogies with financial instruments.

II.A. The Case of Nonrandom Cash Flows

Let's start with a very simple financial instrument, such as a U.S. Treasury bond. The bond has no default risk, so you know the cash flows with certainty. The value of the bond is the present value of the cash flows, discounted at the appropriate rate. Since the cash flows have no default risk, you know that the appropriate discount rate for these cash flows should be the risk-free interest rate, R_f. In other words, you know the risk–return relationship for the type of risk inherent in the bond's cash flows.

---

[2] See Trigeorgis (1988) for a general discussion of the different types of embedded real options.

If CF_t is the cash flow at time t, then the present value, PV, is:

$$PV = \sum_{t=1}^{T} \frac{CF_t}{(1 + R_f)^t} \tag{8.1}$$

You know the cash flows, and you know the appropriate discount rate, so it's simple for you to find the value of the bond.[3] The discounted cash flow approach works quite well for certain types of financial securities, and it works equally well for certain types of real projects.[4] In general, the approach works well for securities that have predictable future cash flows such as bonds and preferred stocks. The approach also works well for projects with relatively predictable future cash flows such as many types of equipment replacement projects. For example, the lighting and HVAC (heating, ventilating, and air conditioning) systems for most buildings and factories have operating costs that are fairly predictable. These costs typically are invariant with respect to the prevailing business environment; i.e., whether the facility is at full or partial operating capacity, you're going to incur these costs. Therefore, the appropriate discount rate for such a project should be close to the risk-free rate.[5]

II.B. The Case of Uncertain Cash Flows

Now consider a financial instrument with uncertain cash flows. If $E[CF_t]$ is the expected cash flow at time t, and r_{UF} is the appropriate rate for an uncertain cash flow, then the present value is:

$$PV = \sum_{t=1}^{T} \frac{E[CF_t]}{(1 + r_{UF})^t} \tag{8.2}$$

But here's the problem: What is the appropriate discount rate, r_{UF}? In other words, how do you determine the discount rate that is appropriate for the uncertain cash flows; i.e., what is the risk–return

---

[3] If the term structure of interest rates is not flat, R_f would not be constant. Instead, you would use the risk-free rate that is appropriate for each payment date. See Chapter 5 for further details related to the valuation of a multiperiod project.

[4] See Myers (1984) for an interesting discussion of financial tools and their role in making strategic decisions.

[5] The appropriate discount rate might be a little higher than the risk-free rate. For example, there might be some uncertainty in the rate of price increases in electricity purchases, which would imply a cost of capital higher than the risk-free rate.

relationship for the type of risk inherent in the cash flows? The answer depends on the nature of the uncertainty in the cash flows.

II.B.1. Completely Random Cash Flows

Suppose the uncertainty is completely random. This means that you could diversify away the uncertainty by holding a large, well-diversified portfolio.[6] A basic belief in finance theory is that you don't get compensated for holding diversifiable risk, so the appropriate discount rate for this type of uncertainty is the risk-free interest rate.[7]

II.B.2. Normally Distributed Cash Flows

Suppose you can model the uncertain cash flows as though they are random variables that come from a stationary normal distribution. In this case, you could use the capital asset pricing model to determine the appropriate discount rate.[8] Your first step would be to estimate beta (β_{UF}) for the expected uncertain cash flows. Given this estimate of beta and an estimate of the expected return on the market, $E[R_m]$, the appropriate discount rate for uncertain cash flows, (R_{UF}), is:

$$R_{UF} = R_f + \beta_{UF} (E[R_m] - R_f) \qquad (8.3)$$

With the estimate of the required rate of return for uncertain flows, R_{UF}, and the estimated expected cash flows of the financial instrument, you can easily find the value of this financial instrument. It's important to realize that the CAPM is the link between the type of uncertainty and the discount rate. Without this link, you can't get a discount rate, and without the discount rate, you can't value the instrument.

As this example shows, you don't have to know the actual future cash flows of a financial instrument with certainty in order to use the

---

[6] This is the principle that life insurance companies follow. The company doesn't know how much it will pay in claims for any single policyholder, but it can predict with virtually no error the total claim payments for all of its policyholders.

[7] If the term structure itself is not expected to be constant during the life of the instrument, you would not discount all the expected payments by the same interest rate. The simplest adjustment would be to use the yields on U.S. Treasury STRIP bonds whose maturities correspond to the payment dates; see Chapter 5 for further discussion of this issue. An alternative approach is to use a model that explicitly incorporates interest rate risk such as the term structure model of Cox, Ingersoll, and Ross (1985).

[8] Actually, the CAPM may be correct even if returns are not distributed normally. For example, you also can use the CAPM if investors have a quadratic utility function even if returns aren't normally distributed. These technical issues are not addressed in this discussion for the sake of simplicity.

discounted cash flow approach to value the financial instrument. You need to know only the *expected* future cash flows, and those expected cash flows must come from a stationary normal distribution. You also can use the discounted cash flow approach to value certain types of risky projects. For example, if an existing product line has expected future cash flows that come from a stationary normal distribution, you can use the CAPM to estimate the required rate of return for most projects associated with the product line. This would include projects that replace existing equipment or projects that make minor additions to capacity.

II.B.3. Nonnormally Distributed Cash Flows

Finally, consider a third and very different type of uncertainty. Suppose the security that you are trying to value is a call option on a stock. This particular call option gives you the right to purchase a share of the stock for $50 on the expiration date of the option, which is one year from now. This is a "European" option, which means that you cannot exercise the option until the date of expiration. How much will the option be worth on the expiration date? Suppose the price of the stock on the exercise date is only $40. You would let the option expire unexercised; you certainly wouldn't exercise the option by paying the $50 exercise price when you could buy the stock directly for $40. If the price of the stock on the expiration date is less than $50 (the exercise price of the option), the option is worthless. Suppose that the price on the stock is $60 on the date of the option's expiration. You could exercise the option for $50 and then sell the stock (which you just got by exercising the option) for $60: this means that the option is worth $60 − $50 = $10.

Let X denote the exercise price, S_E denote the price of the stock on the option's expiration date, and C_E denote the value of the option on the exercise date. The value of the option at expiration, C_E, is equal to zero if the stock price is less than the exercise price ($C_E = 0$ if $S_E < X$); the value of the option at expiration is equal to the difference between the stock price and the exercise price if the stock price is greater than the exercise price ($C_E = S_E − X$ if $S_E \geq X$).

To use the discounted cash flow approach, you would have to estimate the expected cash flow for each payment date. For this option, payments occur only at expiration, so there is only one payment date. Before you can estimate the expected payment, you have to make some assumptions about the stock's expected returns. The instantaneous rate of return on the stock is the return on the stock over a very short interval of time. Suppose that the stock's instantaneous rate of return comes from a normal distribution with a mean of μ and a standard deviation of σ. In other words, you expect the stock to have a return of μ over any short interval, but the actual return may not be exactly equal to μ.[9]

For illustrative purposes, assume that this stock has an expected instantaneous rate of return of $\mu = .15$ and an instantaneous standard deviation of $\sigma = .30$. The computations are a little complicated, but you can use these assumptions to calculate the option's expected payment on the expiration date.[10] For this example, if the current stock price is $50, the option's expected payment at the time of expiration, $E[C_E]$, is equal to $11.27.

The next step in the discounted cash flow approach is to find the appropriate discount rate, and this is where you run into a problem. The CAPM approach is appropriate only if the uncertain cash flows have a normal distribution.[11] The stock has normally distributed returns, but does the option also have normally distributed returns? If the stock price at the time of exercise is less than the option's exercise price, the option has a return of zero; if the stock price at the time of exercise is greater than the exercise price, the option has a positive return. As this demonstrates, the option's returns definitely are not normally distributed. In fact, the option's returns are skewed to the right.

Because the option's returns aren't normally distributed, you can't use the CAPM to link the option's uncertain returns to an appropriate discount rate. As a matter of fact, finance theory has not established a risk–return relationship for the type of risk inherent in the option. Therefore, *you can't use the discounted cash flow approach to value this option.*

---

[9] The stock's return generating process is defined by:

$$dS/S = \mu dt + \sigma dz,$$

where ds is the differential change in stock price, dt is the differential change in time, and dz is a Gaus–Wiener variable.

[10] The formula for the expected cash flow of the option is: $E[C_E] = S\,e^{\mu T}N\{E_1\} - X\,N\{E_2\}$, where T is the time until the option matures, $E_1 = (\sigma^2 T)^{(-.5)}[\ln(S/X) + \mu T + (.5\sigma^2 T)]$, $E_2 = E_1 - (\sigma^2 T)^{(.5)}$, and $N\{\cdot\}$ is the cumulative probability density function for a standard normal variable.

[11] As note 7 indicates, if returns are not normally distributed, the CAPM remains valid if investors have quadratic utility functions. However, there is no reason to believe that investors have quadratic utility functions.

II.B.4. Valuing the Nonnormally Distributed Cash Flows of An Option

Fortunately, there is an alternative approach that allows you to find the value of this option. You can apply the Black–Scholes option pricing model:

$$C = SN\{d_1\} - Xe^{-R_fT}N\{d_2\} \tag{8.4}$$

where R_f is the risk-free interest rate, T is the time until maturity, $N\{\cdot\}$ is the value of the cumulative standard normal density function, and d_1 and d_2 are as defined below:

$$d_1 = \frac{\ln(S/X) + (R_f + .5\sigma^2)T}{\sigma\sqrt{T}} \quad \text{and} \tag{8.5}$$

$$d_2 = d_1 - \sigma\sqrt{T}$$

If you apply the formula to the option, you will get an option value of \$7.86.

But suppose the Black–Scholes option pricing model had never been invented? Could you use the discounted cash flow approach to find the value of this option? Yes, if you can estimate the appropriate cost of capital. For example, suppose you know the discount rate that is appropriate for the type of risk inherent in the expected cash flows of this particular option. If r_{OPT} denotes this appropriate discount rate, you can find the value of the option by discounting the expected future cash flow, $E[C_E]$:

$$C = \frac{E[C_E]}{(1 + r_{OPT})^T} \tag{8.6}$$

You know the expected future cash flow of the option, which is \$11.27 (see note 10 for the calculation). But how do you choose the appropriate discount rate? In the absence of any other method, suppose you have a Zen-like experience, which leads you to choose a discount rate of 43.38%. Using this seemingly absurd discount rate, you find the value of the option is:

$$C = \frac{E[C_E]}{(1 + r_{OPT})^T} = \frac{\$11.27}{(1 + .4338)^1} = \$7.86 \qquad (8.7)$$

Surprisingly, this is the correct value of the option, as specified by the Black–Scholes option pricing model of equation (8.4). In other words, if you had been able to estimate this seemingly absurd discount rate, you could have used the discounted cash flow method instead of the Black–Scholes model.

Unfortunately, you are unlikely to estimate the appropriate cost of capital. Zen-like experiences are rare, and finance theory fails to provide a linkage between the type of uncertainty inherent in the cash flows of this option and the appropriate discount rate for those uncertain cash flows. Also, it's important to realize that even though 43.38% is the appropriate discount rate for this particular option, 43.38% is not necessarily the appropriate discount rate for a different option.

What does all this have to do with finding the value of a real project? If the project's future returns aren't normally distributed, you can't use the CAPM to find the appropriate discount rate. If you can't use the CAPM, there are very few situations for which you can find an appropriate discount rate. And without the appropriate discount rate, you can't use the discounted cash flow approach.

Unfortunately, projects with embedded real options have nonsymmetric returns, and nonsymmetric returns certainly don't come from a normal distribution.[12] Therefore, you can't use discounted cash flow techniques to value projects with embedded real options.

III. Valuing Embedded Real Options

There is no single method for valuing all embedded real options. In fact, for some types of embedded real options there are no methods at all. A complete description of all approaches for valuing real options is beyond the scope of this book, but it's important for you to know the specific types of real options for which solution techniques exist. Also, there are some qualitative, if not quantitative, statements about value that are valid for all options.

---

[12] See Myers (1984), Kester (1984), and Kensinger (1987) for discussions of this issue.

III.A. Which Real Options Can You Value?

Consider a project with an economic life of 20 years. Even though the project is capable of lasting 20 years, suppose you can abandon this project prior to 20 years if the prices of inputs or outputs change so that the project no longer generates a positive cash flow. Therefore, this project has an embedded real option to abandon. Researchers have long recognized that the option to abandon adds value to a project.[13] The early studies of the abandonment option provide valuable insights, but they don't provide a methodology that you can use to quantify the option to abandon. Recent studies by McDonald and Siegel (1985) and Myers and Majd (1990) do provide techniques you can use to value the abandonment options. Numerical examples by Myers and Majd indicate that the abandonment option can easily exceed 6% of the conventional NPV of the project.

Sometimes you can delay your entry into a new market, particularly if you have proprietary rights to a product or technology. Other times you can delay the rate of project implementation, such as the rate of construction for a new manufacturing facility. During this period of delay, market conditions may change in such a way that you can profitably modify your original plans. Therefore, the embedded real option to defer an investment has value. Majd and Pindyck (1987), Pindyck (1988), and McDonald and Siegel (1986) provide techniques that allow you to value the option to defer an investment. Their numerical examples show that this option often can be quite valuable. If you have a project that has an embedded real option to defer, immediate implementation of the project is equivalent to an early exercise of the option. In many situations you should exercise this option only if the conventional present value of the project is much greater than the cost of the project.

If the project is in the natural resources sector, there are several special techniques for valuing embedded options. For example, Brennan and Schwartz (1985) have developed a model to evaluate natural resource investments such as mining. In addition to providing estimates of project value, their model specifies operating policies, such as when to open the mine, when to suspend operations temporarily, the rate of extraction when the mine is open, and when to abandon the mine. Venezia and Brenner (1979) have a model that allows you to determine when to terminate a natural resources investment, such as when to

---

[13] See Robichek and Van Horne (1967, 1969), Dyl and Long (1969), and Bonini (1977).

harvest a forest or when to bottle an aging wine. Although their model is not specifically limited to the natural resource sector, Siegel, Smith, and Paddock (1987) provide an approach to valuing offshore oil properties, which is also useful for determining bids on property leases.

Another type of embedded real option is manufacturing flexibility. Suppose, for example, you are comparing a dedicated production line that can produce only one product with a flexible manufacturing system that can produce multiple products. Even if both systems begin by producing the same product, the flexible manufacturing system allows you to switch production to the most profitable product should input costs or output prices change. This flexibility is an embedded real option. If the manufacturing process converts a commodity into a higher-order commodity, such as soy beans into soy oil, you can use the exchange model of Kensinger (1987). For noncommodity products, Ehrhardt and Reeve (1991) demonstrate a technique to value a production system that can make one switch in products. Triantis and Hodder (1990) and Kulatilaka (1988) develop more general models for valuing manufacturing systems that can make multiple switches between products. According to their numerical examples, the embedded real option to switch can add significant value to a project.

There are several other option pricing techniques that are related to the valuation of real options. Margrabe (1978) provides a model for valuing the option to exchange one asset for another. Stulz (1982) shows how to value an option on the minimum or maximum of two assets. Trigeorgis (1991) develops a technique for valuing multioption investments. Geske (1977) develops a model to value compound options.[14] Carr (1988) develops a model for valuing sequential exchange opportunities. While these studies do not specifically address embedded real options, many of their techniques are applicable to the valuation of real options.

III.B. The Value of Real Options: Some Qualitative Effects

Except for the specialized cases in the previous section, there are no specific solution techniques that allow you to value most real options. Even though an exact quantitative solution may not exist, there are several general insights that apply to almost all real options. First, the value of the option is higher, the longer the time until it expires.

---

[14] See Geske and Johnson (1984) for a minor correction of Geske's compound option pricing model.

For example, the option to defer an initial investment in a product is worth more, if you have a longer time to decide than if you must immediately accept or reject the project.

In general, you have a cash outflow at the time you exercise an embedded real option. For example, if you decide to extend a project at the end of its original life, usually you will have to add equipment or other resources. If interest rates increase before that date, the present value of your future cash outflow decreases. In other words, it will be "cheaper" for you to exercise the option. Therefore, an increase in interest rates typically causes an increase in the value of a real option.

Strangely enough, the more volatile the underlying source of risk, the greater the value of the real option. Consider the introduction of a new product line with an embedded option that allows you in two years either to abandon the project or greatly expand capacity, depending on the size of the market two years from now. If the market is smaller than a critical size, you abandon the project. Notice that it doesn't matter how much smaller the market is than the critical size. You will abandon the project if the market is barely smaller than the critical level, and you will abandon it if the market is very much smaller than the critical level. In either case, your loss is limited to your investment in the original project. On the other hand, if the market turns out to be very large, your option to expand is quite valuable. In fact, the larger the market is, the more valuable the option to expand. Therefore, more volatility in the underlying source of risk *increases* the value of the option.

As you might expect, more flexibility increases the value of the option. Yet the value doesn't increase at a constant rate. In other words, the value of a flexible manufacturing system that can produce four products isn't twice as high as the value of a similar system that can produce only two products.

IV. Summary

The Deist philosophers of the seventeenth and eighteenth centuries believed that God created the world and also a system of physical laws that subsequently governed creation. They believed these laws were so complete that God never needed to intervene in the affairs of the world. Some projects are like this Deist world view: once the project has been implemented, it needs very little intervention from managers. The discounted cash flow method is a powerful and valuable tool for valuing such a project. This is particularly true for routine projects, or projects that involve replacement of existing machinery with more efficient equipment.

Many projects, however, allow and even require considerable intervention on the part of management. In many ways, this intervention is like the exercise of a financial option. Just as the discounted cash flow approach is not appropriate for valuing a financial option, it also is not appropriate for valuing an embedded real option. Unfortunately, there are no simple and well accepted solution techniques for quantifying the value of most embedded real options. Even if you can't assign an exact numerical value to these options, however, it's important that you consider these options when you evaluate your projects. The successful firms of the next decade will be those that constantly create value-adding projects, and much of that value will undoubtedly be in the form of real options.

References

Bonini, C.P. "Capital Investment Under Uncertainty with Abandonment Options." *Journal of Financial and Quantitative Analysis* (March 1977): 39–54.

Brennan, M.J., and E.S. Schwartz. "Evaluating Natural Resource Investments." *Journal of Business* 58(2) (1985): 135–157.

Carr, P. "The Valuation of Sequential Exchange Opportunities." *Journal of Finance* 43(5) (December 1988): 1235–1256.

Cox, J.C., J.E. Ingersoll, Jr., and S.A. Ross. "A Theory of the Term Structure of Interest Rates." *Econometrica* 53(2) (March 1985): 385–407.

Dyl, E.A., and H.W. Long. "Abandonment Value and Capital Budgeting: Comment." *Journal of Finance* 24(1) (March 1969): 88–95.

Ehrhardt, M.C., and J. Reeve. "Creating Value: The Appropriate Use of Capital Budgeting." *Managerial Finance* 17(5) (Summer 1991): 3–11.

Geske, R. "The Valuation of Corporate Liabilities as Compound Options." *Journal of Financial and Quantitative Analysis* 12(4) (November 1977): 231–232.

Geske, R., and H.E. Johnson. "The Valuation of Corporate Liabilities as Compound Options: A Correction." *Journal of Financial and Quantitative Analysis* 19(2) (June 1984): 231–232.

Kensinger, J.W. "Adding the Value of Active Management into the Capital Budgeting Equation." *Midland Corporate Finance Journal* (Spring 1987): 31–42.

Kester, W.C. "Today's Options for Tomorrow's Growth." *Harvard Business Review* (March–April 1984): 153–160.

Kulatilaka, N. "Valuing the Flexibility of Flexible Manufacturing Systems." *IIEE Transactions on Engineering Management* 35(4) (November 1988): 250–257.

Majd, S., and R.S. Pindyck. "Time to Build, Option Value, and Investment Decisions." *Journal of Financial Economics* 18 (1987): 7–27.

Margrabe, W. "The Value of an Option to Exchange One Asset for Another." *Journal of Finance* 33(1) (March 1978): 177–186.

McDonald, R.L., and Siegel, D.R. "Investment and the Valuation of Firms when There is an Option to Shut Down." *International Economic Review* 26(2) (June 1985): 331–349.

———. "The Value of Waiting to Invest." *The Quarterly Journal of Economics* (November 1986): 707–727.

Myers, S.C. "Finance Theory and Financial Strategy." *Interfaces* 14(1) (January–February 1984): 126–137.

Myers, S.C., and S. Majd. "Abandonment Value and Project Life." *Advances in Futures and Options Research* 4 (1990): 1–21.

Pindyck, R.S. "Irreversible Investment, Capacity Choice, and the Value of the Firm." *The American Economic Review* 78(5) (December 1988): 969–985.

Robichek, A.A., and J.C. Van Horne. "Abandonment Value and Capital Budgeting." *Journal of Finance* 22(1) (December 1967): 577–589.

———. "Abandonment Value and Capital Budgeting: Reply." *Journal of Finance* 24(1) (March 1969): 96–97.

Siegel, D.R., J.L. Smith, and J.L. Paddock. "Valuing Offshore Oil Properties with Option Pricing Models." *Midland Corporate Finance Journal* (Spring 1987): 22–30.

Stulz, R. "Options on the Minimum or the Maximum of Two Risky Assets." *Journal of Financial Economics* 10 (1982): 161–185.

Triantis, A.J., and J.E. Hodder. "Valuing Flexibility as a Complex Option." *Journal of Finance* 65(2) (June 1990): 549–565.

Trigeorgis, L. "A Conceptual Options Framework for Capital Budgeting." *Advances in Futures and Options Research* 3 (1988): 145–167.

———. "A Log-Transformed Binomial Numerical Analysis Method for Valuing Complex Multi-Option Investments." *Journal of Financial and Quantitative Analysis* 26(3) (September 1991): 309–326.

Trigeorgis, L., and S.P. Mason. "Valuing Managerial Flexibility." *Midland Corporate Finance Journal* 5 (1987): 14–21.

Venezia, I., and M. Brenner. "The Optimal Duration of Growth Investments and Search." *Journal of Business* 52(3) (1979): 393–407.

Index

A

Aaa utility bonds, 92
Abandonment option, 219
Accounting changes, 124–125
Accounting information, and cost of capital, 83n, 103–104
Adjusted discount rate method, 136–138
Adjusted net present value (ANPV) approach, 25n, 139, 202–203
ADR. *See* American Depository Receipt (ADR)
Alberts, W. W., 59n
Alexander, G. J., 192
Allowable cost of capital, for utilities, 165–168
American Depository Receipt (ADR), 191n
Amihud, Y., 126
Ang, J. S., 197
ANPV approach. *See* Adjusted net present value (ANPV) approach
A priori multifactor models, 90–91
Arbitrage pricing theory (APT), 88–89
  globalization and, 188n
  "unspecified" approach in, 89–90
  utilities and, 171–172
Archer, S. H., 59n
Arditti, F. D., 26–27
Ashton, D. J., 184n

B

Baker, H. K., 125
Banking consortiums, 35n
Banking industry. *See* Financial institutions
Bankruptcy risk, 70
Bavishi, B. V., 201n
Becker, K., 184, 186
Ben-Horim, M., 39n
Beta
  accounting, 103n
  defined, 52
  equal to one, 93
  estimation of, 52–60, 81
  estimation period and, 54–55
  firm size and, 57n, 59
  frequency of observations and, 57–58
  globalization and, 189n
  for long-term projects, 145n
  market index and, 53, 57
  multiple-regression approach and, 107–114
  pure-play approach and, 104–107

relation between debt and, 115–117
return interval and, 54
risk-free rate and, 54, 57, 60–61
sensitivity of, 55–59
Value Line Investment Survey and, 52
Bhagwat, Y., 108, 109n
Black, F., 85–88, 217
Block, S., 200n
Bonds
  Aaa utility, 92
  below investment-grade, 71, 73
  with sinking fund, 132n
  STRIP, 141, 214n
  U.S. Treasury, 92, 175, 212–213
  valuation of, 140–143
Book value
  estimation of weights and, 73–76
  multiple regression approach and, 108n
  utilities and, 165, 167, 169n
Bower, D., 171–172
Bower, R., 117n, 120, 171–172
Bradley, D., 195
Bradley, M., 120
Brennan, M. J., 219
Brenner, M., 219
Brigham, E. F., 76, 83n, 102n, 169
Burton, R. M., 156
Buy-and-hold strategy, 62

C

Callen, J. L., 39n
Call options, 87n, 215–218
Capital asset pricing model (CAPM), 51–65
  beta in, 52–60
  cost of equity using, 64–65
  cost of preferred stock in, 65–67
  financial institutions and, 174
  flotation costs and, 137–138
  globalization and, 185–188, 193n
  long-term projects and, 140, 143–147, 152
  market premium in, 61–64
  nonstochastic term structure alternatives and, 144
  relationship to cost of equity, 51–52
  risk-free rate in, 60–61
  uncertain cash flows and, 214–215, 216, 218
  use of, 51–65
  utilities and, 168–169
Capital budgeting
  discounted cash flow approach and, 5n